Four Years

Written By:
Lily Rose

For my family, my future, the Creator, my friends, and Shakia.

Table of Contents

Introduction

Joshua sat at his desk in pre-calc with a pounding headache, sore legs, and a grumbling stomach. His eyes struggled to stay open as he wrote endless equations on his worksheet. He used to enjoy math, but now he didn't really care about it. He needed a break.

Then, as if someone had poured ice-cold water over his head, he was awoken from his trance. The sound of creaking floorboards caused him to look up, and he saw *him* standing there. He was no longer falling asleep, but his stomach hurt worse, and he started to feel lightheaded.

His teacher looked up from her computer at the boy standing in the doorway and said, "Hi. Are you looking for Mrs. Childs?"

"Yes. I'm Kole. I'm supposed to be in pre-calc right now."

"Hi, Kole. Welcome to pre-calc!"

"Thanks. Sorry that I'm late. I got lost."

"It's okay; I understand. Find a seat, and I will get you a worksheet."

"Okay."

Kole looked around the room. His eyes laid on Joshua, but just as quickly as they settled, they moved away again. It was as if they had never met each other before.

Joshua's mind was racing for the rest of class, dreading the bell—when everyone would be set free, making him vulnerable.

Chapter 1: New Kids

A true phenomenon: Joshua was actually feeling *excited* about the upcoming school year. He was going into seventh grade, and he had so much potential. When he got to school, he went to his assigned locker and found that two of his best friends, Sam and Aaron, were one away from him. They each greeted him as they checked out their new locker. They were in the middle of talking when they heard someone say, "Excuse me."

A petite girl with light brown hair and green eyes shoved her way through the boys, towards the one locker that was in between them. Joshua's face turned red, and his stomach spun, suddenly frozen in time.

Her name was Reese.

Joshua was nudged by Sam, and he realized that he had been staring at Reese for a little too long, and now it was time to go to advisory. Joshua shut his locker and followed his friends to their class.

Once they were out of earshot, Sam turned to Joshua and exclaimed, "Woah, you've got your locker next to Reese!"

"Yeah, I saw," Joshua said.

"Really? Because you seemed kind of out of it," Sam laughed.

Joshua's face turned red, and it stayed that way as they walked into their advisory. Immediately, they were surrounded by dozens of computers; they were in the Innovation Lab. They were in a unique advisory where they were going to work on the school's T.V. program.

They were just finding seats when Reese walked into the classroom. Sam and Aaron whipped their heads toward Joshua, whose face had turned red again.

***

Joshua went through his school day and was disappointed to find out that he only had one other class with Reese, and it was one that would only last six weeks. He was on his way to science class near the end of the day when a blond boy, who was new to the school, walked up to him and said, "Hey, do you know where Mr. Kreisten's room is?"

Joshua turned to face him and said, "Yeah. I'm heading there right now."

"Okay, great! I'll follow you, then. It appears we have a lot of classes together."

Joshua thought about it and remembered that he was in three of his other classes. "Yeah, I guess we do."

"My name's Patrick."

"I'm Joshua."

They talked a little bit more as they walked. Patrick, as mentioned, was one of five new kids in Joshua's class that year.

They reached Mr. Kreisten's room and went inside. It was a huge room. Around the whole classroom there were counters with sinks, and sticking out from those were two-person lab benches. On the walls, there were animal skulls and science posters.

Joshua found Sam and sat with him. Patrick took a seat at the lab bench in front of them. They talked more during class.

***

At the end of the day, Joshua met two of his younger sisters outside the school: Kendall, who was in fifth grade, and Leah, who was in first grade. They met up with his best friend Carson and his younger brother named Connor. The five of them walked home from school together. Carson and Connor lived just a couple places down, in an apartment building that was about a two-minute walk from Joshua's house.

When Joshua and his sisters got home, they were greeted by their youngest sister, Ava, and their mom. Their dad was still at work.

Chapter 2: Patrick and Kole

The following day, Joshua was going out for recess by himself when he saw Patrick walking out as well. They had talked a little bit more in their earlier classes that day, so when they saw each other, they met up and began a conversation. Patrick asked Joshua, "What do you do after school?"

"Starting tomorrow, I'm going to have cross country practice," Joshua answered.

"Oh. You do cross country? Is that it?"

"No. I also swim. And I used to play baseball, but I'm not really into it anymore. I don't think I'm going to play it again."

"I play baseball."

"Oh, you do?"

"Yeah."

"Oh, well, then...maybe I'll consider it. Are you going to play for the school?"

"I don't know."

"Oh." Now, Joshua was confused, but he said, "If you play for the school, then I will consider it."

"Okay. Why don't you like baseball? And...*how* do you like cross country?"

Joshua laughed. "I do cross country for swimming,

my favorite sport. And...baseball just isn't really working out for me."

"Oh, okay. Do you play an instrument? I saw you carrying something into the school today."

"Yeah."

"What?"

"Saxophone."

"Do you like it?"

"*Yeah.*" Joshua's voice faded as he went through the word.

"I'm not convinced."

"I like it. *But*...I want to play the cornet."

"What's that?"

"It's like a trumpet, but...*better*. My mom played it when she was younger."

"Can't you just play hers if you want to play it?"

"She doesn't know where it is."

"Oh, I see."

"What about you?"

"I don't play any. Instruments aren't really a thing for my family."

"Oh."

"But...if I could play an instrument, I would definitely play the drums." Patrick smiled.

"Oh." Joshua smiled back. "That's cool."

"Yeah, isn't it?"

Joshua nodded.

After recess, Joshua and Patrick sat together with Carson and another new boy. This new boy had black hair and green eyes. He was strong and tall. He looked more like a freshman in high school than a seventh grader. He sat uneasily, not because he was nervous—but because he was unsure where his eminent nature fit in. When they were all sitting down, Patrick introduced the unfamiliar boy to Joshua by saying, "This is my nephew, Kole."

And Kole added, "But I'm older."

"Oh," Joshua said. "Hi."

"Hi," Kole replied.

Joshua then introduced Carson, and Kole snappily replied, "I know," as if it was extremely obvious they had already met.

"Okay," Joshua said, taken aback.

The next day at lunch, Joshua invited Patrick and Kole to sit at his and Carson's usual table where they sat with four other boys named Aiden, Andrew, Daniel, and Caiden. After that day, Patrick and Kole became regulars in the friend group, and they—especially Kole—began to fit right into the group.

One day when Joshua sat down, Kole was telling a story that everyone else was listening very intently to. They all laughed and joked, and Joshua had no idea what they were talking about since he had just sat down. He didn't say anything; he just began eating his lunch, trying to piece things together. Kole had immediately found a high place in their friend group—Joshua could tell.

Lunch was almost over that day when Reese walked past their table. She smiled as she went by. The boys watched her, and once she was back at her table, Kole asked, "Do you know that girl?"

Carson, Aiden, and Andrew were all quick to answer with, "Yeah!"

"What's her name?" Kole asked.

"Reese," Aiden replied. He then quickly turned his head toward Joshua.

"Augh! She's so annoying!" Kole cried.

"Haha!" Aiden laughed. "That's Joshua's crush!"

Joshua's face was the color of a strawberry (but without the seeds and leaves).

Kole looked over at Joshua and said, "How?"

Joshua was quiet, trying to put a sentence together in his head, but he couldn't figure out what to say before Kole continued, "She's so annoying. She's in every single one of my classes, and she is always trying to talk to me. But I just want her to leave me alone!"

"Haha! Yeah! She's so annoying!" Aiden said.

"I went to a different school in middle school, and she was there. Then, I moved here, and she also moved here," Andrew said.

"You guys think she's annoying, too?" Kole asked. He shot a quick glance at Joshua out of the corner of his eyes.

Aiden and Andrew both nodded. The other boys didn't respond.

"Then how does Joshua have a crush on her?" Kole asked.

"I don't know," Aiden and Andrew both replied.

"Wow, you must be crazy," Kole said, looking at Joshua.

"No!" Joshua snapped.

"Whatever," Kole said.

Lunch ended, and everyone went to their classes.

Chapter 3: "Sure"

September quickly came to an end, and October began. The middle school dance was at the end of the month, and since it was only for seventh and eighth graders, it would be Joshua's first. The walls were covered with posters advertising it. Joshua was walking through the hallway with Patrick on their way to class when, noticing one of the posters, Patrick said, "There's a dance at the end of the month, you saw?"

"Yeah," Joshua replied.

"So, what did Reese say?"

"What?"

"There's a dance coming, and you've asked her to go with you, right?"

"Oh...no...I haven't."

"Are you crazy!?"

"No!"

"You've got to ask her."

"I..." Joshua stammered.

"You what?"

"I don't know," Joshua replied quietly.

"Why wouldn't you?"

"What if...she says...no?" Joshua looked directly at Patrick.

"You're a little weird, you know? Of course there's that possibility, but you've just got to suck it up and take the chance."

"Okay."

"You should ask her at recess. We will all be there to help you."

"I don't need help."

"*Okay*. But we will be there to make sure you follow through."

"Okay, I will." Joshua paused, then asked, "But...what about Kole?"

"*What* about Kole?"

"Does he..." Joshua paused again, trying to find the right combination of words.

"Kole doesn't like her," Patrick said, quickly.

"But...they talk a lot," Joshua said.

"Yeah, but Kole doesn't like her. Remember? She's *annoying*."

"Right."

"So, you're going to ask her to the dance then?"

"Okay."

"*Yes?*"

"Yes."

"Good." Patrick lifted his hand to about chest level, changing the subject, and said, "Look at this." There was a purplish-red dried cut on the side of his hand about the size of a smushed pea.

"What happened?"

"I cut it."

"Obviously," Joshua thought in his head, but out loud, he said, "On what? How?"

"I fell out of my bed and it landed on a knife."

"How? Was there a knife next to your bed or something?"

"Obviously," Patrick thought in his head, but all he did out loud was nod.

"Why?"

Patrick shrugged. They entered their classroom before Joshua could ask any more questions, and they split up to go to their assigned seats.

***

Joshua exited the doors alone for recess, but it wasn't long before he was bombarded by his friends. Patrick and Kole were the first ones to get to him, but Aiden, Andrew, Daniel, and Caiden were all with them. Carson walked up to Joshua's side. He also noticed that Sam and Aaron were there, even though the only one of his friends they talked to was Carson. Before Joshua had the chance to say even one word, Kole asked him, "Are you going to ask her now?"

"What?" Joshua asked.

"Patrick said you promised to ask out Reese."

"I didn't *promise*, but yeah, I said I would."

"Same thing."

"No, it's not."

"Are you going to do it or not?"

"Yes, I am."

"Okay, let's go find her!" Patrick chimed in.

"No!" Joshua cried. "I don't need your help!"

"Why? Kole's like really good friends with her. He could get her to come over. He could convince her. In fact, he's already mentioned it to her that you are going to ask her out," Patrick said.

Joshua looked at Kole.

"We're not friends, but yeah, I mentioned it to her," Kole said.

Patrick laughed.

"*You did?*" Joshua asked, narrowly avoiding a voice crack.

"Yeah," Kole answered.

"What'd she say?" Joshua asked.

"She said she would say yes."

"Are you lying?" Joshua squinted his eyes.

"No."

"Look, there she is!" That was Aiden. He was pointing at the top of the hill where Reese was standing with her friend, Zoe. Everyone looked up. The girls were looking down on the group of boys.

"*Joshuaaa,*" the other boys all said.

Joshua's face was as red as the barn his parents used to walk by with him in the stroller when he was little.

Joshua's friends all started walking up the hill toward Reese and Zoe. Joshua had no choice but to follow them. When they got to the top, one of the boys pushed Joshua forward toward Reese as he mumbled, "I said I didn't need help."

Joshua looked at Reese, expecting a face of judgment but none was there. She looked at him intently, waiting for him to speak.

"Ask her!" one of the boys shouted, but Joshua wasn't sure which one said it.

Joshua looked at Reese who looked back at him. His legs were shaking, his heart was pumping fast, and his head spun around a little bit, but he calmed his emotions, took a deep breath internally, then said, "Do you...want to go to the dance with me?"

"Sure," Reese replied, smiling.

"Okay, cool," Joshua said, smiling back. His heart was still moving fast, but other than that, he felt fine. In fact, he felt great! He felt like he did every time he took his overstuffed backpack off his back.

"Joshua and Reese have to sit together at lunch today!" Kole exclaimed. "At some other table by themselves."

"It would be so romantic," Patrick laughed.

Joshua and Reese were both quiet. Joshua's face was red again, and Reese had her arms crossed.

"Sorry, guys. We're just kidding," Patrick said.

"*I'm* not," Kole said.

Joshua looked at Reese, and she looked at him.

"Okay," Reese said. "I'll sit with Joshua."

Recess ended, and they went inside for lunch. Zoe sat with some of her other friends, and Reese sat at Joshua's table. But since there wasn't enough room for her to sit with them, the table got split up. Joshua and Reese ended up sitting with Patrick, Kole, and Carson. Aiden, Andrew, Daniel, and Caiden sat at a different table. After they were all sitting down, Kole looked around the table, then at Aiden's table, then back at his table and cried, "How'd I still get stuck sitting with the two love birds?"

Joshua gave Kole a side-eye, then he ignored him.

Reese hardly talked to Joshua, but she was still probably the loudest at the table. She wasn't talking to Joshua; she was mostly talking to Kole. Joshua didn't say anything until at the end of lunch, when Kole said, "You guys have been sitting together this whole time, and you haven't said one word to each other!"

"Yes, we did!" Reese said.

"*One* word, sure," Kole said.

"No. *Three*," Reese said.

"Still, why don't you guys ask each other about yourselves? You're going to dance with each other. You've got to know about each other. That's why I thought you should sit by yourselves," Kole said.

"No, that's not why," Patrick whispered.

"It's part of the reason," Kole said.

"Okay," Reese said. She looked at Joshua, and he looked at her. They stared at each other, neither one of them saying anything. Joshua feared that Kole was going to intervene again with something cleverly rude, but he didn't say anything. He just watched. *Everyone* just watched, which was probably what made it so hard for them to come up with something to say.

Finally, Joshua managed, "What's your favorite color?"

"*What?*" Reese laughed.

"Oh...is that a bad question?" Joshua asked.

Reese shrugged, then said, "My favorite color is purple. What's yours?"

"Red," Joshua answered.

"*I'm* going to ask a question," Patrick said. "Joshua,

do you like Tony's Taco Bar?"

"Yeah, it's fine," Joshua said. He looked at Reese. "Do you?"

"Yeah," Reese answered.

"You busy tonight?" Patrick asked.

"Me?" Joshua asked.

"No, not you, *Carson*," Patrick said, shooting a quick glance at Carson who looked just as annoyed as Joshua.

"Oh," Joshua said.

"Haha! Yes, you, of course!" Patrick exclaimed.

"I have cross country practice, and...I..." Joshua started to say.

"No, you're not busy," Patrick interrupted.

"Okay," Joshua said. "I guess I'm free after cross country practice."

"Okay, that works. What about you, Reese?" Patrick asked.

"What do you think? I'm never busy," Reese replied.

"You've got cross country practice, too," Joshua reminded her.

Reese rolled her eyes.

"What?" Joshua asked.

"You do cross country?" Patrick asked, looking at Reese.

"Yeah, but I don't like it. I'm not coming back next year," Reese said.

Joshua frowned.

"I don't blame you. Who wants to do a sport where all you ever do is run?" Patrick asked.

"Haha!" Reese laughed.

“That’s why I play baseball,” Patrick said.

“Yeah, same,” Kole chimed in.

“Now, Joshua, I understand why you *really* like cross country,” Patrick said, winking.

Joshua’s face turned red, but he didn’t say anything.

“So Joshua, are you going to ask Reese to go on a date with you to Tony’s Taco Bar tonight? You guys are obviously both free,” Kole said.

“Oh, uh,” Joshua looked at Reese who looked up at him. “Do you want to…go to Tony’s Taco Bar tonight?”

“Sure,” Reese replied. “But…I’m not going to practice tonight.”

“Oh, you’re not?” Joshua asked.

“No,” Reese said.

“Oh, okay. That’s fine. I can come to your house after *I* practice, and we can walk together,” Joshua said.

“Okay, cool,” Reese said.

“You’re going to make her walk?” Kole asked, scoldingly.

“What do you expect? I don’t have a car. I’m 13!” Joshua exclaimed.

“I’m just picking,” Kole said.

Chapter 4: Tony's Taco Bar

Joshua walked home after cross country practice to his mom in the kitchen making supper. Kendall, Leah, and Ava were coloring at the kitchen counter.

"Hey Joshua, how was your practice?" Mrs. Abare asked when he walked in the door.

"Good," Joshua answered. He paused, then he said, "Hey...would it be okay if I went to Tony's Taco Bar tonight? I...uh...sort of have a...date."

"A date?" Mrs. Abare asked. "With who?" Her eyebrows raised up almost to her hairline. At the same time, all three of his sisters' eyes were drawn to him as their mouths dropped open. Their brother, as awkward as he was, had found a *date*?

"Reese," Joshua answered.

"Oh, how nice," Mrs. Abare said. "Sure, that's fine. Do you need a ride?"

"Uh, no thank you. We can walk. It...it might be a little awkward...if you're there."

"Oh, I see."

"Sorry."

"No, no, it's okay. I agree with you. I'll give you my phone. That way if you change your mind, you can call us."

"Okay, thanks."

"What time are you meeting her?"

"Six."

"Okay."

"I'm going to go take a shower." Then, Joshua walked out of the kitchen.

After Joshua had gone up the stairs, Kendall and Leah started laughing with each other.

***

It was still light outside when Joshua left his house at quarter to six. He was wearing a plaid button-down shirt and blue jeans. When he arrived at Reese's house, she was sitting on her front porch. She smiled when he stepped onto the driveway, getting up and walking over to him. "Wow. I'm impressed," she said.

"What?" Joshua's face got hot.

Reese tugged on his sleeve. "You're not wearing a baggy t-shirt and sweatpants."

"Ha." Joshua's face turned even redder than it already had been.

"You ready?" Reese put her hands behind her back, sweetly.

"Yeah."

The two of them started walking. It would take 10 minutes to get there, but they talked the whole time. Not surprisingly, it was a lot easier to talk when Patrick, Kole, and the others weren't around. They arrived at Tony's Taco Bar and were seated. Joshua and Reese continued to talk, never running out of something to say.

As the night was nearly over, and they were almost back to Reese's house, Joshua asked, "Hey, are you doing anything Halloween?"

"I was going to go trick or treating with some of my friends."

"Oh, who?"

"Zoe...maybe. But...uh...Kole, and..." Reese started to reply.

"Kole?" Joshua crossed his arms. "Are you..."

"*Friends.*"

"Right. But...if you guys are..."

"We're just friends, Joshua." Reese paused for a second, then as if a light bulb had turned on in her head, she said, "You could come with us."

"Okay," Joshua replied.

They arrived at Reese's house, and Joshua walked her up to the door. Reese put her hand on the doorknob and looked back at Joshua to say, "Bye."

"Bye," Joshua replied.

Reese opened the door and went inside.

Chapter 5: Dance

The following Friday was the dance. Patrick and Kole were out of town, so they weren't going to be there.

Joshua walked to Reese's house to meet her beforehand. He was holding a bouquet of flowers, and on his way, he walked past some of his classmates who were heading toward the school in the opposite direction.

"Who are those flowers for?" one of them asked.

"I didn't know you had a girlfriend," another one of them said.

"If you're going to the dance, you're going the wrong way," another one said.

One of them stopped in front of him and said, "Who are you going with?"

Joshua stopped in his tracks, his body froze, and his heart beat fast. After a moment's pause, he answered, "Reese."

"Oh, really?" the last one said. "She doesn't really seem like your type. She's loud, and you're...just not."

Joshua shrugged, then they all continued walking. Joshua arrived at Reese's house. When he got there, she was not waiting for him on her porch like she was when they went to Tony's Taco Bar. Joshua went up to the door and knocked on it. He only had to wait for a second before the door was opened, but it wasn't opened by Reese. Standing there in leggings and a cozy white sweater was Reese's cousin, Wendy. She was Joshua and Reese's age. Last year, word got out that she had a crush on Joshua, but it was awkward because he liked her cousin. He hoped that maybe since she knew he was going to the dance with someone else, her feelings had gone away.

"Hey...Wendy," Joshua said, nervously. He looked down at the flowers in his hand.

"Hey," Wendy said. Her voice sounded like sadness. *Nope. She hadn't gotten over it.* "You must be looking for my *cousin*. She's upstairs, getting ready. You can step in if you'd like."

"Okay, thank you." Joshua stepped inside the house. He heard dogs barking in the other room. A cat walked in and rubbed her head on Joshua's leg. Joshua could see into the living room where Reese's younger brother, the only boy in her family, was playing with Wendy's younger brother, the only boy in *her* family (though, her family was half the size of Reese's family).

Wendy walked away from the door, leaving Joshua standing awkwardly and alone in a house that he had never been in before with people he had never met. *Where was Reese?*

Finally, a door opened upstairs, and Reese appeared. She was wearing a light purple dress, and she had her hair in a braid with a bow that matched her dress holding it together. She was standing with her sister who was only a year older and also going to the dance. Her sister was wearing a red dress with a rose barret in her hair that was artificially wavy. Her sister tapped her on the shoulder and then walked to a different room. Reese looked down the stairs at Joshua and smiled. “Hey, Joshua!” she exclaimed. “Sorry, I’m running a little late! I’ll be right there!”

“It’s okay,” Joshua said.

Reese went into another room, then she came back out. This time, she came down the stairs. When she got to the bottom, Joshua handed her the flowers.

“Thank you,” she said.

Joshua smiled. She brought him into the kitchen where she got a vase and put them in. While they were in there, Reese’s mom walked in. “Hi, you must be Joshua,” she said.

Joshua nodded.

“Nice to meet you,” she said.

“You too,” Joshua replied.

“Have fun tonight.”

“Thanks,” Joshua said.

Reese finished taking care of the flowers, then the two of them went out the door. Once they had gotten outside, Reese turned to Joshua and said, “Now I’m *really* impressed.”

Joshua let out a small laugh and asked, “Why’s that?”

“You’re wearing a *suit*. And to think that only just a week ago, all I had ever seen you in was a t-shirt and sweatpants,” Reese said.

Joshua smiled and said, “I dress up for special occasions.”

Reese smiled. “You look good. It brings out your blue eyes.”

"Thanks." Joshua's stomach did somersaults.

The two of them began walking and got to school just before the dance began. They went to the entrance where they had to pay. The dance cost only five dollars, but Joshua gave them 10 dollars. Then, they went into the gym. The lights were off beside the disco lights, music was blaring, and clusters of middle schoolers were scattered throughout the gym. Joshua and Reese went looking for their friends. They found Aiden, Andrew, Caiden, Carson, and Zoe all standing together. Carson's girlfriend, Camilla, was also standing with them.

They all greeted each other and began talking.

The first slow dance came on about half an hour into the dance. When it turned on, all of the couples got together and formed a line down the center of the gym. One person would stand on one side of an imaginary line, the other on the other side. No one danced but on the imaginary line. Friends of the couples who didn't have a partner themselves would stand next to their friends and make fun of them while taking pictures.

Joshua was nervous. He had been talking to Reese for a week now, and they had already gone out twice (one other time besides Tony's Taco Bar), but they had never done more than talk. They hadn't even held hands before. Joshua stood next to Carson. He looked at Reese, who stood on the opposite side of the imaginary line (next to Camilla), and put his hands above her waist. Reese put her hands on his shoulders. They slowly swayed back and forth, but they didn't look at each other. They looked just about everywhere except each other's faces. After about a minute, they both looked at each other at the same time, making eye contact. Then, they let their eyes lay locked together, until the end of the song. When it ended, they both backed away from each other and smiled. Then, they went back to their friends.

The rest of the slow dances after that were less awkward. They were able to look at each other, and they even had a conversation during one.

The dance got done at nine, and Joshua walked Reese home before going back to his house. By the time he got home, it was almost 10 o'clock. All of his sisters had gone to bed, and he wasn't up for very long either because he was extremely tired.

Chapter 6: Halloween

October was quickly coming to an end with Halloween. It was on a Wednesday. Reese had been sitting with Joshua's friends every day at lunch, but ever since the dance, she hardly talked to him. He tried to talk to her during advisory, but she always seemed like she was preoccupied with her work. When he asked her if she wanted to hang out after school one day, she told him she was busy. The next day, he found out she had gone out for dinner with Patrick, Kole, and one of Patrick and Kole's friends from their old school, named Maverick.

During advisory on Halloween morning, Joshua said to Reese, "Am I still going trick or treating with you?"

"If you want. I don't control what you do," Reese snapped back.

"What?" Joshua's face turned red.

"You're your own person. That's what I'm saying."

"Where are you meeting?"

"The south side of Airport Drive."

"Airport Drive? Where's..."

"We're going to Burlington."

"*Burlington?* You're not going *here*?" Joshua crossed his arms.

"No."

"Since when?"

"I don't know."

"I can't go to Burlington. Why aren't you going here?"

"Because Burlington has the better candy. That's what Kole said."

"Oh. I guess I'm not going, then."

"Sorry," Reese told him, but she didn't sound it. She went back to her work.

Joshua turned away, and he went back to his own work, sort of, but he wasn't really doing more than staring at it. Sam and Aaron were sitting next to him, and they looked from him to each other to Reese, looking surprised and confused.

***

When Joshua got home from school that evening, he went to the living room where his mom was putting the final touches on his sisters' costumes. He sat down on the couch next to her, looking at the floor.

"Hey, Joshua," Mrs. Abare said. "What's wrong?"

"Reese," he answered. "I mean, I guess I'm not going trick or treating with them anymore. They're going to *Burlington*."

"Oh."

"I don't get it. Why didn't she tell me that? She said I could go with her, but I feel like that's a pretty important detail to include. Ever since the dance, she's been acting like I don't exist."

"Did you talk to her?"

"No."

"Maybe you should. Find out what's going on."

"Yeah. But it's too late tonight. I already said I wasn't able to go, and even if I talked to her, I don't think I'd be changing their minds anyway. Not at this point."

"Sorry, Joshua."

"I guess I can take Kendall and her friends out now."

"No, don't worry about it. They're already going with Pearl's parents."

"But...my costume."

"You can stay with your grandparents and pass out candy with them if you'd like."

"Okay."

Joshua left the living room and went up to his room. He sat at his desk, which had a view of the road, where he could watch cars drive by and people walk along while he wrote in his notebook. It had been about half an hour when he saw two familiar faces appear in front of his house and walk up to his door.

It was Patrick and Kole.

Joshua got up from his seat and went to the door. He got there just as they were about to knock. He shouted to his mom who was there, then he stepped out to talk to them.

"Heard you're not going trick or treating with us," Kole said, immediately.

"I can't," Joshua said. "You're going to Burlington."

"We don't have to. I mean, yeah, that's where all the

good candy is, but you and Reese have to go together."

"I don't think Reese wants to go with me."

"Why not? Aren't you guys a thing now?"

"Not really. She won't even hardly talk to me."

"You went to the dance together."

"Doesn't matter. She doesn't want to talk to me."

"Did she say that?"

"No."

"Then you're just assuming."

"It *feels* that way."

"You're coming trick or treating with us."

"I already told my grandparents I would pass out candy with them."

"We're not going until eight. Pass out candy with them until then."

"*Eight?*" Joshua's eyes widened.

"What? Is that past your bedtime or something?"

"*No.*" Joshua crossed his arms. "I just...I don't think there will be any candy left by then."

"There will be. Trust me." Kole smiled.

"You're kind of new around here, so..." Joshua started to say.

"It will be okay."

"Okay."

"So, are you coming?"

"I guess...I mean...okay, yeah."

"Good. We will meet at the park around quarter of, and we will go in town, so meet us then."

"Okay."

"See ya," both Patrick and Kole said.

"Bye," Joshua said.

The two of them walked away, and Joshua went back inside. He told his mom, and she hesitantly told him it would be okay if he went with them. She said he had to be back by 10.

Joshua went to his grandparents' at six when his sisters headed out to go trick or treating. It was already nearly pitch black out. At 7:30, Joshua left his grandparents' house to meet everyone at the park. He was nervous that no one would be there, but when he got there, they were. Patrick, Kole, Reese, Aiden, and Maverick (Patrick and Kole's old friend) were all there, and they said that they were waiting for Andrew, Daniel, and Caiden. Carson had gone trick or treating earlier with Zoe and Camilla.

After Joshua greeted them all, he looked at Reese, who looked back at him but didn't say anything. Daniel got there shortly after, and when everyone was greeting him, Reese walked over to Joshua and said quietly, "Are we dating?"

"I don't know," Joshua said.

"Kole thinks we are," Reese said. "But I told him we're not."

Joshua looked over at Kole, then back at Reese, and he said, "If *you* told him we're not, then we're not."

"But...I feel like...you want to."

Joshua was quiet for a minute, then he said, "I don't know what I want. I like you, but I think you like someone else."

"I..." Reese said.

"It's okay, Reese. I understand."

Andrew and Caiden arrived at this time, not

allowing Reese to say anything more because Aiden said, "Okay, let's get going."

The entire night, Reese continually talked to Kole. It seemed like she only felt bad for a minute. But Kole got fed up with her constant conversation and said, "You're supposed to be talking to Joshua, not me!"

"Why?" Reese asked.

"Because he's your boyfriend!" Kole exclaimed.

"We're not dating! I told you that!" Reese snapped.

"Yes, you are," Kole said.

"Kole, stay out of it! We're not dating! We already talked about it," Joshua chimed in.

"Wow! Is that like...the first words you've spoken all night?" Kole asked.

"No," Joshua answered, crossing his arms.

"Then it's the second words, maybe. Did you guys really talk about it?" Kole asked.

"Yeah," Joshua replied. "We did."

"Oh," Kole said, letting out a sigh.

"So, anyway..." Reese said, and she started talking to Kole again about something totally unrelated to Joshua.

Reese was hardly the only one ignoring him for Kole. All of his friends loved Kole, especially Aiden. And it wasn't that Joshua *didn't* love Kole, it was just that...they weren't at the same level of thinking.

Chapter 7: The Beginning

Joshua and Reese never started dating. Joshua still tried to talk to her, and now, after Halloween, she would not completely ignore him, but she made it clear she preferred talking to Kole more than him even though Kole always said how he didn't like her behind her back. Joshua didn't try to get Reese to hang out anymore because he was busy many nights during the week with swim team now (which started the week of Halloween), so he thought why put in more effort than he could ever get out?

By the time Thanksgiving break was around the corner, Joshua was beyond tired and ready for the break. It was the Friday before, and Joshua was sitting at lunch with his new usual table group: Patrick, Kole, Reese, Aiden, Andrew, Daniel, and Caiden. No Carson. Carson sat with Camilla. When Joshua sat down, Kole was just getting over telling them the fact that his birthday was the coming Sunday.

"Are you doing anything for your birthday?" Reese asked him.

"Yes. I'm having 100 chicken nuggets."

"Wow. Are you doing anything with...you know...us?"

"What? With you? Why?"

"Because we're your *friends*."

"Oh. We'll see." Kole winked.

When Joshua got home from school that night, he told Mrs. Abare, who was in the kitchen making supper, about Kole's birthday being on Sunday.

"Oh yeah? Is he doing anything?" Mrs. Abare asked.

"I don't know," Joshua replied.

"You know that's the day of the chastity talk Mr. Landon wants you to go to for class, right?"

"Chastity talk? What's that?"

"It's about refraining from sex out of respect for yourself and future spouse as part of your religion."

"Oh. When is it?"

"One to three."

"Where?"

"The Parish Hall."

"Oh, that makes sense. Guess it doesn't matter if Kole's doing anything then because I won't be home."

"Is that okay?"

"Yeah.".

"Okay."

***

On Sunday, Joshua and Mrs. Abare set off to go to the chastity talk after lunch. Mr. Abare was staying home with Joshua's sisters because they, at least the two younger ones, were too young to sit through the talk.

Inside the Parish Hall at the chastity talk, there

were rows of chairs that formed a semi-circle. There were already teenagers from other churches around town and a few from Joshua's sitting in the chairs. He went and sat with the ones from his church. Mrs. Abare went to the back of the room where there were some parents. Over by the wall, there was a container of hot chocolate and a platter of cookies. Joshua was freezing, so he and three of his religious classmates, Anderson, Gabriel, and Jeremiah (the only ones who were in his grade), went and got some hot chocolate after being told to help themselves. Anderson and Jeremiah were on the cross country team with Joshua.

At one o'clock, the speaker, a petite woman with curly red hair and a teal dress that hung just above her knees over gray leggings, stepped forward to begin her talk.

She told her story, saying that she was adopted. She told them about her life before she was adopted, and it wasn't easy. She said she knew what it was like to skip meals. The family who adopted her was very nice, and they helped her pick herself up. When she was younger, she was broken, and although people may never be able to become fully whole, no matter their life and background, her adopted family helped her to become where she was then. Then, you know, she talked about the chastity portion of her talk. It was very nice.

It ended just before three. Joshua and his classmates helped themselves to cookies, then Joshua walked home with his mom. They got home just before four o'clock. When Joshua got home, he went up to his room, grabbed his notebook, then he went outside and began writing in it. He was writing a story. He was still sitting out there writing, when he looked up and saw Kole walking by. The sun had begun to set, and the air was now gray.

Joshua didn't say anything. He just watched. But when Kole got to his driveway, he looked up and saw Joshua.

"Hey, Joshua!" Kole exclaimed.

"Hey."

Kole started walking up the driveway, so Joshua put down his notebook and pen, got up, and started walking toward Kole. They met about halfway down the driveway.

"What's up?" Kole asked.

"Not much," Joshua said. "Happy birthday."

"Thanks." Kole paused, then he said, "What are you doing?"

"Writing."

"That sounds boring."

"No." Joshua crossed his arms, and his eyebrows pointed toward his nose.

"Whatever. I came by earlier, and you weren't home. Where have you been?"

"I was at a chastity talk."

"A *chastity* talk?" Kole raised his eyebrows in surprise.

"Yeah."

"Isn't that about *sex*?"

"No...I mean...yeah, but...it's about religion, too."

"Oh, you go to church?"

Joshua nodded.

"I'm not really into the whole *church idea*," Kole

said.

"Oh, you're not?"

"It's just a bad world."

"What does that have to do with church? Church is good." Joshua crossed his arms.

"But what's the point? People go to church, but there's still evil in the world. Why's that, Joshua?"

"Because..." Joshua paused, then he continued, "When God created us, he created us to be people, not robots. He gave us a choice, and some people choose evil because there are many temptations around us. Like with Adam and Eve."

"I'm just not buying it."

"Why not?"

"I don't know."

"That's not a very good reason."

"It's just that Christians are kind of hypocritical."

"It's not about the people; it's about God," Joshua said. With Kole's comment, it was like something had been flipped inside Joshua's head. His emotions were bubbling inside. It was like a fire had been lit, and every word that was about to be spoken would be like a log thrown into that fire. Everything that Kole had ever said to him, especially in regards to him and Reese, or that he was crazy or boring or weird, was all adding logs.

"Okay," Kole said.

"What do you want?" Joshua asked.

"I just wanted to say hey."

"Why? You don't even like me!"

"True. You're *too* good. I'm just not into that whole thing."

"What whole thing?"

"Being *good*. And you know, religion."

"Why?" Joshua asked.

"Because I'm not *gullible*," Kole replied.

"I'm *not* gullible!" Joshua snapped, and he pushed Kole.

Kole pushed him back, and Joshua wasn't expecting it, so he fell to the ground. Kole laughed and said, "Or maybe you're *not* the good one." Joshua climbed back up to his feet, realizing he had made a huge mistake. Kole was a good five inches taller than him. Kole pushed him again and said, "Ha, just kidding." Joshua pushed back, and Kole pushed him again. Joshua pushed Kole again, to the ground this time, and Joshua got on top of him, pinning him to the ground.

"Get off of me. I thought you were a good Christian," Kole said.

Joshua suddenly felt guilty and rolled off, staring at Kole, startled again by what he did, but only for a split second because it was a trap. Kole pushed Joshua to the ground as he had done to him a second ago, pinning him down by holding his shirt collar, and Kole punched Joshua across the face. His nose immediately started bleeding.

"Haha. Wow. You unimpress me," Kole said.

Joshua felt like a fool even more now, but he knew he wasn't gullible. He grabbed Kole's arms and pulled them off of him. He pushed him to the ground and pulled himself out from under him. When he was out, he wasn't on top of Kole, but he got up off the ground and kicked Kole in the ribs. Kole cringed.

Kole got up and pushed Joshua again. He didn't fall

to the ground. Joshua punched Kole in the lip. It split, and a drop of blood formed on it.

Kole punched Joshua back in the eye. Joshua punched Kole in the face again, and Kole retaliated. Joshua's face throbbed, and he could feel his eye swelling up, making it hard to see. He pushed Kole this time rather than punching him. Kole fell to the ground, for he was also in pain. Joshua kicked him while he was on the ground, then he stopped because Kole wasn't getting up. Kole was laying there for about 15 seconds before he started to pick himself back up. He stood up and pushed Joshua, but it was weak, and Joshua barely moved. Joshua could tell Kole was losing it, but Kole pushed him a second time in a row, so Joshua pushed him again, and he fell again. This time, Kole bounced right back up and pushed Joshua. It was still weak, but it was stronger than last time. Joshua pushed him back again, but he didn't fall. Kole charged at Joshua, and Joshua dodged it, causing Kole to nearly fall to the ground. He caught himself. Joshua stared at Kole as he stumbled on his feet. It was as if Kole had found his second wind.

The two of them were back into a punching fit, both going for each other's faces, until Kole decided to make a punch right below Joshua's chest, knocking the wind out of him. Joshua couldn't breathe, and he fell to the ground. Kole started kicking him while he was down. Joshua gasped for air, but he couldn't find it when Kole was kicking him.

Somehow, Joshua managed to move just enough out of Kole's range, and he caught his breath a little. He grabbed Kole's foot, causing him to fall. Joshua climbed off his knees, still struggling to breathe a little, but Kole also got up. Joshua pushed Kole with all the strength he had left, and immediately after, someone shouted, "HEY!"

But the boys ignored the shouting. Joshua didn't have enough energy or breath to focus on more than one thing.

"BREAK IT UP! BREAK IT UP!"

The two boys continued punching each other. Joshua's fist now had Kole's blood on it, and the same for Kole's fist and Joshua's blood.

Patrick, Maverick, Aiden, and *Reese* were all running over to the two boys. When they got over, they all grabbed onto Kole's arms, stopping him from punching Joshua. Kole fell limp in their arms, and Joshua fell to the ground. He looked up at the five of them. Kole had his eyes closed, blood all over his face, and the other four boys stood holding him, glaring back at Joshua. He frowned back at them. Without saying anything, Patrick, Maverick, Aiden, and *Reese* all started to walk Kole away. Kole gained some power in his legs, but he still looked pretty beat. Joshua didn't feel so great himself, either. He stayed there on the ground for a moment, watching the boys and Reese slowly walk Kole away.

Chapter 8: Mistake

Joshua looked back at his house, and he saw Ava walking over to the living room window. His face was swollen and covered in blood, so he quickly looked away, not wanting to scare her. But it was too late, she already saw. He could hear her shouting.

The front door opened, and Mr. and Mrs. Abare came out. Kendall, Leah, and Ava followed.

Mr. and Mrs. Abare went over to Joshua, asking him some questions, like *what happened*, but he didn't answer because he was too overwhelmed, embarrassed, and in pain. They grabbed his arms and helped him stand, walking him toward the door, letting him rest his arms over their shoulders.

Joshua looked back towards the road as they carried him. Patrick, Kole, Maverick, Aiden, and *Reese* were still within sight. They all looked back and glared at him, then they continued walking, not looking back again.

Joshua's sisters closed the door as his parents walked him to the bathroom. He cringed in pain as he walked. During the fight, he had too much adrenaline to let the pain hinder him (except, of course, when he got the wind knocked out of him). Mrs. Abare pulled a washcloth out of the cupboard, wet it, and handed it to Joshua.

But Joshua didn't do anything with it except simply hold it in his hand. A tear formed in his eye, and he cried out, "I'm sorry."

"Sorry for what?" Mrs. Abare asked.

"What are you talking about?" Mr. Abare asked.

"It's my fault," Joshua cried. He paused, then he continued, "I started it! I pushed first!"

"You did?" Mrs. Abare asked, surprised.

"Yes," Joshua cried. He expected his parents to walk out, maybe even hit him themselves, even though they never had done that before (but he had never done *this* before). His eyes watered some more, and he tried to get rid of the tears because he didn't want to cry in front of them.

"Why?" Mrs. Abare asked, her voice soft.

"Because I was mad," Joshua said, with a solid, level tone, not raising it or lowering it. It was like a simple explanation.

"What were you mad about?" Mrs. Abare asked.

"He said he wasn't good or religious because he wasn't gullible, and...I had just got done telling him that I was at a chastity talk and go to church, so I felt like he was calling me gullible, and that made me mad. And...also, he just is always belittling me, so I guess all that just came out right then. I know it was wrong, and I'm sorry!" Joshua said, crying at the end.

"Oh," Mrs. Abare said.

"Sounds like Kole's not very nice. He deserved to get beaten," Mr. Abare said.

Mrs. Abare gave her husband a quick look, then looked back at Joshua and said, "I don't know about that, but I'm glad you are defending your religion."

"But I'm not representing it well by starting a fight," Joshua cried.

"What would you do if someone was teasing, say, Ava?" Mrs. Abare asked.

"What if they made her cry?" Mr. Abare asked.

Joshua looked over at Ava who looked terrified. All of his sisters were standing in the doorway of the bathroom.

"Would you push them because they were upsetting her?" Mrs. Abare asked.

"I don't know," Joshua said.

"You might. And if you did, would you feel guilty for it? They were insulting your sister," Mrs. Abare said.

"They were insulting my sister, but I shouldn't have pushed them," Joshua said.

"You're right, violence isn't an answer, but in that moment, you're so mad at them for insulting your sister, don't you think you would feel okay about it because they were *bullying* your sister?" Mrs. Abare asked.

"Maybe," Joshua said.

"What if they were *hurting* her? Then don't you think you would push them?" Mr. Abare asked, adding in.

"Um...yeah, I guess I would," Joshua said.

"See, this is the same thing," Mrs. Abare said.

"So...you *want* me to start fights?" Joshua asked.

"No, no! Not at all! But I'm just saying, he *was* insulting your religion, wasn't he?" Mrs. Abare asked.

"Yeah," Joshua said.

"And that's not right," Mrs. Abare said.

"Yeah, you're right," Joshua said. "But...two wrongs

don't make a right."

"No, they don't," Mrs. Abare said. "But I'm not mad at you just because you started it. It was in defense of your religion, and that's important. What can I do after the fact?"

"But what about God?" Joshua asked.

"I can't speak for God, but I don't think He would judge you too harshly. You *were* defending *Him*," Mrs. Abare said.

"Yeah, I guess so," Joshua said. He was quiet for a second, then he said, "I'm so glad it's Thanksgiving break. I don't want to face those guys ever again."

"I see that," Mrs. Abare said.

Joshua looked at his face in the mirror. It looked pitiful. He couldn't believe it. He had never seen himself that way. His family stepped out of the bathroom and let him clean himself up in private.

But, even after he was done cleaning his face, it still looked pretty bad. Joshua went out to the living room and laid on the couch. His body ached. While he was laying there, he heard the front door open and close, but he wasn't facing it, so he couldn't see why or for who. After a few seconds, he heard it open and close again, then about a minute later, his sisters came and dropped his notebook and pen on the coffee table in front of him. Leah said, "Some boys came by the house and were looking through this. Daddy made them go away. He said they were trespassing. They tried to take it, but he made them give it back, and they actually listened. I think they were scared because you beat someone up, and they thought Daddy might too. So, here it is, so that way no one tries to take it again."

"Thanks," Joshua said.

There was a small pause, and Leah and Ava started to walk away, but Kendall remained standing in the same spot, staring at the floor beneath Joshua. After a moment more, she asked, "What is it like?"

"What?" Joshua asked.

"To be in a fight," Kendall clarified.

"*Awful.* You hurt, but you can't stop because if you do, you will hurt 10 times more than if you were to keep going. You can't stop because then the other person wins, and you get your butt kicked *worse.*"

"Did *you* win?"

"We didn't finish. Some of our friends...well, Kole's friends...came and pulled Kole away."

"Who?"

"Patrick, of course, because that's Kole's uncle. And Aiden..."

"I thought Aiden was *your* friend."

"He was *both* of our friends. At least...that's what I *thought.* I guess not, though"

"But you've known Aiden for a long time."

"Yeah, but that doesn't matter, I guess. When the rest of them are going to defend Kole, Aiden's going to stick with them. And I haven't been that close with Aiden lately."

"The *rest* of them? Who else was there?"

"This boy named Maverick. He went to Patrick and Kole's old school. I never expected him to take my side. I met him on Halloween, but we didn't talk at all."

"Was there anyone else?"

"Yes, one other person," Joshua said, his voice trailing off, as he looked at the ground.

"Who?"

Joshua sighed, then answered, "Reese."

"Reese? Your crush? The person you went to the dance with?"

"Yeah," Joshua replied, his voice cracking.

"And she took *Kole's* side?"

Joshua nodded.

"What? Did they all take Kole's side because you pushed first?"

"No. They weren't there when we started fighting, so they didn't see that I pushed first. They don't know what it was about, either. Maybe if they knew, then maybe at least Reese and Aiden might take my side. They both go to church."

"I'm sorry, Joshua."

Joshua shrugged, but then he cringed in pain. After a pause, he continued, "Worst part—probably the main reason they took Kole's side without knowing the full story—today is Kole's birthday. In the moment that I pushed him, I completely forgot. It doesn't matter though because I probably would have pushed him even if I had remembered. I was mad. He insulted my religion."

Chapter 9: Trick

Thanksgiving came, then it went. In between the fight and then, Joshua didn't speak to or see any of his friends, nor Reese. He stayed at home either writing, playing the saxophone, or trying to learn the cornet (his mom had just found it about a month ago!). He hadn't gone on his daily run since the incident in fear that he would meet one of the boys or Reese while he was out. It was the day after Thanksgiving, and he was sitting in his room, jamming on his saxophone, his bruised body still suffering from the fight, when he heard a knock on his door. Well, at first, he didn't hear it, but then he heard pounding. He wanted to finish the song he was on because he didn't like to be interrupted in the middle, but he knew he couldn't ignore whoever was at the door. He stopped playing, *mid-song*, and said, "What?"

"There's someone at the door for you."

It was Kendall.

"Okay, I'll be right there," Joshua said. He had been so busy playing he didn't even notice someone came. Usually, he could see them enter the driveway from his bedroom window. At this point, they were already on the porch, so he couldn't see them anymore.

When Joshua opened the door, Kendall was still

standing there, so he asked her, "Who's here?"

"Aiden," she answered.

"Oh," Joshua said, frowning. Still, he went down the stairs and into the kitchen where Aiden was in fact standing (the front door was in the kitchen).

Joshua and Aiden greeted each other.

"Hey," Aiden said a second time, but this time softly. "I just wanted to say that I'm sorry I took Kole's side over yours. You were my friend first, and I should have taken your side."

"Oh," Joshua said. He wasn't sure what he should say. He could've said it was okay, but it wasn't. He could have said that it wasn't okay, and he could explain how he really felt, but he didn't think that was the route he wanted to take either. Instead, he waited to see if Aiden said anything more.

He did.

"I was wondering if...you wanted to go to Tony's Taco Bar," Aiden continued.

"I don't know."

"I understand that you're mad, but I'm sorry."

"I know you say you are, but I just don't know..."

"Please, Joshua."

Joshua sighed. "Fine."

So they went.

The two boys didn't talk much on the way. Joshua would have thought something was up if it weren't for the fact that he (Joshua) was always quiet and always struggled with conversation. They got to the taco bar and went inside.

As they were stepping in the door, Joshua asked,

"Should we get a table?"

"Um...yeah...sure," Aiden said. But he seemed to be looking around for something other than an empty table. His hands were fidgeting with each other, and he was tapping his foot.

Joshua looked around, and suddenly a horrible feeling was in his stomach. "Aiden? Is something wrong?" Joshua's voice trembled.

But Aiden didn't have to answer for him to see what was wrong because he saw it. Aiden was staring at it.

One of the tables near the front of the place sat Reese and Maverick. They both had a taco in front of them, and they looked really happy. Joshua felt trapped, and he froze. So Reese wasn't lying when she said she didn't like Kole, but she did like someone who wasn't Joshua. *She liked Maverick?*

But then, Kole stood up nearly right in front of Joshua. He had been sitting at a table right next to the door, but because it was a booth, and he had his back facing Joshua, he hadn't realized Kole was there until he stood up. Suddenly, Joshua realized that Reese *didn't* like Maverick. It was a...*trick.*

Sitting beside where Kole had been sitting was Patrick.

Joshua quickly knew that Reese and Maverick weren't his worst problem (not because Patrick was sitting there but because of everyone). Joshua looked at Aiden who honestly looked just as surprised as he did, but yet, Joshua cried out loud to him, "I thought I could trust you! You said you were sorry!"

"I *am* sorry, Joshua! I didn't know Reese was going

to be here! I *really* am sorry," Aiden said.

"Reese? What about Kole? Did you know *he* was going to be here?" Joshua asked.

Aiden looked at the ground and paused for a moment, then he said, "Yes."

"You didn't tell me Kole was going to be here!" Joshua snapped.

"Because he told me you wouldn't come if you knew," Aiden said.

"Yeah, I wouldn't have," Joshua said. He turned around and went out the door. He started to walk away, but Kole followed him out. Patrick and Aiden came out after them. Maverick and Reese didn't seem to notice that the commotion had begun.

Kole ran up to Joshua and grabbed the back of his shirt to stop him. Joshua turned around and glared at Kole, but he just stood there, not doing anything else.

"Look, Joshua. You pushed first. If you didn't want trouble, you shouldn't have done that," Kole said.

Kole still had his hand on Joshua's shirt. Joshua looked towards the door and saw that Reese and Maverick had now gotten the memo and were also standing outside. Neither of them looked at all disturbed, though Patrick and Aiden did look like they were a bit upset. Joshua looked back at Kole.

"I'm sorry," Joshua said. "I didn't want to start a fight, but you were insulting my religion, and I was mad."

"I'm entitled to my own opinion, aren't I?" Kole asked.

Maverick butted in and said, "Maybe you shouldn't get so defensive, Joshua. Did you see me and Reese?"

Those were the first words that Maverick had ever said to Joshua.

Joshua looked at Maverick, who smirked. Then he looked at Reese, who now had a little bit of a smile on her face.

"It's clear that God loves me more than you because I'm better looking than you. He made you ugly, but He made me handsome. Reese chose me, not you because God made it that way. Because He loves me more," Maverick said.

"God didn't make it that way. Kole made it that way because he's mad at me," Joshua said. "God doesn't love you more, and He doesn't love me more, either."

"He doesn't love you more because you're ugly. You're a good Christian, but you start fights and are ugly. That's why He loves us the same, not you more," Maverick said.

"No, that's not true. God loves everyone the same because we all come from the same place, breathe the same air, and live under the same sun," Joshua said.

"We are *not* the same. *I* am *better* than *you*," Maverick said. "You think this is Kole's doing? Let's ask Reese." Maverick looked at Reese who hadn't said anything yet, and he asked her, "Who do you choose? Me...or Joshua?"

"You," Reese said, avoiding looking at Joshua.

Maverick looked back at Joshua and said, "See? She chose me."

It felt like Joshua had just got punched in the stomach. He looked at Reese, and then she finally looked at him, but she still didn't say anything to him.

"I don't get why you're so upset," Kole said. "You guys aren't dating. Remember? You guys talked about it. Remember?"

"It's not just about that," Joshua said.

"Then what *is* it about?" Kole asked.

"You don't even like her at all, yet..." Joshua looked at Reese who suddenly didn't look so pleased anymore. "...she takes your side."

"Maybe that's a sign," Maverick said. "That we're better than you."

"A sign? *Or a test?*" Joshua asked.

"What?" Maverick asked.

"You are *not* better than me," Joshua said. He was looking at Maverick, but out of the corner of his eyes, he could see Reese. She stood with her arms cradled in each other, and she was looking at the ground out of the corner of her eye.

Joshua's focus was fixed back on Maverick, who stepped close to him and pushed him. Joshua didn't fall, but that was probably because he was pushed right into Kole. Kole immediately grabbed him and put him into a headlock. Joshua tried to break free but couldn't.

Maverick punched Joshua in the face. It hurt 10 times as bad as the first time he had been punched in the face because he was still sore from the fight with Kole.

Kole took his other fist, the one that wasn't connected to the arm which held Joshua in a headlock, and he punched Joshua in the stomach. He punched hard, and Joshua lost his wind again, spit instinctively falling out of his mouth.

Patrick, Reese, and Aiden watched, feeling stunned,

scared, surprised, and *impressed.*

After more punches to his stomach and face, he couldn't feel anything anymore. He went limp in Kole's arms, and suddenly, Kole let go. Joshua fell to the ground, and he stayed there for a minute.

No one moved. They watched Joshua on the ground, and he could feel their eyes staring at him. He couldn't bear them all seeing him like that, so he used whatever strength he could gather together and picked himself up. He stood on his feet and looked at Kole, then at Maverick. Reese was now standing next to Maverick. It felt like that night at his house, when all of Joshua's friends stood in opposition to him. But now, it was just Maverick and Reese standing in front of him.

Maverick started laughing and said, "Look at you. You're a mess. See? God *does* love me more."

That was it. No more holding back.

"Don't say that!" Joshua shouted. He said it sternly, not cowardly, not whiny.

Kole came from behind and pushed Joshua who let out a small cry that went, "Oof!" He turned around and punched Kole in the face, then he punched Maverick and started running. His stomach hurt—and really his whole body—as he ran. He could feel Kole's fist imprinted on his stomach...and face. He could feel blood dripping from his nose and down his chin. He could hardly see as his eyes were swollen again, *and* it was getting dark. But still, he ran. He could hear the others running after him, which made his need to go fast even more crucial. He was sick of the pain and the insults and the guilt that made it so hard to defend himself. He kept running, as fast as he could, despite all of the suffering. It was like the cross country state meet all over again. He was in so much pain, but he wanted to do well. But this penalty for running slow was far worse than that of the state meet.

Joshua, since he did cross country, was able to outrun all of the others. Not even Reese and Aiden, who also did cross country, caught up to him, but he wasn't sure if the two of them followed him or not. Even when he knew that he had lost the others, he kept running as fast as he could. He didn't stop until he was on his front porch opening the door.

The second he entered his house and closed the door behind him, he dropped to the floor, breathing heavily. His whole family was sitting in the dining room, eating supper, and they all jumped from their seats when they saw him. Mr. and Mrs. Abare got to him first, and they lifted him up to see his face. Fresh blood. Fresh bruises. Fresh cuts in his skin, on his lips. Salty tears, which he couldn't prevent, started to run down his cheeks and burned as they ran across the cuts.

"What happened?" Mr. Abare cried.

"It was a trick. It was just a stupid trick!" Joshua cried, remembering when Aiden stood in his kitchen and told him he was sorry. He interrupted his playing *mid-song* for that.

Kendall, Leah, and Ava stood behind their parents looking at Joshua. He cried for a moment more, then he decided he didn't want his family to continue looking at him like this, so he went upstairs to his room. His saxophone was still lying on his bed where he left it, and the music stand still sat in front of his chair with his music book open to the page he had been playing. He gently moved his saxophone, then he plopped onto his bed. He felt the pain in his stomach and face, just laying there.

After a few minutes, his sisters brought him some ice. He thanked them, then he told them that they could go finish eating. He could explain later but not right now.

Chapter 10: Tree Lighting

There was an annual tree-lighting festival the weekend after Thanksgiving on Joshua's street. It was less than a five-minute event, but it attracted many people throughout the town. Usually, Joshua would peek out his window when it happened. Sometimes, his family would go sit on their front porch and watch, but it was pretty cold that year, so they didn't.

Joshua was sitting by his living room window with his sisters as people outside were getting ready for the tree lighting. They had turned off the living room light so that they could see clearly outside. Right now, the streets were dark, as the lights hadn't been lit yet. They could see figures of people as they positioned themselves so they could see.

It was five minutes until dusk, and that's when the trees would be lit. As the time got closer and closer, Joshua saw a group of people his own age walk to the back of the crowd right in front of his driveway. There were two of them who stepped into his driveway and stood at the end with their backs to the Abares' house. The rest of the group stood on the sidewalk with the rest of the crowd.

The two who stepped into the Abares' driveway were holding hands, and Joshua recognized them immediately. He stood up and backed away from the window.

"What's the matter?" Kendall asked.

All three girls turned around to look at Joshua. As they had their backs to the window, the lights turned on, and suddenly, the event was over. The girls all turned back around, seeing the reflection in Joshua's eyes, before he could respond.

"Aw, we missed it!" Ava cried.

"Aw," Leah said.

"Oops," Kendall said, and she looked back at Joshua who was still staring out the window. "What's the matter?" she asked.

Joshua still didn't respond. He was still staring. He had a frown on his face, and his arms were crossed. Kendall looked back out the window, and she saw what Joshua was staring at. At the end of the driveway stood Maverick and Reese, their hands held together. They currently still had their backs to the Abares' house, but as the crowd started to leave, the two of them looked back and smiled.

The Abares' living room was still dark, but they could see Joshua's outline staring at them. They giggled and turned around, then the whole group walked away, disappearing into the crowd. After they had gone, Joshua walked away.

"Joshua!" Kendall cried.

Joshua stopped. He was standing at the bottom of the stairs, about to go up.

"Joshua," Kendall said again. "They're just trying to make you mad."

"I know," Joshua replied. "But...that doesn't make it any better. In fact, that makes it feel worse."

"I know."

"I just...can't believe it. I can't believe *Reese*."

"I can't either. It seems like she's not very nice."

"Seems so. Guess I was wrong about liking her."

"That's too bad, Joshua."

"Yeah, it is."

Then, Joshua turned around and walked up the stairs. He went into his room, closed the door, and plopped onto his bed. He buried his head in his arms and started to cry.

Chapter 11: Back to School

Going back to school was miserable. That morning, Joshua stood in front of the mirror for a solid 10 minutes trying to convince himself that the bruises on his face weren't that bad and that they weren't that noticeable. But he just couldn't do it. They were still awfully bad and noticeable. The original ones, from the first incident, were fairly faded, but they were still noticeable, so he knew that Kole would also be walking into that school with a full presentation of their fight.

Joshua had advisory first, which was with Reese. He dreaded that, but it wasn't as bad as the rest of his day. He had Patrick in all of his classes, and although Patrick wasn't the one he had the fight with, he was Kole's uncle and was undoubtedly going to take Kole's side, or so Joshua believed.

When Joshua got to advisory, Reese was already in there, and so were Sam and Aaron. Reese was still sitting at the same table that she usually sat at, which was the one with Joshua, Sam, and Aaron. She had begun sitting with them after Joshua asked her to the dance. Usually, Reese sat right next to Joshua, and she was still in that same seat that morning when Joshua walked in. He didn't want to sit next to her, so he sat on the opposite side of the table.

Usually, he sat next to Sam, but that morning, he sat next to Aaron.

Initially, when Joshua sat down, Reese didn't say anything.

Sam and Aaron were both already there as well. He hadn't seen them since before the fight, nor had he talked to them much afterward. He didn't tell them about it ever because it was simply just embarrassing. Sam and Aaron weren't friends with the others. Patrick and Sam talked sometimes, but only because they were in all the same classes together *with Joshua.*

Sam and Aaron's eyes were immediately drawn to Joshua's face when he sat down, even though he tried not to attract attention. He didn't want to talk about all that had happened, especially with Reese's ears in the room. But, what could he do? His face was like a screaming witness to the whole incident.

He looked down, not looking up, hoping that his friends wouldn't comment on anything, but Sam asked, "Hey Joshua. What's up? Is there something you'd like to tell us about?" And Joshua knew that he was hinting at his bruises.

"Not really," Joshua replied, honestly.

"Okay," Sam said. "If there is anything...I'll listen."

"Me too," Aaron added.

"Okay," Joshua said, and he decided he should just give in before their hints got more persistent. "I got into a fight."

"Really?" Sam asked, sounding both surprised and concerned.

"Yeah," Joshua answered, looking at the table in

front of him.

"When?" Sam asked.

"Over break."

"Obviously," Sam thought to himself, but he could tell Joshua was distraught, so he simply just asked, "But what day?"

"Sunday."

"With who?" Aaron asked.

Joshua shot a quick glance at Reese, who appeared to not be paying attention, then he looked back at his friends and answered, "Kole."

"About what?" Aaron asked.

"Was it..." Sam said quietly, jerking his head toward Reese.

Joshua shook his head.

"Then what?" Sam asked.

"Religion," Joshua said. "But I don't really want to talk about it."

"Okay," Sam and Aaron both said.

Their teacher, Mr. Hendrick, came over. When he saw Joshua's face, he looked like he wanted to say something, but he politely didn't. He figured it wasn't any of his business, and Joshua looked like he didn't want to talk about it. Instead, Mr. Hendrick gave them all instructions on what to work on. Joshua, Sam, and Aaron did their usual: worked on the weekly calendar. Reese did whatever she usually did; Joshua wasn't really sure what that was.

After Mr. Hendrick walked away, Reese finally looked up from behind her laptop, and she looked right at Joshua. He felt her eyes, so he looked up. She motioned to him with her hand to come over to her. He sighed but did as she gestured.

Joshua sat down next to her, on the side opposite of where he usually did pre-fight so that they were private from Sam and Aaron.

"Are you mad at me?" Reese asked, quietly.

"I don't know," Joshua answered honestly, at the same voice level.

"Why would you be?" Reese crinkled her nose.

"Isn't it obvious? Kole and Maverick are using you to make me mad, yet you still are choosing them over me. What have I ever done to you?"

"Nothing, but neither have they."

"But they aren't very nice, and you're still taking their side *over* mine. Remember what they did at Tony's Taco Bar?"

"You were the first to push."

"No, I wasn't."

"They said you were."

"You were there. I didn't push first!"

"No! At the first fight you pushed first," Reese said. Joshua frowned as Reese continued: "They were never going to inflict violence on you, but then you pushed Kole, so now, war is on."

"No! It's not a war! They were *insulting my religion*, and I got upset!" Joshua cried.

"Don't wars usually start with getting upset?" Reese asked.

"Not after one incident! That would be crazy! I might have made a mistake by pushing Kole, but they shouldn't have dragged me to that taco place just to tease me! I can't believe they used Aiden to trick me, and that he followed through. And that...you *still* chose them."

"To be fair, I chose Maverick *before* they beat you up."

"But they were still insulting me because of my religion. I thought you were religious. In fact, don't you go to my grandparents' church? I'm pretty sure they told me they saw you there."

Reese stared at him, her mouth open slightly, but she didn't say anything.

Joshua sighed, frustrated, then he went back to his new seat.

"Augh," Reese said, but she went back to her work, not trying to call Joshua back.

Advisory ended shortly after their heated conversation. Joshua shut down his laptop the second it ended. He left the classroom as quickly as he could because he didn't want to have to walk back with Reese. He went to band. Aiden was in that class, but they played different instruments, so they didn't sit together, and they never had the chance to talk. Joshua was quick in and out before and after rehearsal. After that, he had math. Aiden was going to be there again, and so was Patrick.

When Joshua got there, Patrick was already there, and Daniel was sitting with him, but Joshua sat at a different table than them, even though before break he would sit with them. He was sitting at Sam's usual table, which had one extra seat. But when Sam's friends got there, they saw Joshua sitting at their table, and they sat at a different table because they didn't realize he was trying to sit with them. That left the table open, and Daniel looked over at him and saw him alone. He came over, and although Joshua wasn't mad at Daniel in any way, he feared that Patrick would follow, and sure enough, he did.

Daniel sat down next to Joshua, and Patrick sat across from Joshua, in perfect opposition. Joshua let out a sigh.

"Why didn't you sit with us?" Daniel asked.

Joshua looked at Daniel, then at Patrick.

"I'm not mad at you," Patrick said. "I've told Daniel about the fight, and he's not mad at you, either. He's just going to stay out of it. And as for me, it's not like I've never gotten into a fight with Kole before."

"Yeah," Daniel agreed.

"How do I know you're not trying to trick me like Aiden did?" Joshua asked.

"Aiden wasn't trying to trick you. Kole tricked him, too," Patrick explained.

"Aiden should have known it was a trick when Kole said not to tell me that he'd be there. And...*you* were there," Joshua said, looking at Patrick.

"Listen, Joshua. Why are you trying to make more enemies? You already have Kole, you don't need me as one, too," Patrick said.

"I'm not trying to make you into an enemy. I just don't feel like getting beat up again," Joshua said.

"I can understand that," Patrick admitted.

"I heard you pushed first." A voice was coming from behind Joshua. He turned around and saw a girl named Violet. She was standing with her friend, Mandy.

"Yeah, that's what Kole said," Mandy said.

"Is it true?" Violet asked.

Joshua sighed, but he answered, "Yes."

"Wow, I'm surprised. I didn't expect that from you. You're kind of quiet, and I never thought you meant any harm," Violet said.

"I didn't! I don't!" Joshua pleaded. "I just...he was..."

"It doesn't matter," Violet said. "You still pushed him first. That makes you fair game."

Joshua opened his mouth to say something, but he was at a loss of words. He turned around and faced the middle of the table. Patrick had a neutral face, showing no emotion. Daniel had a frown.

Sam finally walked into the classroom and saw that Joshua was sitting with Patrick (specifically), so he went over to the table group.

"Hey," Sam said.

"Hey," Joshua said back.

Looking directly at Joshua, Sam said, "Is everything okay here?"

"Yes, thank you," Joshua said.

"Okay," Sam said, then he went and sat with his usual friends.

Aiden walked in shortly after, and he walked over to Joshua, Patrick, and Daniel's table. He stood behind the empty seat and said, "Can I sit here?"

"Yes," Patrick said, quickly.

Aiden looked at Joshua, who didn't say anything, so Aiden sat down, moving slowly and tentatively.

Chapter 12: Lunch

When Joshua got to the cafeteria, he sat down at an empty table. Usually, he looked around for his friends to see where they were. Today, he didn't care. He didn't want to sit with them because he knew Kole would be there. He sat down and began to eat his lunch. He couldn't stand being alone, but with the current circumstances, he felt like being alone was better than being with what he was up against. He tried to persuade himself with the fact that he wouldn't have to listen to anyone complain about the smell of his hard-boiled egg.

Until he did. Well, he didn't have to listen to complaints, but he wasn't left alone.

Caiden, who hadn't been part of the fight, sat down at the table with Joshua. Joshua wasn't mad at him, not for this anyway, but he knew that the others would surely follow. Joshua wanted to get up and move, but he thought Caiden would take it personally.

Soon, they were joined by the whole crew, Kole and Reese included. In fact, Kole got a seat right next to Joshua. But Joshua couldn't bear that seating arrangement, so he put all of his containers in his lunch box and started to move, until Kole grabbed his arm.

"No Joshua, stay here. I have some questions for

you," Kole said. "You know, since you're a know-it-all."

"I don't have any answers," Joshua said. "Because, you know, I'm *not* a know-it-all."

But Kole didn't let go of his arm. In fact, he held on tighter. He tried to tug it away, but Kole tugged back. "Sit down," Kole said.

"No," Joshua said. He tugged his arm again. This time, he broke free, but also this time, his lunch box went flying, and the contents went everywhere because it wasn't zipped.

Kole started laughing.

"Augh," Joshua said, but he picked up the contents. When he finished, he looked out the cafeteria door. Kendall was standing there, staring. He frowned, and when she realized he saw her, she turned around and went into the bathroom across the hall. Joshua walked past Kole, pushed him, then went to sit with Carson, who was sitting with Camilla. Being a third wheel was surprisingly more appealing than sitting with Kole

Chapter 13: Egg

Joshua walked to the art room with Carson. As they were walking there, Kole was coming in the opposite direction. He was walking with Patrick, Reese, Aiden, Andrew, Daniel, and Caiden. The six of them were talking, not noticing Joshua and Carson. But as they began to get closer, Kole looked up. When he saw Joshua, he smiled. All of the others looked up, and their conversation was silenced, mid-sentence. Reese smirked; Patrick and Aiden showed no emotion; Daniel and Caiden looked scared.

When the two groups met, Kole stepped in front of Joshua and punched him in the stomach. His torso curled in pain as he cried, "Oof."

Kole laughed, triumphantly, and he continued to walk on.

"Poor Joshua," Daniel said, but he continued to walk with Kole and the others.

Joshua didn't move for a moment. Carson looked back at Kole as he walked away, glaring. "He's such a jerk."

"Yeah," Joshua said. "I've noticed."

They continued walking. Joshua's stomach throbbed a little, but it was mostly gone by the time he sat down in art.

After art was recess. Joshua and Carson walked

around together, escaping Kole and the others for the time being. When they went inside, the two of them sat together. Camilla had not yet come in to sit down. Joshua figured Kole and the others wouldn't sit with him again because there wouldn't be enough room for them all with Carson there.

Caiden was first to sit down from that group, and he didn't sit with Joshua. When Joshua saw that, he sighed with relief. Seemed like Caiden had caught on to Joshua's attempt to avoid Kole.

When Aiden, Andrew, and Daniel got their food, they all went to sit with Caiden. Patrick, Kole, and Reese came into the cafeteria together but didn't get food and didn't sit with those guys. They sat down at Joshua's table, not next to him and Carson, but across from them.

Joshua sighed, and without saying anything, he got up and left the table. Carson followed him, without questioning.

But so did Patrick, Kole, and Reese. Joshua and Carson sat down at another empty table, but Patrick, Kole, and Reese all sat down with them. This time, they sat right next to them; Kole was right next to Joshua.

Kole grabbed Joshua's apple, which was in his lunch box, and said, "Ooh, this looks good." He took a bite from it and said, "Yum, it is. Honey crisp, my fave. Do you like honey crisp?"

Joshua rolled his eyes. *Of course* he did. Why else would he have brought it to school to eat for lunch?

"Ew, what kind of lunch do you bring?" Reese asked, looking in at the rest of the contents in Joshua's lunch box.

"Can't you always smell his disgusting hard-boiled eggs?" Kole asked, taking another bite of the apple, juice flying everywhere.

"Ew, that's what that is?" Reese asked.

Kole nodded.

Joshua's face was red.

"Leave him alone," Carson said.

"Who," Kole said.

"Asked," Reese laughed.

"Haha!" Kole laughed.

"That's not funny!" Joshua snapped.

"Yes, it is," Kole said. "You just don't have good humor."

Camilla walked over to the table now, with her lunch tray in her hands. She set her tray down at the seat next to Carson, but then she looked at Patrick, Kole, and Reese, and said, "What's going on here?"

"Kole and Reese are being creeps," Carson said.

"What? How?" Kole asked.

"You're following us around," Carson answered.

"That's like a stalker," Joshua added.

"We're not stalkers. We just want to hang out," Kole said.

"Yeah, Joshua!" Reese exclaimed. "I thought that's what you wanted."

"Come on, Reese." That was Camilla now. "Why are you being like this?"

"What are you talking about?" Reese asked.

"We used to be best friends—you, me, and Zoe—but now you won't even talk to us. You've abandoned us for this *guy*, who you just barely met, and he's turned you into a real jerk," Camilla said.

"I'm not being a jerk," Reese said.

"From the look on Joshua and Carson's face, it appears you are," Camilla said.

Reese looked at Joshua and said, "Joshua, am I being a jerk?"

"Yeah, you are," Joshua answered.

"No, I'm not," Reese said.

"You're just jealous," Kole said.

"I'm *not* jealous," Joshua said.

"Then why are you so salty?" Kole asked.

"You've all just been insulting my lunch ever since you sat down! And have you opened your eyes recently!? Look at me! I'm covered in bruises! I look hideous! But forget how it all looks! It hurts! I just want to be left alone!" Joshua cried.

"Look at me, I don't look much better," Kole said.

Carson let out a sound of disagreement but didn't form any words.

"And *you* started it," Kole said.

"But you're the one who keeps coming back for more!" Joshua cried.

"I'm just trying to finish it all," Kole said.

"It *is* finished!" Joshua cried.

"No, it's not. It's far from finished," Kole said.

"Yes, it is! It has been finished ever since Patrick, Maverick, Aiden, and *Reese* carried you away from my house. Now, it's just you making up excuses! But I don't want any of it!" Joshua said.

"No. It wasn't over then. And it's not over now. This is a fight that will go on until one of us wins. Neither of us have won yet," Kole said.

Joshua was silent.

"Wow, Reese!" Camilla exclaimed. "Look what you're getting yourself into! Look at the types of people in this! Whose side do you want to be on?"

"Not yours," Reese said.

Camilla frowned; her face turned red.

"Augh," Joshua said. *"How could she be so cruel?"* he wondered. But he stood up and said to Carson and Camilla, "Come on, let's go eat in the classroom."

"Yeah, let's go," Carson said. The three of them left, and finally, Patrick, Kole, and Reese didn't follow them.

Chapter 14: Sick

Joshua was laying on his couch with the T.V. on. Kendall had a basketball game, so she was at the school with the rest of the family, playing in her game. Joshua stayed home because he was sick. His throat hurt, his nose was stuffed, his head throbbed, he felt dizzy when he stood up, and when he ate anything, he felt like he was going to vomit. Even though he had the T.V. on, he wasn't watching it. He mostly had it on because he didn't like the silence. He had it on a low volume since his head hurt, but he couldn't bear his house being completely silent and being alone at the same time.

He was still lying on the couch when he heard a knock on the door, causing him to jump what felt like five feet off the couch. He didn't want to answer the door, so he quickly turned off the T.V.

There was another knock, then a voice that said, "I know you're there!"

A familiar voice. An unfriendly voice. *Not now*...or ever...but especially not now.

Kole, of course.

Joshua groaned, but he still didn't get up.

There was another knock, but this time it was pounding, and Kole shouted, "I'm not leaving until you open up!"

Joshua sighed, but he decided to get up. Maybe Kole would take it easy on him when he saw how sick he was (which was pretty noticeable). His face was red, his eye lids looked weighed down by lead weights, his nose was running, his lips were chapped, and his words were short and slow.

Joshua's head spun as he walked, but he went to the front door and opened it anyway. Kole stood there, alone.

When Joshua stood in the entrance, Kole's eyes widened, and he said, "Woah, dude! You look awful! Guess this was bad timing."

"Yeah," Joshua agreed.

"I just had something important to tell you."

Joshua could hardly comprehend what Kole was saying.

"I wanted to tell you that I'm sorry for the way I always treat you," Kole said. "I get it. You made a mistake, and I was doing something to upset you. It doesn't give me the right to beat on you and stuff. It's just part of my nature, but I get that it's mean. So, I wanted to say sorry, and I was wondering if you'd want to hang out sometime."

"Uh..."

"Next Friday, there's this thing at the library. We could go to that—make up for rough times."

"Um..." Joshua honestly had no idea what Kole just said because his head was spinning and pounding.

"Just say yes, and I will leave you alone."

"Yes," Joshua said, not thinking about the repercussions.

"Okay, great. See you Monday at school."

"Yeah, yeah," Joshua said, dizzily. He heard that part.

"Do you want me to help you into the living room or something?"

"No, thank you."

"Okay."

He turned around and began to walk away. Joshua shut the door and immediately fell to the floor. He realized he probably should have accepted Kole's help because Kole probably wouldn't have hurt him when he looked like that. But since he didn't, he was stuck laying on the ground. Instead of getting up, he stayed there and fell asleep. He was okay, just sick.

About 10 minutes later, he woke up again, and he got up and resumed his position on the couch, turning the T.V. back on. But he fell asleep again, this time for longer because he was more comfortable. He stayed asleep until his family was back home. He didn't tell them about Kole's visit because he had forgotten due to being pretty out of it.

Meanwhile, Kole walked back to his house. Patrick, Maverick, Des (Patrick and Kole's cousin), and Reese were all there. Kole walked up to the room upstairs where they were all hanging out, and Kole announced to them all, "He said yes."

"Wow," Patrick said. "That was quick."

"Yeah," Kole said. "It actually wasn't that hard."

"We didn't think you would be back before supper," Maverick said. "And we didn't know how many pieces you would be in when you got home either."

Kole smiled.

***

Joshua was walking to his locker Monday morning when he was greeted by Kole, who exclaimed, "Hey, Joshua!"

"Hey," Joshua said, confused. *Why was he so enthusiastic? Why wasn't he trying to punch him?*

"Excited for Friday?" Kole exclaimed.

"What's Friday?" Joshua asked.

"Have you forgotten?"

"Yeah, I guess I have."

"It's the thing at the library we are going to."

"The what?"

"There's this thing at the library, and you said you'd come with me to make up for our rough times."

"The *library*?"

"Yeah."

"I definitely don't remember that."

"Remember Saturday when I came to your house?"

"Augh. I was so sick that day that I didn't know what was going on."

"Nonetheless, you said you would come. If you're a good Christian, you will follow your word."

"Augh. You tricked me."

"I wanted to apologize. How would I get you to listen without tricking you?"

"I don't know. What if I hadn't been sick?"

"I don't know. Guess God was just working in my favor, wasn't He?"

Joshua didn't respond.

The two boys continued on their way. Joshua went to his locker, and Kole went to his advisory. Reese got to her locker when Joshua was still there, and she exclaimed, "Hey, Joshua!"

"Hey," Joshua said, rolling his eyes. Not because of Reese but because of how Kole tricked him, and he figured that was probably why Reese was greeting him the same way Kole had.

"I heard you and Kole are friends again," Reese said.

"*Again?*" Joshua asked. "I don't know if we ever were to begin with, and I don't know if you could say that we are now, either."

"What do you mean?" Reese asked. "I thought you were going to the library together next weekend to make up. You agreed to go."

"Yeah, I agreed to go because I was really sick, and I couldn't comprehend anything. He said he would leave if I just said yes, so I did. I wasn't thinking about how that probably wasn't the best option because I had no idea what he was talking about. I wasn't thinking straight, not thinking about the consequences of my answer," Joshua said.

"So are you not going now?" Reese asked.

"I don't know. I said I would go, but we will see how this week goes."

"It's not going to just be you two. We're all going."

"Oh. Really?"

"Yeah. You could bring Carson or somebody."

"Oh," Joshua said, thoughtfully. "Hmm."

"Kole's not looking to beat you up. He's sincere.

Even though you were sick, and he used that to his advantage, it really was never meant to be a trick."

"If you say he's not going to beat me up, I might consider it."

"Do you trust me?"

Joshua shrugged.

Reese frowned.

"I'll talk to Carson."

Reese smiled.

Joshua left his locker. Reese left a little after.

Chapter 15: Friday

Carson arrived at Joshua's house a little after five Friday night. At that point, Joshua had told his parents about the incident with Kole while he was sick, and they tentatively agreed to let him go as long as Carson was going. The two boys set out walking to the library once Carson got there. They talked the whole time about random things, never anything to do with Kole or Reese. When they arrived at the library, Patrick, Kole, Maverick, Des (Patrick and Kole's cousin), and Reese were all waiting outside. So were Aiden, Andrew, Daniel, and Caiden. When Kole saw that they had arrived, he smiled and walked over to them. The others followed.

The library looked in a way which Joshua had never seen before. Initially, when he found out he agreed to go to the *library* with Kole, he was surprised. The *library* didn't really seem like Kole's cup of tea, if he drank tea, which Joshua couldn't picture either. But...that night, the library was set up with different games like foosball, ping pong, pool, and air hockey. There were arts and crafts, but Joshua knew Kole would probably steer away from those. Outside, there was a basketball hoop, volleyball pit, and later, there would be a bonfire. It was dark outside, but it was still cool. There was food, too. The best part...it was all *free*. Joshua was surprised. He wondered how he had never known about this before and how it took the new guy in town to introduce him to it.

A lady was walking around, saying, “Exchange your phones for a candy bar. You can get your phone back when you leave, but you can keep the candy bar.” She was holding a bin of phones under her left arm, and she was holding a tray of giant candy bars in her other. She set them on the table. All of Joshua’s friends went over and put their phones in the bin, labeling them with their names, then they took a candy bar.

“I don’t have a phone,” Joshua mumbled.

The lady heard him and said, “Then you get a candy bar for free.”

Joshua smiled and took one.

The friends all ate their candy bars, then half of them went and snuck their phones back and hid them in their pockets. Even though it annoyed Joshua, he didn’t say anything because he didn’t want to upset them again, especially since Kole was one of the ones who took it back.

“Let’s play some games,” Aiden said.

“Yeah,” the others agreed.

“I want to challenge Joshua in air hockey,” Kole said.

“I’ve never played air hockey before,” Joshua said, nervously.

“What!?” Kole cried. “You’ve never played air hockey before!?”

“No,” Joshua said.

“How come?” Kole asked.

“I don’t know,” Joshua answered.

“Oh. That’s okay. It’s really not that hard. We can still go play,” Kole said.

“Okay,” Joshua said. His stomach did a somersault because he was in disbelief at how nice Kole was to him. He thought for sure that Kole was going to tease him, but he didn’t.

The two of them walked over to the table. Joshua took one side and grabbed the paddle. Kole went to the other side and grabbed the other paddle. The puck was in Kole’s goal, so he took it out and put it in the middle. Kole briefly went over how to play, and when they were both ready, they went for it at the same time, both trying to hit it towards the other person’s goal.

Joshua hit it first, and it went flying towards Kole’s goal, but it didn’t go in. It landed on the surface of the table, and it slid into the wall, bouncing off lightly. Kole looked surprised, like he was expecting to hit it first. He smacked it back across the table, and it slid and hit the wall. Joshua hit it back. It was about to go into the goal when Kole smacked it away. Instantly, it soared across the table right into Joshua’s goal.

“Yes!” Kole exclaimed. “One point for me!”

Joshua pulled the puck out of the goal, and he pushed it across the table. It zoomed across but didn’t go in. It hit the wall right next to the opening. Kole hit it back, towards the goal. This time, Joshua blocked it. He hit it back towards Kole, and this time, Kole missed, and the puck slid into the goal, crashing down into the slot. Joshua smiled.

“One to one,” he said.

Kole hit the puck back towards Joshua, and Joshua

immediately hit it back, and it went right back into the goal.

"Two to one!" Joshua exclaimed, excitedly.

"Oh no, I can't let a newbie beat me!" Kole cried.

"I think you've won your fair share of events. I think it's my turn now," Joshua said.

"Okay," Kole said, smiling and blushing. He hit the puck back towards Joshua, but this time, it went into the goal.

"There," Kole said. "We're even again."

They continued playing, and they decided to play until seven. Joshua ended up winning seven to five.

When they finished, it was time to eat. As they were waiting in line for food, Joshua asked Kole, "How did you find out about this?"

"My neighbor is one of the people who puts it on, so she told me I should come. I came last time, but it was only Patrick and me. That wasn't fun."

"This happens a lot?"

"Once a month. The first Friday, usually."

"Oh."

"You think you will come next time?" Kole asked.

"Maybe," Joshua said.

They got their food, then they sat down with the others. Joshua and Kole didn't talk at all during the meal, but afterwards, Kole said he wanted to play ping pong with Joshua. Joshua immediately was brought back to a memory from fifth grade when he was playing ping pong with a boy who didn't go to their school anymore. The two of them couldn't keep it on the table. It was always falling on the floor.

"Come on, let's go," Kole said.

"Um...okay," Joshua said.

They went to the table and each grabbed a paddle. "Fair warning," Joshua said. "I'm not very good."

"Fair warning...*I am*," Kole said.

The ball was on Joshua's side, so he picked it up and served. He hit it right to Kole who hit it back. Then, Joshua hit it! He was so surprised with himself. They continued to hit it back and forth. Most of the hits were pretty perfect. A couple of times, one of them would hit it wrong, and it would go flying, but usually, if they dove for it, they could recover it without their hand touching it. They didn't even hit anyone or send it flying...for a while.

They weren't going for points; they were just going to keep it in the air, and they kept it going for about five minutes. Then, they lost it.

Joshua went to retrieve the tiny ball, which had rolled under the food table that was now being covered with desserts. Joshua walked back and Kole said, "You're not *awful*." Then, he smiled, and Joshua smiled back.

They continued hitting it back and forth.

Soon, some other teenagers wanted to come use the ping pong table, so they moved on. Joshua glanced over at the others. He saw Carson was enjoying himself too, and he was relieved because he felt bad for ditching him. Carson was then playing air hockey with Aiden. He also noticed Reese, who did not seem to be enjoying herself. She was watching Joshua and Kole, but she quickly looked away when Joshua glanced over. She looked at the ground for a little while, and Patrick came over and nudged her on the shoulder, then they went outside with Maverick. Des,

Andrew, Daniel, and Caiden must have been outside because Joshua didn't see them.

Joshua brought his attention back to Kole as they arrived at the foosball table. Kole easily crushed Joshua there. Then, they played pool. Joshua had never played that either, so Kole showed him how. But Kole quickly got bored, and they gave up their game. Joshua was pretty sure it partly had something to do with Joshua winning, but he wasn't sure.

At that point, all of the others were outside around the bonfire, so Joshua and Kole went outside to meet them. On their way out, Joshua grabbed his winter jacket and put it on, but Kole went out in his sweatshirt that he was wearing. It was December.

They got to the fire, and it was warm. All of their friends were roasting marshmallows and stuffing them inside graham crackers and chocolate. Joshua and Kole both grabbed a stick and began their own roasting.

The night ended soon after that. Since it was late, Mrs. Abare came to pick Joshua and Carson up. Patrick and Kole had to walk home, but it wasn't as bad for them, Joshua thought, because their walk was only 10 minutes.

Chapter 16: Walk

Joshua was sitting at the table Saturday morning eating breakfast when there was a knock on the front door. He ignored it, and his mom went to answer it.

As soon as Mrs. Abare opened the door, Joshua could see who was there from his seat at the table. It was Kole, who greeted her, and she greeted him back.

"Is Joshua home?" Kole asked, but he already knew the answer, for he was directly looking at him when he said it.

Mrs. Abare looked back. "Yes, he is," she replied.

Joshua got up and walked over.

"Hey, Joshua!" Kole exclaimed. His eyes ran down Joshua's clothing, observing the fact that he was still in his pajamas: a gray t-shirt with black and blue flannel pants. He ignored that, mostly since it was hardly different from what he wore on a regular basis, and continued with, "Do you want to hang out? I'm free all day."

"Um..." Joshua said. He looked at his mom who was staring at him. Her mouth was open like she wanted to say something but couldn't in front of Kole. Joshua looked back at Kole and said, "One minute."

"Okay," Kole said.

Kole stepped inside, and they shut the door. Then,

Joshua and Mrs. Abare stepped into the living room where they could still see Kole, but if they talked quietly enough, Kole wouldn't be able to hear what they said.

"Can I?" Joshua asked, quietly.

"Are you crazy!?" Mrs. Abare cried.

"Kole and I are cool now."

"This is a mistake."

"Mom, we're cool now," Joshua said again.

"Augh."

Mrs. Abare looked over at Mr. Abare who was sitting on the recliner next to their conversation drinking a cup of coffee.

"He said they're cool. People can seek forgiveness. Boys fight each other sometimes," Mr. Abare said.

"This is an awful idea," Mrs. Abare said.

"He walked 35 minutes just to get here," Joshua said.

"Fine," Mrs. Abare caved. "But I'm sending you with my phone."

"Okay," Joshua said.

"And a bubble," Mr. Abare laughed.

Mrs. Abare rolled her eyes. She got her phone, which was sitting on the coffee table in the middle of the living room. Joshua went up to his room to get dressed, then she gave it to him and allowed him to go off with Kole.

The second that the door shut behind the two boys, Mrs. Abare said to her husband who still had his phone, "Text Joshua. See if he's okay."

"He literally just left," Mr. Abare said, annoyed.

"Yeah, and he was in our front yard the first time

they got into a fight."

"Just go look out the window. You will still be able to see them."

Mrs. Abare went to the living room window and looked outside. Indeed, Joshua and Kole were still there talking, not hitting or shoving.

Mrs. Abare let out a sigh of relief.

Joshua and Kole walked along the sidewalk, not having any set destination in mind. They just walked.

Joshua had to admit to himself, *he* was a little bit nervous. He knew that last night had gone fine, but they had been under the supervision of adults. Now, they were alone. He had fun at the library, which was why he could trust Kole enough to go with him, but he still had a sneaking suspicion that this might be another trap.

"Your parents seem real protective of you," Kole pointed out as they were walking.

"Yeah, I guess," Joshua said.

"They must not like me very much."

Joshua shrugged.

"It's okay. You can be honest."

"They certainly aren't *in love* with you."

"Yeah, makes sense. My parents don't really care where I am or what I'm doing. Probably why I'm able to so easily be a jerk."

Joshua didn't respond or acknowledge what Kole said. He just thought about it, unsure of how to react.

They arrived in front of a coffee shop, and Kole said, "Have you been here before?"

"Yeah," Joshua replied.

"Do you want to get something to drink?"

"Sure," Joshua said. A hot drink sounded so great, as he was freezing. He decided to go only in a sweatshirt because he didn't want Kole to think bad of him for wearing a jacket.

They went inside and both ordered a drink. Kole ordered coffee, which he then filled with sugar and cream. Joshua got a hot chocolate. They walked outside, and it was freezing again. Joshua was already regretting his decision to not bring his jacket, but he didn't complain. They continued to walk around. As they did, Joshua felt his pocket buzz. He pulled out his mom's phone, and it was a message from his dad. It said: "Your mom wanted to know if you were doing okay."

"Oh, I've got to answer this," Joshua said, unlocking the phone.

"Okay," Kole replied. "Who is it?"

"My dad."

"Figured." Kole paused. "But I was also wondering if it was Reese."

"Why?" Joshua rolled his eyes in the other direction, looking at the ground.

"I don't know." Kole shrugged.

Joshua didn't say anything more to Kole. Clearly he didn't know it was his mom's phone, but Joshua didn't bring that to his attention. He responded to his dad with: "I'm fine." Then, they continued walking.

There was a Farmer's Market going on in the park, so the two of them went to check it out because they didn't know what else to do. Nothing there really sparked their interest, so they left again. Had it been summer, they would have gone to sit by the fountain, but it was frozen now, and so were they.

When they were leaving the farmer's market, Joshua's pocket buzzed again. He pulled his phone out, and it was his dad again. He said the same thing as last time: "Your mom wanted to know if you were doing okay."

"What? Your dad again?" Kole asked.

Joshua nodded, then he responded to the text.

It was almost noon, so they decided to go out for lunch.

"Do you want to go to Tony's Taco Bar?" Kole asked, smiling and elbowing Joshua lightly.

"No." Joshua frowned and crossed his arms.

"I'm just kidding. I know of a good sandwich place by my house, we can go there."

"Okay."

They walked there and went inside and each ordered their lunch, then they sat down and continued to talk. Afterwards, Kole walked Joshua home, even though their houses were in opposite directions.

They arrived on Joshua's front porch, and both boys were still in one piece. Joshua was about to open the door to go inside when he stopped to face Kole and said, "Thanks."

"For what? I made you pay for all your own food and drink," Kole said.

"Thanks for *hanging out*," Joshua said.

"Ah, it's nothing," Kole said. "I'm glad you came. If you hadn't, I would have been stuck at home with Patrick all day, and that would have been awful."

Joshua smiled slightly.

"See ya," Kole said.

"Bye," Joshua replied, and he turned around and went inside. He walked into the living room where his mom was jumping out of her chair to greet him.

"Oh, Joshua!" she exclaimed. "You're here! You're alive! You don't have a single bruise on your face!"

"Yeah, I'm here and sound," Joshua said. He looked back out the window where Kole was walking away.

"Wait..." Mrs. Abare said. "Did you not wear a coat?"

"Uh..." Joshua said.

"Dude," Mrs. Abare said, knowing the answer without a response.

Joshua shrugged.

He left the living room and went upstairs to his bedroom, walking past his sisters' room. Kendall had gone into Leah and Ava's room, and the three of them were playing with dolls. When Joshua got to his room, he took out his music stand and cornet book, and he set up his instrument and began playing.

Chapter 17: Square

"Are we square?" Reese asked Joshua as the two of them walked together from their lockers to the Innovation Lab.

"Sure," Joshua answered.

"Cool," Reese said, smiling. "So...can I sit at your table again?" Reese had moved to the other table the day after their heated conversation.

"I never said you couldn't," Joshua told her.

"But you were upset with me."

"Okay, I *was* glad you didn't sit with us, but we're okay now, so you can sit with us again."

"Cool."

The two of them got to class, and Sam and Aaron were already in there. Joshua sat next to Sam as he always did, and Reese sat on the opposite side of him.

"Oh, no," Sam said, shaking his head.

"Reese is sitting with us again?" Aaron asked.

"Leave," Sam said sternly, with locked eyes.

Reese frowned.

"Guys," Joshua said.

"What? You're okay with this?" Aaron asked.

"Yeah. I said it was okay," Joshua said.

"Reese is a jerk. We know it, we always have known

it, and we thought you knew it now too," Sam said.

"Reese and I are square now," Joshua said.

"Well, *we're* not," Sam said. He looked at Reese and said, "So leave."

"What have I done to you like what I have done to Joshua? If Joshua can forgive me, certainly you can too," Reese said.

"You haven't done anything to gain our forgiveness," Sam said.

"You have to ask for it first," Aaron said.

"Can I have your forgiveness?" Reese asked.

"Now, you have to *act* on it," Aaron said. "*Show* us you have changed."

"Fine," Reese said.

"Wait...Joshua's only forgiving you because he has a giant crush on you. He's blind!" Sam exclaimed.

"Sam!" Joshua cried.

Joshua and Reese's faces both turned red; Aaron laughed.

"Sorry," Sam said.

"Now look who's apologizing!" Reese exclaimed.

"Augh," Sam said. He looked at Joshua with his jaw dropped slightly, but Joshua just stared back without saying anything.

Chapter 18: Bullying

The same day that Reese moved back to Joshua's table during advisory was the first day of their new choice groups. Joshua had Independent Study, which was meeting in the library. He got there, and he found Reese sitting at a table alone. He went over to her and sat down at the table saying, "Hey."

Reese looked up at him and smiled, also saying, "Hey."

They were silent for a moment, then Reese said, "Cool that you have Independent Study."

"Yeah, you too," Joshua agreed.

"I'm actually really excited for this class. It sounds like it's going to be a lot of fun," Reese said.

"Yeah. I agree."

"Might actually learn something useful for once." Reese smiled.

Joshua frowned in confusion.

"I just don't get it," Reese continued. "Why do I have to learn math all my life? I'm not going to be a mathematician or anything when I grow up. I'm going to be a director. Why do I have to learn math instead of director skills."

"What about advisory? Is that not director skills?"

"It is, but I'm in seventh grade now. I started learning math when I was five."

Joshua shrugged.

"Sorry...if you're thinking about a math major."

"I honestly have no idea. I want to be a writer, but I've been told that's not going to make me enough money to live on."

"It will if you become famous."

"That would be cool." Joshua smiled thoughtfully.

Suddenly, they heard someone shout, "HEY!"

Joshua and Reese both spun their heads to face the voice, and they learned it was Kole.

They both greeted him as he sat down at their table, and Kole said, "Pretty cool that we're in the same class."

"Yeah," Reese agreed. "Are you excited for it?"

"No! It sounds awful! Who wants to spend a whole class *studying*?" Kole asked. "Are you?"

"Nah," Reese said, waving her hand like she was brushing away that idea.

Joshua's jaw dropped.

"What?" Kole asked him.

Joshua looked at Reese, then at Kole and shrugging, he replied, "Nothing."

"Okay," Kole said. "Are *you* excited?"

"It sounds cool," Joshua said.

"Okay, whatever," Kole said. "I hope you're right."

Joshua nodded.

Class began. There were four teachers, and they said that they were going to split into four smaller groups, one group per teacher, so that everyone could have a more individualized experience. They explained what they were going to do: study a topic of their choosing. The teachers acknowledged that this was probably different than anything they had ever done before in school, for they were always given a specific guideline to follow when doing something for school. This class would give them more freedom.

They were almost finished talking when they told them that they would hand out their notebooks, which were for taking notes on their topic. On the notebook, there would be a number in the corner that indicated the group that they were in. The teachers began handing them to the students. When they received their books, they were to brainstorm a list of research ideas on the inside cover.

Joshua was the first at his table to get a book. He was in the first group. Kole got his next, and he was in the fourth group.

"Ah, too bad," Kole said.

Joshua shrugged.

Reese got her book after, and she was in the first group also. Joshua was happy about that, but Reese said, "What if I just changed it to a four?"

"No," Kole said. "Why would you do that?"

"To be in your group," Reese said.

"But Joshua's in your group," Kole said.

Reese looked at Joshua, then back at Kole, and said, "He can just change it to a four, too."

"No, you can't both switch. They'd know. And plus, you know Joshua. He's a good Christian. He wouldn't deceive anyone. Right, Joshua?" Kole asked.

"Uh...right," Joshua said, unsure if that was a trap.

So Reese dropped the idea, and they began

brainstorming. Afterwards, they were instructed to read them to each other.

Joshua, Kole, and Reese all looked at each other, waiting for someone to start. They kept looking at each other until Kole finally said, "I'm not going first."

"Me neither," Reese said.

"Fine, I'll go," Joshua said. He looked at his notebook, annoyed that he had to read them, but then he went on: "Swimming, music, writing, bullying..."

"*Bullying?*" Kole asked.

"Yeah," Joshua said.

"I thought we were cool," Kole said.

"Who said we weren't?" Joshua asked, frowning.

"That's so targeted," Kole snapped, crossing his arms.

"Augh," Joshua said.

"Yeah, it is," Reese agreed.

"I want to know what causes bullies to act the way they do and what makes a victim of bullying," Joshua said.

"You want to know what makes a victim of bullying?" Kole asked.

"Yeah," Joshua replied.

"I'll tell you what."

"What?"

"People who research bullying." Then Kole laughed, and so did Reese.

"No!" Joshua snapped.

"Yeah! Look! I've just done your whole project for you!" Kole exclaimed.

"No! You haven't!" Joshua said.

"Right, sorry. I forgot. I'm supposed to be nice to

you," Kole said. "Research whatever you want."

Joshua leaned back in his chair and crossed his arms, his face red, and he said, "Just read yours!"

"Okay," Kole said, but as he opened his mouth to speak, they were called together to end class. Kole and Reese laughed that they didn't have to read.

As they were leaving, Kole put his hand on Joshua's shoulder and said, "Hey, dude, we're still cool, right?"

"Sure," Joshua said.

"Great!" Kole exclaimed.

Joshua walked behind Kole and Reese slowly, so he lost distance behind them. The two of them were talking and didn't realize that they were leaving him behind. While he was walking, something came to Joshua's mind that made him turn around. When he did, he saw this girl, named Isabella, standing behind him holding her water bottle up in the air. When he saw that she was doing that, she said to him, "Would you like to get hit over the head with this?"

"No, I don't, actually," Joshua replied, and he picked up the pace. *What was that?*

Chapter 19: Newspaper

Joshua was back to sitting with the full group. Carson was sitting with Camilla, so he and Joshua didn't sit together anymore, but they still talked at recess and after school; that meant Joshua was sitting with Patrick, Kole, Reese, Aiden, Andrew, Daniel, and Caiden.

At lunch the day of their new choice class, Aiden said to the table group, "We should start a newspaper."

"That doesn't sound very fun," Daniel said, quietly.

"That would be so cool!" Reese exclaimed, ignoring Daniel.

Daniel's face turned red.

"Who wants to do it? We don't all have to do it, just some of us could," Aiden said.

"Me!" Reese exclaimed. "I want to do it!"

"I will," Joshua said, as he was a writer.

Reese looked at Kole, who said, "Okay, I will, too."

Then, there was silence, and Aiden looked at the others to say, "What about the rest of you?"

The rest of them shook their heads or said no.

So, Joshua, Kole, Reese, and Aiden all agreed to meet that weekend, and when the time rolled around, they all got together to work on their articles. They each decided to work on an article that was pressing to them.

They made a shared document but wrote their articles in a separate one. When they finished, they would copy and paste it into the shared document.

Joshua wrote his on bullying. Since he had been researching it for Independent Study, it was hot on his mind. He was first to finish, since his mind was just flowing like a stream in the spring. Kole was next to finish. Kole pasted his at the top of the document after Joshua, which made it go before Joshua's. When Reese and Aiden finished, they put theirs before Kole's. After Kole pasted his article on the document, he found a quote and posted it among his words, right before Joshua's article. The quote said, "Bullying is a part of life, and it is meant to prepare us for our future."

As soon as Joshua read it, he snapped, "Kole!"

"What?"

"You can't put that there!"

"What?"

"That quote! It totally defeats the purpose of my article!"

"But it like...totally supports *mine*." Kole smiled.

"Augh! Your article is so stupid! How could you say that!"

"That's not very nice."

"Your article isn't very nice! You can't put it on here!"

"Why should I take my article out just because it contradicts yours? Why does everything have to be your way? Why don't you take *your* article out? Write about something else."

"It's not simply because it contradicts mine. My

article is right; yours is wrong. Yours is being mean; mine isn't. Bullying isn't a good thing; it's a bad thing."

"Why? Because a bunch of losers think they're so entitled that they deserve to have an easy life? Life isn't easy, Joshua."

"I never said it was. But that doesn't make bullying right or good. Do you know the statistics of mental illnesses, suicide, and other issues that stem all from bullying?"

"Yeah."

"And you still think it's good?"

"No. I just think it's a part of life. When are you going to admit it?"

"I just want to raise awareness about why a bully is a bully."

"Then what's wrong with mine? I'm not saying anything against that."

"Because no one is going to care to help bullies if they think bullying is good."

"Bullies can't be helped. *No one* can be helped."

"Augh!" Reese cried, slamming her hands onto the table and standing up. "I can't take this! You guys can't stop arguing even just for a second!"

"We're not arguing," Kole said. "We're just having a friendly conversation."

"This doesn't sound very friendly. Why can't you guys just be friends?" Reese asked.

"We are friends, right Joshua?" Kole asked.

"Yeah," Joshua answered.

"See?" Kole asked. He put his arm around Joshua, but Joshua quickly pulled himself away. Then, they both smiled.

"Sure, you say you're friends, but you don't act like them! Joshua, just let Kole keep his article there. If you don't like it, then change yours. You can't make Kole do anything," Reese said.

"Augh! Why are you taking Kole's side?" Joshua asked. "You like being bullied?"

"I'm *not* bullied," Reese said quietly, blushing.

"Oh yeah? Don't you remember last year? Remember those girls? Remember what they did on ChatChat?" Joshua asked, crossing his arms.

Reese's face got red.

"What happened on ChatChat?" Kole asked.

"Did you like that?" Joshua asked, ignoring Kole.

"How did you know about that? You don't even have ChatChat," Reese said.

"No, but my friends showed me," Joshua said. "Do you really want things like that to continue?"

"No," Reese said, quietly.

"Then why do you side with Kole on this?" Joshua asked.

"What happened on ChatChat!?" Kole cried. "Isn't anyone going to tell me!?"

"No!" Reese shouted. "This is stupid. All stupid! I'm not going to be a part of this stupid newspaper anymore!" She got up and stormed out the door. As she did, she was shouting, "Joshua! I can't believe you went so far as to bring that up!"

"Wow, nice going, Joshua. Who's the bully now? What made you do that?" Kole asked.

"I wasn't being a bully. I was just trying to prove a

point," Joshua said.

"Is one of the reasons for a bully to be a bully trying to prove a point?" Kole asked.

"No!" Joshua snapped.

Kole laughed.

"Augh!" Joshua cried. He pushed Kole, then he walked out, too.

"Wow," Kole said, but then he kept laughing.

Aiden stared at him, his eyebrows facing downwards toward his nose.

"I guess it's just me and you now," Kole said to Aiden, and he stopped laughing. "I guess we are just going to have to write an article about gay rights and pro-bullying. That's what happens when you walk out—your voice doesn't get heard anymore."

"Was that your plan? To make him walk out?" Aiden asked.

"No. It just worked out that way. I'm going to delete their articles so we can just submit ours."

"Forget it." Aiden looked at the ground and crossed his arms. "This whole idea was just stupid. Why did I think any of you would do just one thing together?"

"Don't get mad at me. I didn't storm out like a baby."

"No, but you caused them to storm out."

"I didn't cause Reese to storm out. Joshua did."

"But you *caused* Joshua to get mad, and you *knew* it would make him mad, but you did it *anyway*."

"Joshua's just writing about anti-bullying to make *me* mad. But you aren't mad about that?"

"It's what he believes in. You couldn't honestly

believe in bullying, could you?"

"Have you met me?"

Aiden rolled his eyes.

Meanwhile, Joshua had gone outside and ran up to Reese. She had her hands in her pockets, for she wasn't wearing any gloves. When he got to her, he stopped running and said, "I'm sorry I brought that up."

Reese turned her head to look at him, slowing her pace, and she said, "I'm overreacting. I'm sorry. It was a long time ago."

"No, no. You're not overreacting. I shouldn't have brought it up. I was just trying to prove a point, that's all."

"Well, it worked."

"I didn't realize it was going to upset you this much. Or maybe I did. I don't know. But still, I wasn't trying to offend you."

"It was just an awful time for me. And I guess...I don't think I've quite left that behind me yet, even though it was last year."

"Oh, I see."

"Sorry I took Kole's side. I don't get him sometimes."

"I don't ever get him. But I'd rather be on his good side than his bad side because his bad side isn't very fun."

"Yeah, you would know."

"I wonder how much longer until I'm on his bad side again. Augh...I pushed him again." Joshua covered his face with his hands in embarrassment.

"Joshua! Oh, Joshua. I think you just entered it!"

"Augh." Joshua uncovered his face and looked at the sky. "I'm so stupid. I should have just ignored it. Let it happen. Now, Aiden's probably mad at me too for sabotaging his newspaper."

"I admire that you can stand up for what you believe in, even though you often don't handle it well, and it ends up stinking," Reese said. She was quiet for a minute, then she said, "Even if Kole and you aren't cool, can *we* at least be cool?"

"Sure," Joshua said.

"Cool," Reese said, smiling.

Chapter 20: Kendall

"Augh! I'm so sick of her stupid rules! I can look after myself! And it's not like she cares anyway! She doesn't even pay attention half the time!" Kole cried, throwing his hands into the air. He was standing next to the frozen fountain in the park with Patrick, Reese, and Maverick.

"Sick of who?" Reese asked, confused.

Kole looked at Reese but didn't say anything.

"No one," Patrick said.

"It doesn't matter to you," Maverick said, stepping closer to Reese.

"Maybe I can help," Reese said.

"No! You can't help!" Kole snapped. "No one can! It's all stupid! Everything is stupid!"

"What?" Reese cried.

"Just stop talking, Reese," Patrick said, annoyed.

"I just want to..." Reese said.

"Augh!" Kole shouted, and he started walking away.

"Great going!" Maverick snapped at Reese.

"Augh," Reese said, upset. "Why won't you tell me anything?"

Patrick and Maverick followed after Kole, who was walking very quickly, and Reese followed after them.

It was almost sunset, and the Christmas lights were

yet to turn on. Off in the distance, Kole could see that Joshua was at the park with his sister, Kendall, who he didn't know.

When Kole got closer, Joshua turned around to see him and said, "Hey, Kole."

"Don't talk to me," Kole said, pushing Joshua.

"Hey!" Kendall snapped.

"Augh! What did you do that for!?" Joshua cried.

"Don't talk to him right now," Patrick said.

Joshua looked at Reese who shrugged. For the first time ever, she looked just as confused as he was, and it wasn't like she was in on Kole's insanity.

Kole stopped walking. He turned around to Joshua and said, "I'm sorry. That was mean, wasn't it?"

"What is going on?" Joshua asked.

"It's just, you act like I'm so mean, like I'm the one who has to apologize. Yet, you don't even know what it's like. You're fun, but you're clueless, and you know, I thought maybe you were okay, but now I remember. You're perfect. You have it perfect. Everything about you is just perfect. Me...I'm a mess. And you say God can fix it? But I can't even find God. So how is He supposed to fix it?" Kole asked.

"Is this about the newspaper?" Joshua asked.

"No! It's not about the newspaper! That's nothing compared to this! It's your cluelessness! You have a loving family, so how could you really not be clueless? Look at your sister! She's here with you now! *Alive.* I have two little sisters at home, but what about the third? Where is she? Not there. That's for sure. She's dead," Kole said.

Joshua's stomach suddenly hurt.

"What...happened?" he said, gulping.

"It's this thing...called S.I.D.S. No one really knows what happens, except that the baby stops breathing," Kole said.

"I..." Joshua said.

"Didn't know?" Kole asked. "Of course, you didn't. I never told you. There's a lot that I haven't told you, actually. That's because I just don't trust you. You think everything is good, but it's not. You are still the same as you were and so am I. So how could anything change?"

Kole pushed Joshua again, but he didn't push back. Joshua's stomach already hurt. He didn't know that about Kole, and now he felt guilty because even though Kole had been a jerk, he wouldn't want that for anyone.

"So...you know...next time you think I'm the bad guy, just remember who's life is better," Kole said. "You always rebuke me for not caring about religion, but tell me that you still would after losing your baby sister."

"You think that we haven't lost anything?" That wasn't Joshua, but Kendall adding in. Kole looked at her and raised his eyebrows. "You never told him that, and he never told you something! Our mom has had two miscarriages! One of them was twins. So...you think that our life is perfect? Don't you know we could have turned away from God, but we *didn't*! We lost *three* baby siblings!"

"That's different," Kole said. "Because they weren't born yet."

"What makes that different?" Kendall asked. She pushed Kole, real hard. He wasn't expecting it, and he lost his balance, nearly falling to the ground. Patrick let out a laugh. "They had a beating heart full of love and life before they died!" Kendall pushed him again. "Maybe Joshua can fall into your endless traps, but I know you for who you really are! Don't try to find pity from us because you have a hard life! Everyone does, and I'm sorry it's an 11-year-old that has to inform you that! Maybe you and Joshua have your differences, but I can't take seeing him walk in our front door covered in blood, eyes swollen, aching from head to toe. I can't stand every night when he sits at the table unable to eat because his stomach hurts from the way you treat him! When I heard that you were friends again, I was mad at his decision because I knew you were evil."

Kole was silent: bewildered and impressed. But Maverick couldn't take the silence and said, "You know that your brother was the first to push?"

"Yeah, I do, but Kole deserved it," Kendall said.

"You don't know anything," Maverick said.

"Yeah, I do!" Kendall snapped.

"Don't talk to my sister," Joshua said, looking Maverick in the eyes. He looked at Kendall and said, "Let's go."

The two of them walked away, and they weren't followed, not even by Reese. When they arrived at their house, Joshua thanked Kendall, and he told her she had quite the nerve, but he was glad. She responded with, "It wasn't that hard. I understand now why you pushed Kole. It's easy to fight someone with confidence when you are fighting for something you really care about."

"Yeah, see? I'm glad someone gets it. I feel awful all the time for what I did," Joshua said.

"I know," Kendall said.

"I guess Kole probably doesn't like me again. But I think he was already heading in that direction after the newspaper we tried to do," Joshua said.

"Are you kidding? He *never* liked you," Kendall said.

Joshua shrugged.

Kendall paused for a minute, then she asked, "What happened with the newspaper?"

"Augh, the usual: we fought," Joshua told her.

"Of course you did," Kendall said, frowning.

"I just don't get it," Joshua said. "We can't agree on *anything*. I bet that if I said it was winter, he would say that it's summer just to cause an argument."

Kendall didn't say anything, and they went inside their house.

Chapter 21: Stairs

Things were back to the way they were, and Joshua filled Carson in on everything. When Kole saw Joshua again for the first time after that, he pushed Joshua into the wall but just walked away. Reese was not with Kole at that time, but Joshua still saw them together later. He wasn't sure what to think of her. He wanted to abandon her again, like he had Kole, but something inside him made him latch onto her, like when a little kid can't let go of their thumb-sucking addiction.

Joshua was on his way to band when he heard two familiar voices speaking in an unfriendly manner. Joshua immediately stopped and went into the nearby stairwell where he heard the voices and found Kendall and Kole. Kendall was in tears, and Kole had a smirk on his face.

"Kole!" Joshua shouted. "Get away from my sister!"

"Oh, hey, Joshua. Why such the heat?" Kole asked.

Joshua went over to Kendall and said, "Did he hurt you?"

"No," Kendall said, but she still had tears running from her eyes.

"Come on," Joshua said to her. "Let's get away from him."

"Why?" Kole asked. "Are you afraid of me? I

thought Christians didn't get afraid of people?"

"It's not that I'm *afraid.* You just have a track record of hurting Abares, and...I don't want my sister to feel the effect of that," Joshua said, leading his sister away. After they were out of earshot, Joshua said to Kendall, "What were you doing, anyway?"

"The bathroom upstairs was full, so I came down here, and on my way, Kole came over to me," Kendall said.

"What did he do?" Joshua asked.

"He just said mean things. I don't want to say them," Kendall said.

"That's okay," Joshua said.

"Next time the bathrooms are full, I'm waiting upstairs. I'm never going to walk through this hallway alone again," Kendall said.

"Don't be afraid of Kole. I mean, stay away from him, but don't let him guide your life," Joshua said.

"How's that working for you?" Kendall asked.

Joshua shrugged.

Joshua walked Kendall to a different staircase, and she went up it. Then, he went to band. He didn't play well because he couldn't stop thinking about the way he found Kendall and Kole. *Kendall.* He couldn't get the image of the tears running down her face out of his head. That stupid smirk Kole wore. It fit him so well. It scared Joshua, even though he told Kendall not to let Kole scare her.

Suddenly, band was over. Joshua packed up his saxophone and was on his way out when he heard his band teacher, Mr. Goodwell, say his name.

Joshua stopped and turned around to look at Mr. Goodwell.

"Is everything okay?" Mr. Goodwell asked him.

"Yeah," Joshua replied.

"Are you sure? You weren't playing your usual today," Mr. Goodwell pointed out.

"I don't know, actually," Joshua admitted. "But it's okay. It will be okay...I hope." Then, he quickly walked away before Mr. Goodwell could ask him any more questions. He loved Mr. Goodwell, which was exactly why he *couldn't* tell him what was going on.

Joshua went to his locker and then hurried on to his math class. Patrick was in there, but thankfully, Joshua was able to sit at Sam's table where there wasn't any room for Patrick to sit at. Patrick looked over at him and made an annoyed look, but he didn't do anything further.

Joshua still couldn't concentrate well in math. By the time he got to his next class, he was able to concentrate better, but his teacher could still tell something was up. She asked him if he was okay, and he told her he was fine.

But he wasn't fine after his class finished because all of the security he managed to find was wiped away. He was hardly out the door when he met Kole in the hallway.

"Hey, Joshua," Kole said. "Have you seen Kendall lately?"

"No," Joshua replied. "Why?"

"Oh, I don't know. You might just want to...you know...check on her," Kole said.

Joshua's stomach dropped. He stopped walking, feeling dizzy. Kole kept going, laughing. Joshua sprinted through the hallway until he got to the nearest staircase. He ran up it, then he went to the fifth grade hallway. He had no idea what class Kendall was in, but he knew where all three of the fifth grade rooms were, so he walked past them to look in. First, he looked into Miss Mangum's room, which was the closest classroom to the staircase. He didn't see her, and that caused his heart rate to pick up even more. He went to the next room, and he let out a deep breath. Ah, she was in there and looked fine. She was doing her math work, and she seemed to be able to concentrate. Joshua stood there, and she looked up because she could feel his presence.

Kendall's teacher, Mr. Dattillio, who Joshua had when he was in fifth grade, looked over. He waved and smiled at Joshua, and he waved back. Then, he continued walking.

He was walking away when he heard someone call his name. He turned around and saw Kendall standing there. He walked back over to her.

"Are you okay?" he asked.

"Yeah."

"Did Kole bother you again?"

"No. Just this morning when you were there."

"Augh! That jerk!"

"Why? Did he say he did?"

Joshua sighed. "He made it seem like he did. So...I had to come make sure you weren't unconscious on the ground somewhere."

"What if I had been in the bathroom?"

"I would have gone and gotten Reese to go look for you."

"Reese is one of them."

"Reese is friends with Kole, but I know that when Kole isn't there, we're cool."

"That's not right."

"No, but it means I could get her to go looking for you."

"Whatever. But really, you don't need to worry about me. I'm only two years younger than you. I have like...basically the same experience as you. I can take care of myself just as much as you can take care of yourself...and me. Don't worry yourself about me. School is hard enough. You told me not to be scared, so I'm not, but now it's your turn to not be scared."

"I can't stop. You're my sister, and I love you. And Kole...it's different with you."

"Listen, I've seen the way you come home from encounters with Kole, and I don't think I could be much worse. Now, I've got to go back to class, and so do you."

"Yeah...I'm going to be late." Joshua looked at the ground.

They both said goodbye, then Joshua turned around and walked away. Kendall went back to her class and sat down at her table with her friend named Miranda.

"Was that your brother?" Miranda asked Kendall as she picked up her pencil to get back to work.

"Yeah," Kendall replied.

"What did he want? He looked upset."

"He was just seeing if I was okay." Kendall paused. "And I am."

"Wow," Miranda said, dreamily. "He's so caring of you."

"Yeah," Kendall said, but she gave Miranda a grossed out look.

Joshua got to the bottom of the staircase and went

through the doorway to get to the hallway. As he stepped out, he suddenly felt the force of hands pushing against him, and someone said, “Boo!”

Joshua looked over and saw Kole standing there, laughing.

“You’re so gullible!” Kole laughed.

“That’s not funny!” Joshua snapped.

“Yeah, it is. You’re funny. Haha! So funny!” Kole laughed.

“Augh,” Joshua said, and he walked away.

He showed up late for class.

Chapter 22: Worried

"Joshua," Kendall said, sitting him down onto the couch. Joshua had come in the door going on a nervous rant about Kole hurting Kendall, and when Kendall put her hands on his arm, she realized he was shaking. His face was red, his words were quick, and his tone was distraught. It had been days since the incident in the staircase.

"He hasn't come near me since that first day when you found us. He's just trying to scare you. But don't let him. He's not going to hurt me. He just wants you to think he's going to. *Don't let him trick you.*"

"I just can't get the thought out of my head," Joshua cried. "If he hurt you, it would be all my fault. I shouldn't have pushed him. I should have never become friends with him again. I should have never gone to the park that night."

"Joshua, stop blaming yourself!"

"But it's all my fault. That's why I definitely can't let him hurt you. I couldn't bear that. I don't want to see you hurt."

"He's not going to hurt me. He's manipulating you into thinking that, but he's not."

"You're right! You're right! You have to be right!"

“I am. When are you going to learn? Girls are always right.”

“Not *all* girls.” An image of Reese danced through Joshua’s head.

“You’re right, but *I’m* always right.”

“I hope so, but I still don’t think I can stop worrying.”

“I get it.”

“But I can’t take this anymore. What is it going to take for Kole to just quit it? Maybe I should try apologizing.”

“For what?”

“Whatever I did to make him mad.”

“He’s not mad at you. That’s the problem. He’s mad at something greater than you. Apologizing is what’s right but only when you have something to apologize for.”

“But what about when I pushed him?”

“Yeah...no...this isn’t about that. And plus, you’ve said you were sorry a countless number of times.”

“Augh! It’s a lost cause.”

“No, it’s not. You’ve just got to show him he’s not bothering you.”

“But I can’t do that because he is. I’m not a very good actor.”

“You don’t have to be a good actor. Just don’t let him get to you.”

“Okay. I’ll try.”

“That’s all I suggest.”

Chapter 23: Test

"Oh, Joshua. I didn't know you had another sister who went to our school. I thought the other two were younger."

Joshua turned around and so did Kendall and Leah. Behind him was Patrick and Kole; Kole was the one who spoke. Kendall rolled her eyes and turned back around, but Joshua stopped walking and so did Leah, grasping her hands around Kendall's. Kendall turned back around. They were on their way to school, and Carson and Connor were both home sick that morning.

"Leave us alone, Kole," Joshua said.

"Why? I'm not doing anything," Kole said. "I haven't done anything."

"Yeah, Joshua." Patrick butted in. "He hasn't done anything.

"See? I told you," Kendall said.

"Oh, look! Your sister's on my side!" Kole exclaimed.

"Oh, no! I'm definitely not!" Kendall exclaimed.

"I'd be careful about that," Kole said, through gritted teeth. Then, he looked at Joshua and winked.

Kendall looked up at Joshua who looked horrified. His jaw was hanging open slightly. His face was red, and it wasn't just from the cold. His eyes were locked on Kole's face. Kendall sighed and shook her head. "Come on," she said to Joshua and Leah. "Let's keep going."

But Patrick and Kole followed behind them all the way to the school. They had to, it's not like they had a choice, because they were going to the same place.

Joshua didn't talk at all during advisory or band. He got to math and when his teacher, Mr. Henry, told everyone to take out their homework so that he could check it, Joshua realized he hadn't done it. His tablemates didn't tease him, though. They looked concerned. Joshua *always* did his homework. They learned that in fifth grade. That's what caused Joshua to become closer with Sam, who was one of the ones sitting with him. *Homework.* Can you believe that?

It was pretty bad that Joshua didn't do his homework, besides the fact that it negatively impacted his transferable skills grades. He hadn't done a single sheet of homework that week, and they had a test that day. Joshua didn't remember any of the content.

He spent the whole class staring at his test. The first couple of questions were multiple choice. He tried to do the problem the way that seemed most logically possible, but he just couldn't get the answer, so that's what led to his endless staring. Finally, there wasn't any time left, so he just went through and circled all of the Cs. Then, for the non multiple choice questions, he wrote 22 on all of them because that would be his age when he got to graduate college and never have to go to school again.

"Wow," Mr. Henry said when he collected Joshua's test and read the first non multiple choice question. "She swam for 22 hours on Monday?"

"Uh..." Joshua said, confused.

Mr. Henry walked away, and Joshua put his head on his hand, disappointed.

It was a long day after that, and it was even longer when he got home from school. Joshua was sitting at his desk doing homework in his room when his mom gently knocked on the door. He wasn't doing math homework since he didn't have any after the test; he was reading a chapter from his book in literacy. He had fallen way behind in it and was trying to catch up.

"Come in," Joshua said in response to her knocking.

Mrs. Abare opened the door and walked in. Joshua turned around to face her, throwing his bookmark into the page.

"Joshua," she said, sitting down on his bed. "I saw that you got a 1 on your test today. And your transferable skills have dropped a lot: from a 4 to a 2.5." (Grades were from 0-4, with 2.5 as the overall grade needed to pass.)

"Oh," Joshua said. "That's pretty bad." He was looking at the ground.

"Yeah, I agree. What happened?"

"It's just...I...well...I didn't do any of the homework for the past week."

"Why?"

"Because...I just...couldn't. I tried, but...I was just...distracted."

"Is this just in math class? Or is it in every class?"

"Every class."

"Why haven't you been able to concentrate?"

"Lots of reasons. Kole, mostly."

"Kendall told your dad and me that you're worried

about *her*. Are you?"

"Yeah. Because of Kole."

"Listen, you can't let what Kole's done ruin your grades. Don't let a rough week lead to a rough life. It might not seem like a big deal now, but when you're struggling later on, you will realize."

"I know, Mom. I'm not *trying* to fall behind."

"I know. So, let's make a plan on how you're going to fix this."

"I could ask Mr. Henry if I can make up my math test. I could explain to him the situation, and ask if I could make up the homework. If I do my homework, then maybe he will say it's okay."

"Is that allowed?"

"Yeah, people make up tests all of the time."

"Really?"

Joshua nodded.

"Fine. That works, but just know, in the real world, you don't always get to *make things up*."

Joshua looked at the floor and said, "I know. Believe me. I know."

"What about your other classes?"

"Right now, I'm reading my book for literacy. I don't have a lot of homework in humanities and science."

"Okay. And what about with Kole?"

"Oh...I don't know. I can't get him to leave me alone. I don't know what to do."

"Is he really going to hurt your sisters?"

"He says he is, but Kendall says he's just trying to trick me. I want to believe Kendall, but I also can't risk Kole being truthful."

"Uh-huh, I see." Mrs. Abare looked like she was thinking more, but she didn't say whatever it was. Instead, she told Joshua that she would think about it and leave him to finish his work for the time being.

By the time Joshua was called downstairs for supper, he had only finished one more page because his mind was everywhere but in the book. He had 80 pages to read since he hadn't done any reading that week. The next day, he would get 20 more pages.

After supper, he lay in his bean bag and read some more, but it was so comfortable that he fell asleep after reading only 40.

Chapter 24: Make-Up

The next day during math, after Mr. Henry had given instructions and sent everyone off to do their worksheet, Joshua walked over to him and said, "I was wondering..." Out of the corner of his eye, he could see that Patrick was looking at him. Patrick did not look away when he saw Joshua looking at him. Instead, he crossed his arms. But Joshua looked back at Mr. Henry and continued, "...if I could make up the homework that I missed so that I could retake the test we did yesterday."

"Yes, sure, that sounds fine. You're usually a pretty good student, so I will give you a second chance. Is something going on?" Mr. Henry asked.

Joshua sighed and said, "I'm just...I don't know how to explain it."

"Okay," Mr. Henry said.

Joshua and Mr. Henry made up a plan for Joshua to retake the test next Friday, a week later. He also made sure Joshua had all of the homework. Then, Joshua walked back to his seat, where he was sitting with Sam and his friends. Joshua did his current homework, and he finished it early, so he started working on his makeup homework.

Joshua had literacy next, and sure enough, he was

given 20 more pages to read, making him have 60 in total. During class, he only read 10 pages. It was like an endless cycle of debt. Every time he made more money, more expenses would come in.

As he stepped out of his classroom, another expense came in. Joshua was walking to independent study when he felt someone grab his shirt, pulling him backward. He dropped his binder, which hit the ground with a loud, ear-piercing thud.

"Haha."

It was Kole.

Kole pulled Joshua backward again, this time using both hands, and he caused Joshua to fall to the ground. Kole quickly reached down and grabbed Joshua's binder.

"Hey!" Joshua snapped as Kole started to run away with his binder. He jumped up, back onto his feet, and he followed after him. They ran down the long hallway.

They got to the first classroom, which was the elementary art room. Kole swung the binder sideways, and it flew into the classroom, hitting the floor loudly and sliding across the ground. Kole laughed again, then he kept going. Joshua groaned, and, cheeks red, he walked into the classroom.

Joshua knew the art teacher; he had her himself in elementary school. When he stepped into the classroom, she was picking up his binder. She stood up and faced him, holding it in her hands. Joshua stood there, somehow feeling ashamed, even though he technically hadn't done anything wrong.

"Joshua?" she, Mrs. Haines, said, surprised as if it was a question.

"*Yeah*...hi," he said.

"Is this your binder?"

"Yeah. Sorry about that."

"Did *you* throw it?"

"No. I didn't."

"JOSHUA!?" a high-pitched voice exclaimed.

Joshua looked up, and sitting at one of the tables was Leah. She had a paintbrush in her hand and a smock over her shirt. The smock had fresh green paint streaked down the front of it.

"Hey, Leah," Joshua said. He felt his cheeks get a little redder.

"What are you doing in my classroom?" Leah asked. Her voice sounded utterly shocked.

"I'm just getting my binder," Joshua told her.

Leah held up her painting and said, "See this painting I'm making? Isn't it beautiful?"

"Yes. It is," Joshua replied.

"Thank you," Leah said, putting her painting back down and continuing to paint it.

Joshua looked back up at Mrs. Haines, and she insisted that he tell her what happened. Afterward, he left and continued on his way to Independent Study.

He was late again, and when he sat down, Reese leaned over to him and asked him why.

"It doesn't matter," Joshua replied.

"Please, Joshua," Reese said.

"No."

Reese opened her mouth to speak, but no words came out, and she went back to her work. Joshua put his head on his hand, and he opened up his computer.

Chapter 25: Swim Meet

Joshua had a swim meet the following Saturday that was two hours away, so he already knew how he would be spending his whole day. He would leave before the sun woke up, and he would get home just before it went to bed. But it was worth it...usually.

The past week had been a hard week when it came to swimming. He had physically been at practice, but not mentally. During practice, he was just going through the motions without much care for swimming because his mind was somewhere else. He feared how this would show when it came to the meet.

When he arrived on the pool deck, he told himself that he was going to leave everything that went down with Kole outside. He wasn't going to bring it into the pool with him; he was going to drop it into the cold snow outside. He tried to remind himself that he had been swimming since he was eight years old, and the past week was only a small fraction of that time.

When he first got to the pool, it was empty because he was in the first warm-up. It was giant: 25 yards by 25 meters. Such a giant pool, which Joshua had rarely seen completely empty—completely still—was now just that.

Being that it was so early in the morning, it was quiet on the pool deck, much different from the sound it was during the meet when everyone was screaming, cheering, whistling, and splashing around. The pool gave a tranquil vibe that Joshua had been longing to grasp since that November night.

But when Joshua jumped into the pool for his warm-ups just 10 minutes after his arrival, that tranquility was broken. Suddenly, the pool was filled with swimmers and more people began to arrive. It was no longer quiet, no longer still, no longer empty. And just like that, Joshua's mind was filled with all of the negatives from the recent past, and not the positives of his past as a whole. After swimming just 25 yards, he was out of breath, and he couldn't even stay with his teammates. He was set to do the 200 IM that day, so he could already see that it was going to be a struggle. In addition to that, he had another 200: breaststroke. Plus, he had the 100 butterfly and 50 freestyle.

Thankfully, he had a break after warm ups while other teams warmed up, but his 100 butterfly was the first event. Butterfly was his favorite stroke, but it was in no way *easy*. Before he knew it, he was standing on the block, and the starter said, "Take your mark."

He reached down and grabbed the front of the block. Then, the buzzer went off, and he dove in. He began swimming butterfly. Each pull felt like someone had tied a brick to his forearm, or to his waste, or to his legs, or to his whole body.

Each 25 felt like more bricks were being tied on. By the last 25, there were so many bricks tied around his waist that his hips were sinking.

Finally, he reached the final wall and drew his eyes toward the scoreboard. His eyes set on J Abare who got 1:30. That was 15 seconds added to his personal best. After the next heat started, he climbed out of the pool and walked sadly back to his team, fearing that his coach might comment. He wanted to walk out and not face them immediately after, but he had to get ready for his next race, which was only four events away.

Thankfully, his coach didn't say anything. There was another one of their swimmers in the next heat, and he was winning, so they were shouting his name and cheering.

The rest of the meet continued to go downhill for Joshua. In his 200 breaststroke, he added 15 seconds again, which wasn't as bad as adding that much in a 100, but it was still upsetting to him. In his 50 freestyle, he only added two seconds, but in such a fast race, that made a huge difference. Finally, in his 200 IM, he added 20 seconds. He was bewildered, impressed, and upset all at the same time at what one week of inadequate practice could do. But really, it was beyond just that. The past week wasn't just bad practicing; it was fear, worry, distraction, confusion, and so on.

Joshua got changed after the meet, then he met his mom in the lobby. His dad and sisters had stayed home.

"I'm sorry," were the first words that Joshua said to his mom when he met her.

"Sorry? For what?" Mrs. Abare asked.

"For wasting your time."

"Wasting my time? What do you mean?"

"I've wasted your whole Saturday."

"Says who?"

"I made you come all the way down here just to add a total of 52 seconds. That's almost a whole minute just in one meet!"

"Woah," Mrs. Abare said, surprised. "I mean...it's okay. We all have off days...off weeks...off times, and we can't control when they come. Sometimes, they will come on the day of a swim meet. Sometimes, they will come on the day of your job interview, or your first day of college, or the day of a big exam. They come at the worst of times, always. I'm not mad, and I'm not resentful."

"Okay," Joshua said. "Thank you."

Mrs. Abare nodded.

When they stepped outside, the hairs in their noses froze together, and they waddled to their car as quickly as possible before their legs froze. It was especially cold for Joshua since he was still wet from the pool. When they sat down in their seats, it was like they had just sat down on a hockey rink.

Chapter 26: Again

Joshua was walking to the bathroom by the school lobby during Independent Study. That was the bathroom that the second through fourth graders used, but also the kindergarten and first graders who were in art, and at that time, Leah was in art. It was the one Joshua would use when he was in Independent Study—it was the bathroom *everyone* used when they were in Independent Study.

When Joshua got to the outside of the bathrooms, he found Leah standing in front of the girls' bathroom door. Standing in front of her was none other than Kole Jackson. Leah was looking up at him, and she had a frown across her face. She stood still, without moving at all. Joshua had never seen her so still. Kole was talking to her, standing up straight. But shortly after Joshua got there, he kneeled on the ground so that he was at Leah's eye level. Now, she moved, stepping back. Kole leaned forward.

At this moment in time, neither Leah nor Kole had noticed that Joshua was there. He was frozen in disbelief. When Kole talked to Kendall, it was scary, but Kendall wasn't that much younger than Joshua. She was only two years younger. When Joshua saw Kole talking to Leah, it brought upon him a whole new level of fear. Leah was only six years old, and Kole was 13.

Joshua unfroze, and all of the emotions inside of him rushed over him like a wave rising up from the ocean.

"KOLE!" Joshua shouted. "What are you doing!?"

Leah looked over at Joshua, and immediately, she started crying. She ran over to him and wrapped her arms around him.

"What are you doing with my little sister?" Joshua cried.

"We're just having a conversation," Kole said, standing up.

"He said he's going to come to our house tonight!" Leah cried. "And he said he's going to beat us all up. He said he will win because you're weak, and I'm a girl, and Kendall's a girl. He says he's going to hurt us really badly!"

Joshua looked at Kole and said, "What is wrong with you? Why can't you leave my sisters alone? She's six, Kole! She's six!"

"All I was doing was going to the bathroom. I can't help it that your sister was walking past me at the very same exact time," Kole said.

"You could have just kept walking, but you didn't!" Joshua snapped.

"Listen, Joshua," Kole said. He stepped close to him. "I've got to get back to class. We can discuss this tonight...at your place."

Then, Kole walked away.

Joshua looked at Leah who looked up at him. Her eyes were wide, and she was frowning.

"It's okay, Leah," Joshua said. "Kole won't hurt

you."

"I'm scared!" Leah cried.

"Did he hurt you?"

"No! But I'm scared he will!"

"I won't let him. Here, let me walk you back to class."

"Okay," Leah said, and so he did.

Chapter 27: Up Late

Joshua got home from school that afternoon with a lot of homework to do, but instead of taking it up to his room, he left it in his backpack that he threw into the cubby area. He and Leah went upstairs, and Joshua said to her, "Did Kole say when he was coming?"

"No, he just said tonight," Leah told him.

"Okay," Joshua said. "We have to make sure that he can't come in, and we can't go outside."

"But Kendall and Ava are going outside," Leah said.

"Oh...we can't let them. We have to make them come in, and then we have to lock all of the doors," Joshua said.

So, the two of them went downstairs and put their jackets on, then they went outside. When they got out there, Kendall and Ava were building a snowman. They were each rolling out their own snowball. Kendall's was much bigger than Ava's, and her trail extended much farther.

"Guys! You need to come inside!" Leah exclaimed.

"Yeah," Joshua reiterated.

"Why?" Kendall asked.

"Because," Joshua said. "We will explain when we get inside. But you need to come in right now."

"What's your problem?" Kendall snapped.

"Kendall, come on," Joshua cried.

"Just tell me now, and we can get this done a lot quicker," Kendall said. She stood up and crossed her arms. Ava mimicked her.

Joshua sighed, then he explained, "Kole said he's coming over tonight, and he wants to hurt us."

"Seriously, Joshua? Kole!? That's your problem?" Kendall snapped.

"Come on, Kendall! You've seen what he can do!" Joshua cried.

"I've seen what he can do? Yeah! I have! He can *scare* you! Don't you know that he's not really going to come here?" Kendall asked.

"What are you talking about?" Joshua asked.

"He's just trying to make you scared!" Kendall snapped. "He does this all of the time! You know that!"

"But he does hurt us sometimes," Joshua said.

"But he never warns you first. Come on, Joshua, be realistic. You know the way he is. He's not coming," Kendall said.

"Yes, he is, Kendall!" Leah cried. "He told me he was!"

"He's just trying to scare Joshua," Kendall said.

"He's scaring me, too," Leah said.

"Don't let him get to you. I've tried to get Joshua to see that, but he just won't," Kendall said.

"Why can't you come inside just in case?" Joshua asked.

"Because Ava and I want to build a snowman," Kendall said.

"Not anymore," Ava said. She was no longer standing with her arms crossed, but she stood still with a worried face. "I don't want to play outside anymore. I want to go inside."

"Yeah, come on Ava, let's go," Leah said, and the two of them skipped through the snow and went back in the door.

Kendall looked at Joshua with a frown and said, "Nice going."

"I just don't want you to get hurt," Joshua said.

"Okay, I get it. I'll come inside. But let's say this..." Kendall said. "If you're right, and he comes, then I owe you something. It can be whatever you want. I don't care. But if I'm right, and he doesn't come, then you owe me something. *Something big.*"

"Okay, whatever! I don't care! As long as you come inside!" Joshua cried.

"Fine," Kendall said.

The two of them went inside, and when they got in, Leah and Ava were standing in the kitchen in front of their mom, tears running down their faces.

"Joshua," Mrs. Abare said sternly. "Why are your sisters scared out of their minds that someone is coming to hurt them?"

"It's Kole! He told Leah that he was coming here tonight to hurt us," Joshua explained.

"When?" Mrs. Abare asked.

"Earlier, at school," Joshua answered.

"How?" Mrs. Abare asked.

"He saw her when she was in the hallway going to the bathroom, and he told her that," Joshua said.

"Why was he even near her?" Mrs. Abare asked. "I thought seventh grade was on the opposite side of the school as first grade."

"It is, but he was in Independent Study, and she was in art," Joshua explained.

"Is Kole really coming?" Mrs. Abare asked.

"I don't know," Joshua answered, fighting tears.

"He's not," Kendall butted in.

"This needs to stop," Mrs. Abare said.

"That's what I'm saying!" Kendall exclaimed.

Mrs. Abare walked over to the phone and picked it up.

"Wait...what are you doing?" Joshua asked.

"I'm calling the school," Mrs. Abare said.

"But...that's embarrassing!" Joshua cried.

"Look at your sister! Look at *you*! This can't go on any longer!" Mrs. Abare exclaimed.

"Calling the school isn't going to help anything. Kole's everywhere," Joshua said.

"He's right, Mom. As much as I think this is ridiculous, calling the school certainly isn't going to help anything," Kendall said.

Mrs. Abare sighed, then she said, "Listen, I'll leave your name out of it. I'm just going to say that the middle schoolers shouldn't be going near the younger kids. Kole shouldn't have been anywhere near your sister."

"What about Kendall?" Joshua asked.

"I'm fine!" Kendall exclaimed.

"Why do you act like Kole's so harmless!?" Joshua cried. "Do you think he's hot or something?"

"Why would you even suggest that!? I think he's a

real jerk, and he's certainly not harmless! But you're playing into his traps! That's why I say what I say!" Kendall snapped, and she stormed away.

Joshua walked away, too. He went to the front door, where he locked it, including the deadbolt. Then, he grabbed his backpack and went upstairs to his room, where he began his homework. But he didn't get very far before he started feeling bad for what he said to Kendall, so he got up and went looking for her.

She was sitting in her bedroom, with the door cracked open, on her bed with her own homework spread out in front of her. Joshua stood in the crack and knocked on the door. Kendall looked up at him, then down at her homework in front of her and said, "Come in."

Joshua pushed the door open, went through, then put it back to the way it was before: partially open. He walked in, and he sat down on Leah's bed, which was about three feet away from Kendall's—the only thing in between was their nightstand which had a lamp and an alarm clock on it. Kendall looked at Joshua, who began to speak: "I'm sorry."

Kendall didn't respond.

"I shouldn't have suggested that you were being swayed by Kole's looks," Joshua said. "And I'm sorry that I'm getting all worked up over him."

"Joshua, I understand," Kendall said. "You've never met anyone like him before. You've never met someone so mean or persistent. You just don't know how to handle him. To be honest, I don't either, but I'm trying. I'm sorry I suppress your feelings because to be honest, I really am afraid of him. Maybe you should worry. At least...enough to not be stupid, but not to lose sleep over. Maybe you're right. Maybe he will come tonight, but I don't think so. You know what? If he doesn't come tonight...you don't owe me anything. I'll just be glad that he's not trying to hurt you," Kendall said.

"And if he *does* come, you certainly don't owe me anything," Joshua said. "Except...maybe a visit when I'm in the hospital."

"*Joshua*," Kendall said, but she laughed a little.

They suddenly heard the sound of footsteps running up the stairs, and pretty soon, Leah was pushing the door open to announce: "It's time for supper!"

"Okay," Kendall said.

Leah walked back out. Kendall turned to Joshua and said, "We've made it until supper without Kole coming."

"Yeah, I guess so," Joshua said.

The two of them went downstairs and ate. Afterwards, Joshua went back upstairs to his room to continue working on his homework. It had been about 10 minutes when he saw two figures walking on the sidewalk along the road. They were just barely in view when Joshua saw them, about 20 yards away from their driveway. The second Joshua saw them, he shouted, "KENDALL!" But she didn't come right away because she was downstairs, so he shouted again, this time louder, more desperate, his voice cracking, "KENDALL!!!"

"COMING!!!" Kendall shouted, and she came running up the stairs.

She entered the room, and Joshua was trembling as he made out the words, "Look!"

Kendall walked across his room and over to the window, and she saw the two figures.

"Oh my gosh," Kendall cried, looking at him.

"Do you think that's Kole?" Joshua asked.

"I don't know. I can't tell. It's too dark," Kendall said.

"What do we do?" Joshua asked.

"I don't know," Kendall said. She stepped backwards and turned around, then she came back and put her hands on his desk, saying, "Just watch them. See if they keep walking or not."

So, they kept watching. The two figures got closer to the driveway, but they didn't stop at it. They kept going, and they continued on until they couldn't be seen anymore. After they were out of sight, Joshua relaxed, sitting back in his chair, and Kendall did the same, stepping away from the desk.

"Wooh," Kendall said out loud. "Not Kole."

"Ahhh." Joshua let out a sigh of relief. "Sorry."

"It's okay! I was believing it, too!"

"I'm so on edge."

"I guess I'm a little, too."

"Yeah. Looks like it."

"I'm going to get going."

Kendall turned around and walked out the door. Joshua continued on with his homework for a few more minutes, then he saw the motion sensored light over the garage turn on. He couldn't see the garage from his window, so he couldn't see if anyone was actually there, only that something had set it off. Joshua sprung up from his seat and ran downstairs. He ran into the living room where Kendall was sitting on the floor at the coffee table, and Mr. Abare was sitting in his chair, and Mrs. Abare was sitting on the couch. Joshua stood in the entrance and shouted, "The light over the garage is on! Someone's here!"

"No one's here. It's just the wind," Mr. Abare said.

"Oh," Joshua said.

"What's the matter?" Mr. Abare asked.

Joshua looked at Kendall, then at his dad, then at his mom, then at the love seat which was empty. He walked over to it and sat down. "Kole said he was coming here tonight, that's all. I wasn't sure if it was him," Joshua explained to his dad.

"Kole?" Mr. Abare asked. "Why?"

"He said he wants to hurt us. He told that to Leah, and I walked in on their conversation," Joshua explained.

"Is that why you and Leah have both been acting so weird tonight?" Mr. Abare asked.

"Yeah, I guess so," Joshua answered.

"Why was Kole anywhere near your little sister?" Mr. Abare asked.

"Because he's a creep," Joshua explained.

"He was going to the bathroom, and he saw Leah in the hallway," Kendall butted in, clearly dissatisfied with her brother's description. "Kole likes to scare Joshua by talking to me and her. He's not going to hurt her...or me...but he just wants Joshua to think that so he can be scared out of his mind."

"Is this why you failed that math test last week?" Mr. Abare asked, looking back at Joshua.

"Yeah," Joshua replied, looking at the ground.

"Okay, I see," Mr. Abare said.

Joshua went back upstairs, where he continued to struggle with his work.

Joshua had finished his homework and studied a little bit for his math test when he decided that he was too tired to continue, so he went to bed. But as soon as he was laying in his bed, he couldn't sleep. He was thinking about Kole. What if Kole tried to come during the night? He wasn't sure. He was still laying awake when he heard his parents going to bed, and he was still awake after about another hour.

Suddenly, it was two o'clock. Joshua was pretty sure that he had fallen asleep at some point, but not for very long. He couldn't sleep. He was awake for about another hour before he decided to go to the bathroom. After he flushed the toilet, he heard a loud scream coming from the bedroom on the other side of the wall. He quickly washed his hands and ran into the room: Kendall and Leah's room. Leah was sitting up in her bed, and Kendall was standing next to her. The lamp was on.

"KOLE'S HERE!!!" Leah cried.

"No, he's not. That noise was just Joshua," Kendall said.

"ARE YOU SURE!?"

"Yes."

"HOW DO YOU KNOW!?"

"Because Joshua just walked out of the bathroom. Here, let's ask him, just to make sure."

"Okay."

"Joshua," Kendall said. "Did you just go to the bathroom?"

"Yeah," Joshua replied.

"See?" Kendall asked.

"Oh...yeah," Leah said.

"You can go back to sleep," Kendall told her.

"Okay," Leah said, and she laid down.

Mr. and Mrs. Abare appeared at the door and said, "What's going on?"

"Leah just thought she heard something, but it was only Joshua," Kendall explained.

"What are you doing up, Joshua?" Mr. Abare asked.

"I just had to go to the bathroom, that's all," Joshua said.

"Okay," Mr. Abare said. "Is everything okay now?"

"Yes," Joshua answered.

"Okay," Mr. Abare replied. He and Mrs. Abare went back to bed.

Joshua was left standing in the doorway of Kendall and Leah's room. Kendall walked over to him and said, "Have you slept at all?"

"Yeah."

"You don't sound like you're sleeping."

"What do you mean?"

"I keep hearing you roll around in your bed. You don't usually do that—not when you're sleeping."

"Oh."

"So...have you slept at all?"

"I think I fell asleep...at some point, but...not much."

"Kole's come after you a lot, but has he ever come after you this late at night?"

"No."

"Then, you're okay. And plus, he can't get in. The doors are locked."

Joshua shrugged. "What about you? You heard me rolling around."

"I often wake up during the night, so it's nothing new for me. That's how I also know that you're usually silent."

"Oh."

"I'm tired, so I'm going back to bed."

"Okay, me too. At least, I'll try," Joshua said, and he did what he said. He fell asleep for an hour, but then he woke up again and couldn't sleep, so he decided to just get up. But that was a decision he quickly regretted.

Chapter 28: Too Tired

Joshua's eyelids were heavy during advisory. He was already 15 minutes into class, and the only progress he had made was simply pulling up the calendar, when Sam pointed out to him that he seemed tired. Joshua replied, "That's because I am."

"Did you not sleep well?" Sam asked.

"No, not really," Joshua replied.

Reese leaned in toward Joshua after Sam finished talking to him and said, "Is something wrong?"

"I didn't sleep well."

"Is that all?"

Joshua stared at his computer screen, not wanting to answer, but Reese said, "Did *Kole* do something?"

"It doesn't matter."

"Clearly it does, since you're losing sleep over it."

Joshua sighed, and he thought about whether or not it was a good idea to tell Reese about what happened. He decided not. "I don't want to talk about it," he admitted.

"Okay, fine." Reese turned back to her computer.

Joshua spent the rest of his day fighting sleep. Independent study came, and he was in class with Reese again. At the beginning, their teacher announced that if anyone had to use the bathroom, they had to use the bathrooms up by the cafeteria—they weren't allowed to use the ones by the lobby anymore because they weren't allowed to go near the elementary students. Joshua heard, but he didn't show any emotion. He knew exactly what the reasoning was. Reese looked at him, wondering if he had to do with it, but Joshua didn't notice that she looked at him, since he was too tired.

Joshua left Independent Study after class with Reese, and since Kole was in the same general area, he caught up to them. He put his hand on Joshua's shoulder, stepping in between him and Reese.

"Hey, Joshua," Kole said.

Reese looked up at Kole, but Joshua kept his line of vision forward.

"I heard we're not allowed to use the lobby bathrooms anymore. That wouldn't have anything to do with you, would it?" Kole asked.

"No, actually, it has to do with you," Joshua said, stepping away from him so that his hand wouldn't be on his shoulder anymore.

"Really? I didn't say anything," Kole said. He stepped closer to Joshua, but he didn't put his hand back on his shoulder.

"No, you didn't *say* anything. You are bothering the elementary kids. *That's* why it has to do with you."

"So were you."

"No, I wasn't."

"You were talking to that girl."

"You mean my *sister*?"

"Yeah, whatever."

"I was talking to her because you were bothering her!"

"So, you admit it? You ratted me out." Kole smirked.

"I didn't tell the school anything. But my sister was scared out of her mind because of you."

"And *you*? How about *you*?"

Joshua was quiet.

Kole pushed Joshua into the wall, then he walked ahead. Reese kept walking too, leaving Joshua behind. He stood against the wall and watched the two of them together. Joshua said out loud, but so only he could hear, "And that's why I didn't tell you what happened, Reese."

That night, when Joshua got home, he went up to his room and took a nap. But he didn't wake up until 10, so he ate supper then went back to bed.

The next morning was Friday. Joshua got up early and did some homework, but he realized that he had not finished all of his make-up math homework that he said he would do, and now, he was going to fail the test *again*.

Mr. Henry sent Joshua to Mrs. Wheeling's office to take his test during math class. She was the middle school disciplinary person, but she used to be a substitute teacher. She kind of scared Joshua because she could be pretty harsh, but Joshua never caused her any trouble, so she was nice to him. In fact, he was pretty sure she thought fairly high of him...for a guy, anyway.

Joshua sat down and began to take his test. Even though he hadn't finished all of the makeup work, his test was going a lot better than the first one. He was able to understand most of the problems. He was about half done when a familiar face walked in the door.

"Hey, Joshua!" they exclaimed.

Kole.

"Don't talk to him; he's taking a test," Mrs. Wheeling said, sternly.

"A test? Oh, I thought he was in trouble. I thought that he might have started another fight or something," Kole said, smirking.

Joshua glared at Kole until Mrs. Wheeling told him to continue working. Kole sat on the opposite side of the room as Joshua, and Mrs. Wheeling asked Kole what he was doing there. They spoke quietly in an attempt to not distract Joshua, but Joshua couldn't help but be distracted.

"I came in here because I am all done with all of my work, and one of my classmates was distracted by me," Kole said.

"I can understand why," Mrs. Wheeling said.

"It wasn't my fault. This classmate of mine won't stop talking to me. I don't get why. I don't even like her. I wish she'd just leave me alone, and believe me, I've tried multiple times to get her to talk to someone else, but she's just so persistent," Kole said.

Reese.

Joshua was writing things down on his paper, but he was hardly sure what. He finished his test, and he went back to class, but he didn't check over his answers because he didn't even imagine doing that when he was in seventh grade. He handed Mr. Henry his paper, and he immediately started grading it. He didn't give it back to Joshua until the end of class when he came to him and said, "Joshua, your test started out good, but by the end, you were getting a lot of wrong answers. Was there a problem?"

"No."

"Really?"

Joshua thought about it, then he replied, "I was a little distracted."

"I can tell."

"Someone came into Mrs. Wheeling's room, and I couldn't concentrate. Can I just take the test again?"

"No, sorry. I can only let you make it up once."

Joshua sighed, then he said, "What did I get?"

"Two."

"What!?"

"It's better than last time."

"Yeah, but barely! It's still not passing!"

"Is there something going on that I can do something about?"

"No. I don't think you can do anything." Joshua sighed. "Thanks for the opportunity. Sorry I blew it."

"*Joshua.*"

"I'm sorry," Joshua said, quietly.

"What is it?"

Joshua looked at the ground for a moment, then he said, "No. I'm okay."

But Mr. Henry wasn't convinced.

Joshua looked up at Mr. Henry, gave him a distant smile, then walked out of the classroom. To his dismay, he arrived at the door just as Kole was coming in. Kole seemed pretty excited and exclaimed, "Hey, Joshua!"

"Leave me alone," Joshua snapped, and he pushed

Kole.

"Woah," Kole said, but then he pushed Joshua back. Joshua hit the door post.

"Boys!" Mr. Henry snapped.

Joshua blushed. He lost it, again. He could hear some of his classmates giggling. One of them even had the audacity to say, "Wow, it looks like Joshua really is the one who started the fight. I never would have believed it." But Joshua didn't look back. He just kept going. He had only made it a couple of steps before he saw that Reese was standing there, no doubt having seen the whole thing. But she had no idea, so all she saw was that Joshua pushed Kole *first*. Joshua sighed as he walked past her, but they didn't speak to each other.

Chapter 29: The Park

That afternoon after school, Joshua went to the park with Carson. After the long week that Joshua had had, Carson asked him if he wanted to go and just let off steam. At first, Joshua was nervous about that idea because he feared he'd see Kole, but Carson said that they wouldn't. He wasn't sure that Carson really *knew* that, but he accepted it anyway.

They walked around, and even though they were both very cold, it felt nice. The two of them talked about things they would have talked about over the summer before they met Kole. Minus the girls. They talked about girls a lot over the summer, but right now, Joshua was feeling a little bit salty about the girl he used to talk about.

Around supper time, the two of them walked to Joshua's house where Mrs. Abare invited Carson to stay. Kendall made hot chocolate. Meanwhile, Mrs. Abare popped a frozen chicken pot pie into the oven.

Carson left shortly after supper. Joshua walked him to the door, and as Carson put on his jacket and shoes, Joshua said to him, "I feel good."

"Oh yeah?" Carson asked.

"I mean...like...I don't feel stressed or upset. I just feel good...like I did before."

"You mean...before Kole came?"

Joshua nodded, but he didn't look at Carson. Then, he looked up at him and said, "Thank you."

"That's what friends are for." Carson smiled. "We should hang out again."

"Yeah, definitely." Joshua smiled back.

They told each other goodbye, then Carson opened the door and went out. When he got home, he called Joshua, and they talked some more, until they both went to bed.

The next morning was Saturday. Joshua had a relaxing weekend. He stayed at his house the whole time, except to go to Church, and Carson came over again. It was nice to have a break from Kole and *homework*. Joshua had done so much homework that week trying to catch up that he hadn't done anything for himself, which only added to the stress. When Carson wasn't at his house, he was either writing or playing his instruments.

But Monday came around, and that meant back to seeing Kole again. Joshua had never had such a hard time getting out of bed. His alarm went off at 6:30, but he didn't get out of bed until seven. He still had to shower and eat breakfast before leaving for school.

Carson and Connor met up with Joshua, Kendall, and Leah, and they all walked to school together as usual. When they got to the school, Joshua and Kendall took Leah to the first grade and Carson and Connor went with them. Joshua started going with her ever since the incident with Kole by the bathrooms. They were on their way back from the first grade, Connor had already gone to his classroom, when Kole stepped out in front of them from a doorway they were about to walk past.

"Awe, that's cute," Kole said, standing in front of them. "Walking your little sister to her classroom."

Joshua looked terrified, but in reality, it was just the happiness from the weekend leaving his body; Kendall glared; Carson spoke up: "Go away, Kole."

"*Go away, Kole*," Kole mocked. "Such losers. I know why you're bringing your sister to her class. It's because you're scared."

"If we were scared, then why did Joshua push you first?" Kendall asked.

Joshua blushed. Kole laughed and said, "That's real bold of you." He paused, looked at Kendall, then at Joshua, then at the group as a whole and said, "I can't even with you guys. You're too uncultured to realize that you're so stupid." Then, Kole looked at Joshua and said, "You're such a coward." Kole pushed Joshua lightly, so he didn't fall or slam into anything, then he walked away, leaving the three of them—Joshua, Kendall, and Carson—standing there.

Carson looked at Joshua and said, "How can you just stand there? I feel like you've given up trying."

Joshua was silent at first, then he replied, "I have."

"What?" Carson asked. "So you're just...cool with it?"

"No, I'm not cool with it, but what can I do? When I let him bother me, he ruins me, so how about I just ignore him?" Joshua asked. "Isn't that what we're always told? Ignore the antagonizer?"

"Antagonizer?" Kendall butted in.

"What?" Joshua asked.

"Who says that?" Kendall asked.

"Why don't you just call him for what he is? A bully!" Carson exclaimed.

"Because I just can't do that. *I* was the first to push—like Kendall said—so *he* can't be the bully," Joshua said.

Kendall sighed and covered her face for a minute, then she uncovered it and looked at her brother, saying, "You might've been the first to push, but he's taken it too far. That makes him the bully. Don't you know that not all victims of bullies are innocent? Bullies have to have some reason for picking a target. It's like buying a house. Someone who needs a house needs to buy one, but there's got to be something about that house that they like. They're not just going to buy an awful house. A bully needs a target, but they're not just going to pick a random person. They're going to pick someone who stands out. Sometimes, it's someone who they find annoying, weird, or different, and well, sometimes I find you to be all three of those things, but...that's not why Kole chose you. Sometimes, bullies pick their victim because the victim is mouthy, or unknowingly rude, or...because they pushed first! But regardless, the bully is a bully!"

"But I've still provoked him," Joshua said.

"That's what I'm saying! That's what makes a bully choose their target!" Kendall exclaimed. "Bullies target those who provoke them!"

Joshua was quiet. There was a moment of silence, but it was clearly too long for Carson, and he said, "She's right."

"Of course I'm right!" Kendall exclaimed. "I

wouldn't go on about it and make myself late for class if I didn't think I was right!"

"Augh," Joshua cried. "I can't be late for class. It will ruin my perfect attendance."

"Perfect attendance?" Carson asked, smiling.

"Yeah," Joshua answered as they started to walk up the hallway again.

"Maybe you pushing first isn't the only reason that Kole bullies you," Carson laughed.

Joshua rolled his eyes.

"You also just, like, don't have perfect attendance," Kendall said.

"It's never too late to start trying," Joshua said.

Now Kendall rolled her eyes.

Chapter 30: Caiden and Daniel

The day only got worse between Joshua and Kole, so after school, Carson asked Joshua if he wanted to hang out again, and Joshua *did* want to. They went to Carson's house that afternoon. Carson lived in an apartment building with two of his brothers and his parents. On top of that, his parents ran a daycare. It was a tiny little place, so it was crowded. The two boys just stayed long enough to have a snack, then they went for a walk. It was cold, but they didn't mind. They walked up to the park: a place of peace.

When they got there, it was snowing lightly. It was supposed to snow harder later, and when that happened, they would go home. For now, they just walked around, talking. There weren't many other people in the park, since it was not only snowing but a Monday afternoon.

When the snow began picking up, the boys started to walk back home, cutting across the park. As they walked past the fountain, they were met by a group of boys coming from the side. Patrick, Kole, and Maverick all stepped out from behind the frozen water and giant statue in the middle.

Joshua's face immediately dropped to look like he had just faced a great disappointment, which he had.

Carson grimaced.

"Wow," Kole said. "Funny we would meet here."

Joshua tried to walk away, but Kole grabbed the hood of his jacket and yanked him backward.

"Where are you going?" Kole asked.

"Home."

"Why? We just got here."

"It's snowing hard."

"That's kind of rude! Leaving...just because I got here. Why don't you want to hang out?"

"He didn't say that!" Carson butted in. "Don't you listen? He said because it's snowing hard."

"That's just an alibi," Kole said.

"You live farther than me," Joshua said, chiming back in. "Don't you want to go home, too? Before it's dark?"

"The dark doesn't bother me," Kole said quietly, in a deeper tone.

"Yeah, I guess I could have figured that," Joshua mumbled.

"Kole, leave him alone," Carson pleaded.

"Why do you always assume the worst? Am I really that bad?" Kole asked.

"Yeah, you are," Carson said.

"Oof, that wasn't very nice," Kole said.

"It's the truth," Joshua said. "But you're afraid of the truth. That's why you are the way that you are."

Kole punched Joshua in the face.

"SEE!?" Carson cried. "That was uncalled for!"

Kole stared at Joshua to see if he would react. Initially, Joshua just stared back, but then he said, with a slight smile, "Point proven."

Kole went to punch Joshua again, but Joshua quickly ducked. Sadly for Joshua, he slipped in the snow and fell to the ground. But he used that as an opportunity to attack. He wrapped his arms around Kole's legs and stood up, causing Kole to fall. Then, Joshua was on top. He was about to kick Kole when he caught Carson looking at him out of the corner of his eye, and he decided he would let Kole go.

Joshua started to walk away quickly, but he was stopped by Maverick, who threw him into a headlock. Joshua tried to break free, but he couldn't. Now, Kole was back on his feet again, and he punched Joshua. That time, he split Joshua's lip, and blood trickled out. Maverick let him go. Joshua wiped the blood onto the back of his glove, and then he looked at Kole who laughed.

Joshua wanted to attack him, make him pay, though he decided not to. But he didn't know how to walk away without being attacked again. After a few seconds, he decided that he couldn't just stand there, so he looked Carson in the eyes, then they both started to run. But Carson wasn't on cross country like Joshua was. Joshua ran until he heard someone behind him cry, "Oof!"

He looked back and saw Kole had just caught Carson and was holding his hands behind his back so he couldn't get away. Maverick punched Carson across the face, but no blood came *yet*. Joshua's eyebrows raised, and he shouted, "NO!" He ran back over, and Kole quickly let go of Carson who fell to the ground. Kole pushed Joshua, but he didn't fall. Joshua realized that he couldn't walk away from this, so he pushed Kole back. But Kole pushed

Joshua to the ground and pinned him there. Kole punched him twice while he was pinning him to the ground. Joshua's face began to sting and his vision was blurry. He laid on the ground motionless under Kole's weight. For a minute, he was drawn away from reality, half unconscious. Carson saw that Joshua's eyelids were fluttering, and he ran at Kole and pushed him off of Joshua.

Joshua felt that Kole was no longer on top of him, so he slowly climbed to his feet. He thought maybe it was over, but it wasn't. Kole punched him again in the face. Joshua could hardly see, then he took a blow to the throat, and he could hardly breathe. He fell to the ground, on his hands and knees, gasping for air.

Kole stood in front of Joshua, like he was going to hit him again, but Patrick said, "Kole! That's enough!" Carson looked over at Patrick upset. *Why had he waited so long to chime in?*

Carson looked at Kole, who appeared to be ignoring Patrick.

"Kole, leave him alone," Carson cried.

Kole looked at Carson and said, "Fine." But he went over to Carson and pushed him.

Joshua tried to get up, still gasping for air, but Maverick kicked him, making him fall over, still weak from the blow to the throat.

Joshua looked up, and he saw Patrick was walking away quietly. After he got about 10 feet away, he started running. Joshua didn't comprehend it though, for he suffered another blow to the stomach from Maverick's knee. He gagged, spit dropping out of his mouth.

Carson had managed to escape Kole, and he pushed

Maverick away from Joshua. Maverick fell and hit the ground hard.

Joshua was left alone only for a second. He finally got to his feet, and then he was faced by Kole, but he hardly realized it because he was hardly able to concentrate. Carson was shouting, "Don't touch him!" Joshua stood still, unable to fight for himself, so he was at the mercy of Kole. Not a situation he would have asked to be in at any point.

Kole didn't listen. He pushed Joshua. It wasn't that hard, but Joshua was already weakened, so he fell to the ground. Carson attacked Kole, but Joshua didn't realize. He hardly realized that after a few minutes, two people had picked him up.

Everything was blurry, and he didn't feel well. The two people who had picked him up off the ground were putting his arms over their shoulders so that they could carry him. He realized they were Daniel and Caiden after a little while. He looked in front of him as they were positioning him, and he saw Kole and Maverick standing in opposition to him. Aiden and Andrew were standing next to them. Reese was not there, he noted. Carson was standing, not near the rest. He was covered in blood, but he could hold himself up.

"Come on," Daniel said. "Let's go to your house."

"Losers!" Kole shouted as Daniel and Caiden walked away with Joshua slumped over their shoulders. Carson followed them, but he didn't help carry Joshua.

Joshua felt his legs move as they went toward his house, but he knew he wasn't doing any of the work. It was all Daniel and Caiden. They had nearly arrived at Joshua's house when he cried, faintly, “My family can’t see me like this.”

“What did you say?” Daniel asked him.

“My family,” Joshua said, his throat throbbing. “Can’t see me.”

But the boys didn’t listen to him: partly because they couldn’t understand him fully and partly because they just didn’t care. He had to go home, like it or not. They would find out eventually. Better to get it over with while he was barely in it than when he was fully conscious.

They arrived at the Abares’ front porch. The kitchen light was on. Kendall was in there, serving herself a helping of mac and cheese, when she heard the noise of them struggling up the steps. Turning around, she dropped the spoon. It missed the pot, bounced off the table, and fell to the ground, mac and cheese flying from it onto the counter and floor. She ran over to the door and opened it, crying, “Joshua!”

Joshua coughed. His throat was red, and his face was swollen and bloody. And if that wasn’t enough to show Kendall he had just gotten beaten up, she could tell just by the fact that he was being carried by Daniel and Caiden.

The rest of his family ran to the door, too. Daniel and Caiden brought Joshua into the living room, tracking snow, mud, and blood through the house, and laid him on the couch. Kendall shut the door.

Leah and Ava kept looking from Joshua to Carson, for Carson was also covered in blood.

Mrs. Abare cried, as she always did. Kendall got ice, annoyed and mad and just everything that wasn’t happy. She gave her brother some ice, then she gave Carson some ice. Carson explained everything. Daniel and Caiden were silent, listening, for they hadn't shown up until the end and didn't know the whole story.

Joshua sat up during Carson's explanation, but he didn't say anything. He mostly just coughed. It hurt to lay down. Mrs. Abare decided it would be the best decision to take him to the hospital to get it all checked out. Mr. Abare brought Carson home, for it was only a two-minute walk away (though he drove). Daniel and Caiden stayed with Kendall, Leah, and Ava until Mr. Abare got back from bringing Carson home.

Joshua only ended up having a minor injury, but breathing was still uncomfortable for the rest of the night and next morning. He didn't sleep at all, and his mom laid in the living room with him all night in case he needed anything. Though she fell asleep a lot. By three in the morning, Joshua decided that he wasn't going to fall asleep, so he just turned on the T.V.

The next morning, Joshua didn't go to school. He wanted to go because if he didn't, Kole would know he had *won*. But his mom told him he was in no shape to go. So it was over. Joshua called Carson before Kendall and Leah left, and Carson said he wasn't going to go either. With that, Mrs. Abare drove the girls to school. Ava sat in the living room with Joshua all morning. Whenever he coughed or made any noise of distress, she would quickly say to him: "Are you okay?" And he would always answer with: "Yes, thank you."

Chapter 31: Independent Study

Joshua didn't go back to school until Thursday. That morning, he never saw Kole until Independent Study later, but before that, he saw Reese in advisory (as always). When she saw him walk in, seeing his cuts and bruises, her eyes widened, but she didn't say anything. He walked over to his seat and began working, as if he hadn't just missed the past two days.

When his teachers saw him, they asked if they could talk to him. They went out into the hallway and asked him if everything was okay at home. He said yes, and he told them this didn't happen at home, but he didn't tell them where it happened or who did it. He didn't tell them much, just that it didn't happen at home. When Joshua came back into the room, Reese finally spoke to him.

"What was that about?" Reese asked.

"They just..." Joshua said. He looked up at the ceiling, trying to figure out what to say. "...were curious."

"About..." Reese said, nodding towards his face.

"Yeah," Joshua said. The tone of his voice made it clear he thought that should have been an obvious answer. He rolled his eyes slightly.

"Kole did it, didn't he?" Reese asked.

"Yeah," Joshua said, with the same tone. *Who else*

did she think did it? Kole was the only person awful enough to him to do that.

"I don't get it. Why do you guys always fight?"

"You couldn't really call it a fight. A fight makes it sounds like it was mutual, but it wasn't. It sounds like I wanted it to happen, but I didn't."

"What do you mean?"

"It was more like I got my butt kicked, and I didn't even want to fight. I tried to go home, but Kole persisted."

"Oh."

"But it doesn't matter anymore. It's over."

"Have you looked in a mirror today? It doesn't look over to me."

Joshua crossed his arms, then he snapped, "Why do you even care? He's your friend."

"Because you're my friend, too."

"But he's your friend more than I am."

"Says who?"

"No one, but no one has to. You make it pretty clear."

"Oh," Reese said, quietly, and she looked down at the keyboard in front of her.

"Even just acting like there are two sides makes it clear. Kole is being so unreasonable. I want a break," Joshua said, then he turned away.

Independent Study came around quickly. One of the other groups' teacher was absent, so instead of having a sub, they got sent into Joshua and Reese's room. The group came in the door all at once, and amongst them was Kole. Reese looked at him and made eye contact, so he came over to her.

"Real convenient," Joshua said as Kole walked toward them.

"It was like this yesterday, too," Reese told him.

"I can't do this," Joshua said, starting to stand up.

"It will be okay. Just stay here," Reese said.

Joshua continued to get up to leave, but Kole got there before he could get away. Seeing Joshua, he said, "Where are you going, Buddy? You going to run from me *again*?"

Joshua sat back down and said, "No."

"Where have you been the past two days, Joshua?" Kole asked.

"Where do you think?" Joshua asked. He looked at Reese and gave her a face that said, *"You said this would be okay, huh?"*

Joshua looked back at Kole who said, "You were hiding from me."

"I wasn't hiding from you. I could hardly *breathe*," Joshua said.

"Why?" Reese butted in.

Kole ignored her and said, "But you've hid from me before, right?"

Joshua shrugged.

"Why couldn't you breathe?" Reese asked.

Joshua looked at Reese but didn't answer.

"*Joshua*," Reese pleaded.

"Tell her, Joshua," Kole said, smiling.

Joshua looked at Kole and glared. *How could he smile?* Then, Joshua looked back at Reese. He was wearing a turtleneck to cover up his throat, but he pulled it down to reveal the giant bruise on his throat.

"Oh...wow," Reese said, surprised.

Joshua let go, and the collar slid back over the bruise.

"I was going to say...you don't usually wear turtlenecks," Reese said.

"No one does," Kole said. "You're such a weirdo."

"You did that?" Reese asked, looking at Kole.

"Yeah, who else did?" Kole asked.

"I don't know," Reese said. "Could have been anyone."

"No, it couldn't have," Joshua mumbled, quietly.

"It's impressive, right?" Kole asked. "Don't mess with me! Right, Joshua?"

Joshua rolled his eyes.

Chapter 32: Square...Again

Kole came with Patrick and Reese and sat down next to Joshua, who was sitting with Carson and Camilla, at lunch, saying, "Hey, Joshua!"

"Hey," Joshua replied.

"Don't try to run away from me," Kole said.

"I'm not."

"You're not?" Kole's voice sounded surprised.

"Nope. What? Do you want me to?"

"No."

"Because you always tell me not to, but that look you just gave me, it almost seemed like you wanted me to."

"No, no. Stay, stay!"

"Okay."

"I'm just...confused. You hate me."

"I don't *hate* you."

"You certainly don't think I'm your bestie."

Joshua laughed and said, "Nope. Not besties. But...I don't want to fight with you anymore. I want to make things right. Let's...call a truce."

"A truce?" Kole asked, confused.

"Yeah!" Reese butted in. "A truce sounds great!"

"See? Reese thinks a truce is a great idea!" Joshua exclaimed.

"Okay," Kole said. He spit into his hand and stuck it out at Joshua who gave him a disgusted look, leading Kole to make another surprised look, saying, "What?"

"No. Not with spit," Joshua said.

"It's how you make a truce," Kole said.

"I...I didn't mean that way," Joshua said. "Because I'm not touching your spit. Sorry."

"Okay, whatever," Kole said, wiping his spit on his own pants. "We can just make a...um...okay. Whatever. We will make a truce without shaking hands."

"Okay, great," Joshua said, smiling.

Kole nodded.

"Wow," Joshua thought to himself. *"Didn't think that would be so easy."*

After lunch, Carson took Joshua aside privately and said, "Why would you make a truce with him?"

"It's either make a truce with him or be abused by him," Joshua said. "I would rather have a truce."

"He's a bad guy," Carson said.

"I'm sick of getting beat up. I thought I could end it by wrapping up our disagreements," Joshua said.

"It's a bad idea to befriend him."

"I said it already: we're not besties. We're just going to be friendly with each other. There's nothing wrong with that."

"You're just asking to get hurt again."

"No. I'm asking him to stop, actually."

"Whatever. I just think this is a bad idea."

"It's not. I know *he's* not going to stop torturing me, so *I* have to make a difference. I can't wait for *him*."

"Okay. I get it. I guess."

Joshua smiled.

Chapter 33: Indoor Recess

Indoor recess. Kole and Reese sat on the window sill waiting for the rest of their friends to come in, and Reese said, "I'm really glad that you and Joshua are getting along again."

"Yeah, but it won't last long because I just know that I will do something to make Joshua mad again...or he will do something to make me mad," Kole said. "And then it will all be over again."

"I think Joshua wants to be cool with you. He's the one who tried to make things better," Reese said.

"Yeah, but sometimes we just don't get what we want," Kole said.

Reese didn't respond, nor did she have to because Joshua, Patrick, and Aiden all walked in the door together, coming from their class. The rest of their friends weren't able to come in because of what class they were in.

The three of them went and sat with Kole and Reese. Reese smiled, but Kole just looked at them.

"Hey guys, guess what," Aiden said with excitement.

"What?" the others all asked him.

"It came today!" Aiden exclaimed.

"What came?" Kole asked, annoyed.

"My flags!" Aiden exclaimed.

"Your gay flags?" Kole asked.

"Yes! I'm coming out to my parents tonight!" Aiden said.

Kole looked at Joshua who was looking at Aiden and listening. His eyebrows were slightly scrunched up, but he wasn't saying anything. Kole wondered, *"Why does he always argue with me over stupid things? But he doesn't argue with Aiden ever. Am I really that bad?"*

"That's good," Reese said in reply to Aiden.

"Yeah, I know! It will be so good to get it off of my chest. I can't take keeping secrets," Aiden said.

"What if they aren't accepting?" Reese asked.

"I think they will be. I've asked them questions before to decide whether or not I should come out. They've been generally accepting of the whole thing," Aiden said.

"But don't you go to Church?" Kole asked. He shot a look at Joshua who was still silent.

Aiden stared at Kole.

"The Bible says gay people go to hell," Patrick added in.

Aiden crossed his arms.

"Are you still going to tell your parents?" Reese asked.

"Yeah," Aiden said. "Why wouldn't I?"

"Because...I don't know," Reese said.

"I didn't buy the flags for nothing. I'm not rich," Aiden said, snappily.

"Okay, sorry," Reese said. "And neither am I. I have five siblings."

The next day, Aiden told the group about his parents' reaction. He said that they weren't jumping for joy, but they didn't kick him out either, so he considered it a win. Joshua never said a word about the whole event, even though Kole continuously looked at him, wondering if he'd speak, trying to figure out what he was thinking about.

Chapter 34: Excluded

It was the Monday before Christmas break—only five days left of school. The time since Thanksgiving had been painful...and unusually long. Carson was sick, so Joshua hung out with Patrick, Kole, Reese, Aiden, Andrew, Daniel, and Caiden at recess. He said that he wasn't *friends* with Kole, just cool with him, but since Kole hung out with people that he wanted to be hanging out with, he found himself hanging out around him when he didn't have to worry about getting beat up.

Aiden was talking about something he did Saturday night, and it sounded like everyone had been there.

Joshua looked at Aiden, confused. What was Saturday night? He had been at home, alone. He wasn't even hanging out with Carson. Saturday night wasn't bad. He worked out a really hard part on his saxophone piece for band, and he got to do lots of writing. But still...what was Saturday night?

Then, the group started making plans to do something together again. Even Caiden was a part of the conversation! Caiden was like, part of the friend group, but Patrick, Kole, Maverick, Reese, Aiden, and sometimes Des had formed a second friend group that was a part of that group. The two groups hung out at school, but outside of school, they didn't hang out with them. At least, that's what Joshua thought. But now he wasn't so sure. What were they doing on Saturday? He thought they were friends. Guess not. He wondered if Carson was there. They weren't together, and he didn't know where Carson was either. Joshua suddenly felt excluded, but he didn't say anything.

Apparently, they had eaten tacos.

"We should book a reservation this time," Reese said, beginning to make plans. "It was pretty full last time, and we almost didn't get a table. The closer we get to Christmas, the fuller I think it will become."

"Yeah. That's a good idea," Kole said.

Kole thought an idea Reese had was a good one? What had Joshua missed?

"I can make the reservation," Patrick said. "For seven?"

"Yup," the others said. Joshua quickly counted the group in his head. There were eight, if they counted him, but they apparently weren't.

"What about Maverick?" Kole asked.

"Okay, eight then," Patrick said.

"And Des," Reese said.

"I guess," Patrick said. "Nine."

"Does Friday work?" Patrick asked.

It did, for everyone.

"Okay. I will make it when I get home," Patrick said.

"Kole, make sure he does," Reese said.

"Augh!" Patrick snapped. "How dare you doubt me."

Reese shrugged.

None of them looked at Joshua, but he wanted to go, so he said, "What about me?"

"You wouldn't want to go," Caiden said.

"Yeah, we're eating at Tony's Taco Bar," Kole said. "That's not a place we go together."

Joshua frowned. So, it was settled. He just wasn't going. Joshua told Carson the next day when he was back at school, and Carson asked him, "Why would you want to go? Kole's going to be there."

"We're even," Joshua replied.

"For now, but you never know when he's going to turn on you again. You can be friendly with him when you have to see him, but you shouldn't go looking to see him. You know that, right?" Carson asked.

"Yeah, you're right." Joshua paused. "It's just...Reese is going to be there."

"You still like her?"

"I don't know."

"I wouldn't. After all that she's done to you."

"But...you never liked her to begin with."

"No, but I also wouldn't even like Camilla after that."

"Yeah, maybe I shouldn't. But it's just hard to stop liking her."

"That's why people get themselves into bad, abusive relationships. It's hard to stop liking someone just because they wrong you."

Joshua crossed his arms.

"Please, don't be upset that you can't go," Carson said. "Be glad. It's for your own good. How about you come over to my house instead."

"Okay," Joshua said. "That sounds fun."
"Yeah," Carson agreed.

Chapter 35: Blue Lights

Friday afternoon, Joshua and Carson walked Kendall and Leah home. Then they walked together with Connor to Carson's apartment. When they first got there, the daycare kids were there, so it was loud, but they decided to go to Carson's room. They weren't going to the park again, even if Joshua and Kole were cool, and even though they knew Kole had plans elsewhere.

Connor hung out with them. They stayed there until the daycare kids left. When they went out, Carson and Connor's mom, Mrs. Montey, said that she would order pizza. So, Joshua, Carson, and Connor all picked out the kinds of pizza they wanted. Mrs. Montey called, and it was supposed to arrive in 20 minutes. While they waited, Mrs. Montey threw together a brownie mix and baked it.

When the pizza delivery man arrived, Mrs. Montey asked the boys to go get it, saying, "Grab the money. It's on the counter."

Carson grabbed it, and the three boys went to the door. They opened it, and there was a young man, barely 18, standing there, holding four pizzas. Joshua took the pizzas, and Carson handed him the money.

"Thank you," the boys said.

"No problem," the young man said. He turned

around, running briskly back to the car. As Connor began to shut the door, they heard sirens, and two police cars zoomed by with flashing blue lights. Connor shut the door.

Joshua carried the pizzas into the kitchen and set them down on the counter. The boys all helped themselves. Afterwards, they ate brownies, then they watched a movie. It was late when they finished, so Joshua ended up spending the night.

Meanwhile, the police arrived at the scene of Tony's Taco Bar. There was a group of nine seventh graders out front. Two of them were girls. One of the girls was tall with red hair, but the other one was shorter with brown hair. She stood in the grass with a drop of blood dripping from her lip. Two of the boys were fighting each other when the police arrived. They were pushing each other. One of them fell to the ground as the police arrived. The-boy-who-was-in-the-fight-but-still-standing saw the police and pointed at the one on the ground and exclaimed, "That's the one!" The one on the ground looked up, terrified and betrayed.

Chapter 36: Different Sides

Joshua went running the next afternoon. It was cold, and the sidewalk was covered in icy snow on the sides, but he went anyway, being careful to watch his step. He did this because he hadn't gone in a while. After only a few minutes, he was well warmed up, unphased by the cold.

He had gone a little over a mile and was about to turn around soon, when he saw Patrick, Kole, Maverick, Des, and Reese walking towards him. He partially wanted to turn around right then and there, but something made him keep running, right toward them.

Joshua reached them, and they all greeted him. Reese was biting her fingernails.

"What are you running from?" Kole asked him.

"Huh?" Joshua was breathing slightly heavy. "I'm not running from anything."

"Then why are you running?"

"Because I'm on the cross country team."

"Cross country is over," Reese reminded him behind her hand, whose fingernails she was still chewing.

"Yeah, but I have to keep training for next year. Plus, running helps me with swimming," Joshua said.

"Oh," Kole said. "Weird."

Joshua crossed his arms.

"Anyway," Kole said. "We were just talking."

"About what?"

"Aiden."

"Why?"

"He's so gay but can't stand it when we call him for what he is."

"I don't get it. He doesn't like when you call him gay?"

"We didn't exactly call him *gay*, for say, but...I just don't get it. He's proud to be gay, right? So why does he get so insulted?"

"What happened?"

"Nothing." Kole paused. "I mean, a lot, but nothing. Everything's great. You should just continue your run, you know, to help you with cross country and swimming and everything."

"I just don't get it. You called him gay, but you didn't? What does that even mean?" Joshua asked.

"Nothing! It means nothing! Gosh! You're being so nosy! Get back to your stupid, lame, weird run!" Kole snapped.

"Um...okay," Joshua said, and not wanting to get beat up, he listened. He turned around and ran home. The whole way, he was left wondering what happened because Kole's explanation left him with more questions than answers. When he got home, he took a nice, long, warm shower.

He came out from his shower, wearing sweatpants and a sweatshirt, yet he was still cold. His mom was in the kitchen. His sisters were all sitting at the counter, drinking from a cup with a straw. His dad was in there too, drinking from a cup. Mrs. Abare was pouring an orange liquid into another one. She set down the pitcher which had one serving left of the liquid. She put a cover on the cup she had just filled, took a sip, then she looked up at Joshua and said, "Joshua, I made smoothies. You can help yourself."

"Okay, thanks," he replied.

His three sisters all got up from the counter. They filled their cups up with water and set them into the sink. Then, they went into the living room and played with toys. Joshua got himself a cup and filled it with smoothie. He took a sip, and his tongue danced with joy. It was so good and so refreshing. He sat at the counter. His parents both went into the other room, leaving him alone at the counter. He was still sitting there, drinking his smoothie, when he heard a knock on the door. He looked over and could see Aiden's face through the privacy glass. He got up and went over, opening the door. Aiden was there with Andrew, Daniel, and Caiden.

"Hey, guys," Joshua said, surprised, for their visit was unexpected. "What's up?"

"Hi," Aiden said. "Have you spoken to Kole or anyone today?"

"Yeah," Joshua said. He gestured for them to come inside, and they did. He shut the door behind them. "Why?"

"Did he tell you anything?" Aiden asked.

"No...I mean...a little. What do you mean?"

"Did he tell you about the fight?"

"No! There was a fight? Between who?"

"Me and them, mostly." When he said *them*, he was

talking about Kole and the others, not the ones who were standing in Joshua's entryway.

"Wow. I'm surprised. Kole got into a fight with someone other than me?" Joshua asked.

"Yeah, weird, right?" Aiden asked.

"Yeah," Joshua agreed. He looked at Aiden's face. He didn't appear to have any bruises. Neither did any of the others. Joshua recalled Kole and the others when he saw them. He didn't think he saw any bruises on any of them, either.

"The fight wasn't the bad part, really," Aiden said. "There was a little bit of pushing. It was mostly just pushing. One punch was thrown."

"If that's not the bad part, then what is?" Joshua asked.

"He called me the f-word," Aiden said.

"Like the..." Joshua started to say.

"In some places, they call a cigarette this," Aiden said.

"Okay," Joshua said. "That's pretty rough."

"Yeah, it was. But then they act like I was the bag guy."

"Why? It sounds like they were being pretty rude."

"They were...which is what caused me to act like the bad guy."

"What do you mean by that? Everyone keeps trying to talk to me with riddles, but I wasn't there, so none of it makes sense."

"It was a bad event, so no one wants to say it out loud," Andrew chimed in.

"Oh," Joshua replied.

"*I* was the one who threw the single punch," Aiden admitted. He was looking at the ground, and he said it quietly.

"Oh? Why? Who'd you punch? Kole?" Joshua asked.

Aiden shook his head.

Then, Joshua remembered...*Reese* was biting her finger nails. She never did that. It was like she was trying to hide her mouth.

"Who...who did you punch?" Joshua asked, hesitantly.

Aiden didn't answer, so Andrew answered for him: "Reese."

"Did you come over here just to tell me that you punched Reese?" Joshua asked, his voice rising slightly.

"She deserved it," Andrew said, his voice also heated.

"But she's..." Joshua said.

"A girl? Is that the problem?" Aiden snapped. "Before you go on about that, just remember, she was hate criming me! I couldn't refrain myself! You would know how that goes! But don't worry, they handled it just fine. They called the police on me. Thankfully, since they were hate criming me, I got off the hook."

"Wow," Joshua said. "Wait...so that must be what those police cars I saw last night were for."

"You saw them?" Aiden asked.

"Yeah," Joshua said. He thought in his head, *"Hm...why did I never think to call the police on Kole myself?"* But he didn't share that thought out loud. Rather, he said again, "Did you come over here just to tell me this?"

"Yeah," Aiden said.

"Why?" Joshua asked.

"Because we wanted you to know our story. We thought Kole would probably tell you, and we wanted to make sure you knew our side because he would probably try to make us look like the bad guys," Aiden said.

"Did he try to make *me* look like the bad guy?" Joshua asked.

Aiden was quiet. All four boys looked at him. Then, he said, "Yeah, he made it pretty clear to Andrew and me that *you* were the bad guy."

"And you believed him," Joshua said, his voice shaking. He crossed his arms and turned his head slightly.

"I don't anymore," Aiden said.

Joshua was upset and wanted to let that out, but instead, he took a deep breath and said, "They didn't tell me that you got into a fight."

"Good," Aiden said. "Kole is a jerk. I can't believe him. I will never talk to him again."

"I could have told you that much," Joshua said.

"And Patrick's a snake. Reese...she's been an idiot this whole time. And the others, Maverick and Des, they're just pawns. But I just can't believe Kole. I thought we were friends," Aiden said.

"You see...that's the thing about Kole," Joshua said. "He's not who he appears to be."

"I can't believe we were ever friends with him. We're all so stupid," Aiden cried.

Joshua had been waiting a long time for this day. Aiden could have topped it all off with an apology or something.

...

But he didn't.

That was fine. Aiden might have realized Kole's falseness, but he still didn't realize how awful Kole had been to Joshua, even when he laid it right out in front of him. And if he did, he didn't—he couldn't—realize how oblivious he had been before, how he had added to Joshua's misery by always taking Kole's side over his. Would he ever know how miserable Joshua felt for weeks on end? With all of this in mind, Joshua had a hard time understanding Aiden's side of the story.

The boys complained about Kole. Joshua didn't say much, mostly because he wasn't sure what to say. After about 10 minutes of ranting, the boys left. Joshua went back to the counter and finished his smoothie, thinking about the fight. When he finished, he grabbed the phone and dialed Reese's number. He still had it from when they nearly dated, from when Joshua thought he had a chance with her, from the time they went to the dance together, from before the fight at Tony's Taco Bar.

"Hey," Reese said, picking up the phone.

"Are you home?"

"Yeah, why? You want to come over?"

"No, no. I was just..."

"It's okay if you do. Patrick and Kole are here with Maverick and Des."

"No. I just...heard about the fight. I heard you got punched. I heard the police got called."

"Oh, yeah. Aiden punched me, and the police did get called, but you don't have to worry about it. We're all fine."

It was silent for a moment, then softly, Joshua said, "Aiden told me that you called him the f-word."

"Oh, yeah, not me. That was all Kole and Maverick...not me," Reese said.

"No, it wasn't," Joshua heard a voice in the background say. It was definitely Patrick, the bystander.

"So...it's true, then?" Joshua asked.

"We were just saying things. We didn't do anything. Aiden pushed first," Reese said.

"*I* pushed first," Joshua said, his voice trembling, a tear fighting its way out of his eye.

Reese was silent. Joshua heard someone, this time Kole, from the background say, "Let me talk to him."

"Kole wants to talk to you," Reese told Joshua.

"Okay," Joshua said. In his head, he thought, *"I don't want to talk to him."* But he didn't say it because he was trying to be polite.

Reese handed the phone to Kole who said, "Hey."

"Hi," Joshua replied.

"Why don't you just mind your own business? I thought I made it clear earlier that everything was fine," Kole said.

"To be fair, I wasn't calling you. I was calling Reese. I just wanted to know if she was okay, since she got punched," Joshua said.

"Awe, how sweet," Kole said, snarkily.

"Stop."

"Why did you care what we called Aiden then...if you were just wanting to see if she was okay?"

"Because...I wanted to know...if it was true."

"But why do you care? Aiden's gay; you're Catholic. That doesn't mix."

"It was still not cool, whether I'm Catholic or not."

"So...you're taking Aiden's side, then?"

"I just wanted to know if it was true. That's all. Now put me back onto the phone with Reese! I don't want to talk to you!" Joshua snapped. *That didn't last long.*

Suddenly, it was silent, and Joshua realized that Kole had hung up on him. Joshua groaned, but he didn't bother calling back. He put the phone back and went up to his room where he wrote.

***

Two days later, it was Christmas Eve. Joshua tried but couldn't forget about all of his troubles even for the next two days. He sat in his grandparents' living room full of his family, who loved him, opening presents, but he couldn't stop thinking about everything that was going on. Not just about what happened between Kole and Aiden...but also everything that had happened between him and Kole. He remembered the very first fight he had with Kole. Aiden arrived. Joshua was beaten. It was the first time he had ever gotten into a fight, so he was overwhelmed. He was also mad that Kole had insulted his religion. Aiden stood next to Kole, against Joshua. Clearly in opposition. As Joshua looked at Kole in defeat with Aiden by his side, it didn't matter to him that Aiden was gay. Aiden had been his friend, and then, he was standing with Kole, who had just fought with him. It made sense now why Aiden took Kole's side all the time over Joshua's. It had nothing to do with their friendship—it was the topic of the argument. But now...Aiden was in his shoes, and Joshua was in Aiden's shoes. Joshua still liked Reese, despite everything she had done to him. He just couldn't get rid of the feelings. It was like Carson said about abusive relationships. Reese wasn't abusive, just a traitor...which I guess is abusive in its own sense. Joshua couldn't understand why the feelings he felt for her wouldn't go away. He also couldn't get over the fact that Aiden *punched* Reese.

Suddenly, Joshua realized it was his turn to open a present. He hadn't even realized what was going on because he was so lost in thought. He didn't want this on *Christmas* of all times.

After presents and supper, they went to Church to celebrate the birth of Jesus. The Church was so packed that they almost had to stand in the back. They ended up getting split up in order to sit. Joshua sat on a side row with Kendall, his dad, and his religion teacher. His other sisters and mom were sitting in the middle row three seats in front of them, diagonally with their grandparents and a young couple. But it didn't matter. At first glance, it looked like they were getting split up from their family on Christmas. But at second glance—better glance—it was made apparent that they were all family in Christ. It felt nice to Joshua, after everything that had gone down, to be in a place where everyone was there for the same reason: to *celebrate* Jesus—not to criticize the religion. Some of these people only ever came twice a year: on Christmas and Easter. And they were often teased for only going those two days. But Joshua used to be one of those people, at one point in his life. It didn't matter, though. Whether they only went twice a year, or they went every week, they were still showing an acknowledgement to the importance of Christmas (and Easter). It showed that they had some recognition for the faith, for Jesus, for God. Even just two days was better than nothing. Kole certainly wasn't there even for just two days. For once in the past month, Joshua didn't have to be at war with anyone.

The next day, Christmas morning, Joshua took his sisters outside to play with their new toys. They had gotten some to make snow ornaments, so they wanted to try them out while their parents made breakfast and showered. Joshua sat on the front porch in a winter coat and slippers, frozen into a popsicle. He was sitting there when Kole walked by alone. He had his head down and his hands in his pockets. He didn't say anything. He didn't even look up, even though he must have known Joshua was sitting there. Joshua figured Kole must have had decency enough to not try and ruin his Christmas. Joshua wasn't sure that he and Kole were square anymore, after the phone call. He wondered though, why was Kole alone on Christmas? He didn't look happy in the least. And by walking by Joshua's house, was he trying to show him something? Joshua wasn't sure. He watched him walk by, but Kole never looked up. Kendall continuously looked from Joshua to Kole. Leah and Ava didn't notice.

Joshua spent the rest of his day thinking about the way he had seen Kole. He also thought about the night at the park when Kendall was there. Kole was upset about something. He didn't know what. He knew part of it, but not all of it. *Why was he alone on Christmas?*

Chapter 37: Story

Joshua walked out of the Church basement with his classmates who were also in seventh grade. There were only four of them total left: Joshua, Anderson, Gabriel, and Jeremiah. Jeremiah was the son of the religion teacher. They were going to have their Confirmation the next year with the eighth graders, who would be freshmen in high school at the time of their Confirmation. There were six in the grade above.

The four seventh graders were talking together as they walked home. They were going on a retreat in February that was over night, so they were talking about that. They got to the street that Gabriel lived on, so he turned down and left them. Jeremiah's road was the next, then Anderson's. Joshua lived on the main road, on the opposite side of town from the Church. He was about halfway home but alone, when he came across Reese, who was also alone. It was like finding a ruby. He couldn't remember the last time that he had seen Reese without Kole besides during class, which didn't count.

The two of them greeted each other, and Reese asked, "What are you doing?"

"I'm walking home from religion class," Joshua explained.

"Oh. On a Thursday afternoon? I always had it on Sundays."

"Yeah. This was a different kind of class. We're going on a retreat in February, so we were just talking about it," Joshua explained.

"Oh," Reese said.

"What about you? What are you doing?" Joshua's voice sounded defensive because he thought Reese was judging him like Kole.

"Just going for a walk." Reese paused. "I don't know why." Her voice sounded genuine.

"Oh." Joshua's voice cooled.

"I'm just...bored," Reese concluded.

"Oh. If you want, we could hang out. You could come over to my house."

"Okay. I've got nothing better to do."

Reese turned around and started walking to Joshua's house. They talked the whole time, then they arrived at Joshua's house. His parents were surprised to see Reese over, but they didn't look concerned like they did whenever they found Joshua hanging out with Kole.

The two of them went into the dining room and sat at the table. They started out by talking, but then they ran out of things to talk about, so Reese said, "Can I read one of your stories that you've written?"

"Uh...sure," Joshua said. "Can I read one of yours?"

"Yeah," Reese replied. Reese pulled out her phone where she pulled up her story. Joshua went upstairs to get his laptop. He brought it downstairs to the dining room and pulled up one of his stories. He sent it to Reese, and he went to his mail where he found her story she had sent him.

Reese opened up the story and said, “Hm...is this about bullying?”

Joshua blushed.

“Of course it is.” Reese rolled her eyes. “Is it targeted? Did you send it to me for a reason?”

“It’s just the story I’ve been working on lately, and you asked me to send you a story.”

“Why have you been writing a story about bullying?”

“I’ve been studying it in Independent Study, so I thought I’d put a book together about it.”

“Was *that* targeted at Kole?”

“Why else would I want to write about bullying? I want to understand Kole. But at the same time, everything I said was true. I want to understand *bullies*.”

“So...you say Kole’s a bully?”

“Do you disagree with me?” Joshua crossed his arms.

“You don’t get it.”

“But I’m trying to get it.”

“I feel like you want to be his enemy.”

“I don’t.”

“Then why won’t you drop it?”

“I think *you* don’t get it. You know, the best way to get rid of problems between you and another is to understand the other’s point of view.”

“Okay, whatever.”

The two of them were quiet and began reading each other’s stories. Reese’s was about an old western bar fight. At least, that’s how it opened up anyway. After about 10 minutes of silence, Reese suddenly said, "Wait a second...is Mav, your character, based on Maverick?"

Joshua was silent.

"Is he?"

"I needed a name that started with *M*. Mav starts with an *M*."

"Yeah, but so does...Marvin, Marc, Matteo, Matthew, Mason, so many names. Mav is the nickname of Maverick!"

"*I've* never called Maverick Mav."

"But *we* all do."

"But *I* don't, and *I* wrote this story, not *you* guys."

"Is Mav based on Maverick?" Reese asked, again.

"Why do you ask to read my story then criticize it all? First the subject, then the name of one of my characters."

"I don't know. Sorry. But...can't you just answer me?"

"I already did."

"Mav's mean in your story. I know it was based on him. Why did you send me this?"

"Because I forgot that there was someone named Mav, and it's just the story that I'm writing right now."

"That's weird."

"What's weird? That Mav starts with an *M*? Where did you get the name Ava from? I could say that's the name of my sister, couldn't I?"

"Yeah. But I didn't name her after your sister. I don't really even know your sister."

"It's just a name. It's not copyrighted. It's a name that many people have. Where else do people think of names other than names that they've heard before?"

"Okay, whatever."

Reese continued reading for a few more minutes, then she said, "It's getting dark, so I'm going to go home."

"Okay," Joshua said. He crossed his arms.

Reese walked to the door and left. As soon as she had left the driveway, Joshua went to the share setting of his story and deleted Reese's access. As he did that, Mrs. Abare walked into the dining room. Without realizing her presence, he buried his face in his hands and sighed.

"What's wrong?" Mrs. Abare asked.

Joshua looked up at her, then at his story, then back at her. He paused, then said, "Remember that story I told you I was writing where the characters' names all spelled something out?"

"Yeah," Mrs. Abare replied.

"I used Mav for an *M* name as a bully, and I made the mistake of showing it to Reese. She made a connection to Maverick. She got all defensive about it. But it doesn't mean anything! It's just a name! There are so many people named Mav! Or Maverick! It's a *name*! I don't get why she got so defensive," Joshua cried. "I shouldn't have shared that one with her."

"Why did you?" Mrs. Abare asked.

"Because she asked to read one of my stories, and that was the one I've been working on. In the time being, I forgot that I named one of the characters Mav. And I wasn't really thinking anything of it. We share our stories with each other a lot. I feel so...I don't even know!" Joshua cried.

"That's a tough one. But I agree, it's just a name."

"Yeah." Joshua crossed his arms. "But I'm so stupid. Why did I send it to her? Why couldn't I have remembered?"

"I don't know, but there's nothing you can do about it now."

"Yeah. I guess so. Now, I'm going to have to just live with the consequences."

Mrs. Abare didn't say anything because she was still thinking about the whole situation. She walked into the kitchen and said, "What do you want for supper? Chicken tenders or 20-minute stew?"

"Chicken tenders," Joshua said, smiling slightly. *Was that even a question?*

"Of course. I knew you would say that," Mrs. Abare said.

Chapter 38: The Consequence

The next day was extremely cold with temperatures being nearly zero. The sky was gray and snow was falling. Joshua was home alone, laying on his bed with a headache. He heard the phone ringing, but to answer it, he would have to get up, and when he got up, his head hurt even more. So, he stayed in his bed and let the phone finish ringing.

After about five more minutes, the phone rang again, and Joshua thought to himself, *"What if it's Mom or Dad calling? I should have answered it when I heard it ring. They're going to think something's wrong."*

Joshua got off of his bed, his head throbbing, and he went downstairs to get the phone from the kitchen. When he answered it, he said, "Hi."

"Hello."

It wasn't his mom. *Stupid old fashioned phone,* Joshua thought. Otherwise, he could have read the caller ID.

"Reese?" Joshua asked.

"Hi," Reese said. "Um...this is Joshua, right?"

"Yeah. Who else would it be?"

"I just wanted to make sure I got you, not your dad or someone."

"Okay." Joshua put his hands on the counter next to him and laid his head down on his arm. That made the throbbing feel a little bit better.

"Maverick wants to talk to you."

"I don't really feel that great. I have an awful headache, so I'm not really in the mood for talking."

"It can't wait. I'm handing you over."

Joshua sighed.

Maverick took the phone and immediately said, "I want to read the story."

"Augh," Joshua said, and he hung up the phone. He set it down, and then he began to walk away.

He was about to go up the stairs when the phone rang again. He went back to answer it, and although he would have ignored it, since his parents weren't home, he couldn't. Even though he was about 95 percent sure it was Reese (or someone else with her), the last five percent is what made him answer the phone.

"Joshua."

"What?" Joshua asked, annoyed. That time, it was Kole.

"Send us the story."

"No."

"Reese told me about it. I'm trying to be better. I want to read it to learn something about bullying."

"You're trying to trick me."

"Listen. I know you've got something to hide if you deleted Reese's access."

"I deleted her access because I knew this would happen after I saw her reaction. But I don't understand why you're so upset. It's just a name."

"So...you're admitting to using Maverick's name?"

"I didn't."

"Sorry, you used the name *Mav*. Are you admitting to that?"

"Yes. So what?"

"That's Maverick's name!"

"So?"

"It's clear that you took it from him."

"He doesn't own it, so it's fair game to me if I want to use it in my story."

"I just want to see what you wrote. *Please*, Joshua, send it to me."

"No! Give the phone to Reese. I have a message for her."

"Oh, so you *do* want to talk now?"

"I want to talk to Reese. I have something to tell her. Can you *please* give her the phone?"

"Fine."

Joshua heard the shuffling of the phone, then Reese said, "What?"

"You are a traitor," Joshua said. A tear fell from his eye.

"What?" Reese asked. "You said it's not wrong, so why do you care?"

"Because you *know* Kole and Maverick. They don't like me, and this is just one more thing to make them against me," Joshua said. He was trying not to show that he was crying.

"Then why did you do it?" Reese asked.

"I've already told you that! And I didn't realize *you* were going to take it this far," Joshua said. "I thought we were friends. I invited you into my house, and you asked to read my story. I let you, and you found all of the negatives about it. That's the last time that I will share anything with you."

"Fine," Reese said. Joshua was almost positive that there was a shakiness to her voice, but he didn't acknowledge it. Instead, he hung up. He set the phone down, then he went to the medicine cabinet and popped two Ibuprofen into his mouth. He went upstairs into his room, and he watched out the window from his desk. His headache was starting to get better—about 35 minutes later—when he saw Patrick, Kole, Maverick, Des, and Reese entering his driveway. Reese appeared to be tugging on Kole's arm, but he pulled it away. The five of them walked up the driveway and went up to the front door and knocked on it.

Joshua didn't go downstairs but instead ducked down under his desk. Though, he didn't last long there, for he heard Kole shout, "Hey, Joshua! We know you're in there, and we know you're home alone! So come and open the door! We're not leaving until you do!"

Joshua ignored them. He didn't want any trouble. *"Just go away,"* he thought. He wondered, as he was on his hands and knees below his desk, *"If I had never pushed Kole in the first place, would this be happening right now? Or would he have found some other excuse to track me down? Is this my fault?"*

With that thought in mind, and Kole beginning to bang on his front door, Joshua stood up. He looked out the window at Kole's mean face and his little minions. Patrick, Maverick, Des, and Reese. They all had jackets on, even

Kole.

Joshua walked towards his bedroom door. He opened it and went downstairs, leaving the door open. He walked down the stairs and went to the front door. He didn't open it, but he looked at Kole's blurry face through the privacy glass.

"Go away," Joshua said in one last desperate attempt to avoid whatever was coming for him.

"No," Kole said. "Open the door."

Joshua sighed, but he knew he didn't have a choice. He opened the door and suddenly, a cold draft of air overtook him. *"Woah,"* he thought. *"They must be really desperate to hunt me down in this weather."*

Kole grabbed Joshua's shirt collar and pulled him out the door, wearing socks and a t-shirt.

Kole held Joshua's shirt down low so that he couldn't stand up straight.

Maverick looked at Joshua and said, "This is my last straw. I've had it with you!"

Maverick took a swing at Joshua's face. It was the worst punch Joshua had ever experienced. Things hurt worse in the cold. Even Maverick looked like he thought it hurt a little bit.

"Come, now," Kole said, standing Joshua up. "Have a little walk with us."

Kole started dragging Joshua along. Joshua tried to turn around as he saw Reese closing the door. He tried to break free from Kole, saying, "Let me at least get my jacket, my shoes...or something."

"No. I don't think so," Kole said.

Maverick grabbed Joshua's other arm, and they

started carrying him away. Finally, Joshua gave up, and he began walking, but he didn't do it happily. His socks quickly soaked up the snow, and his feet instantly froze. His arms were numb. In fact, nearly his whole body was numb. The good news: his head didn't hurt anymore.

"Let me go," Joshua said. "I'm cold."

"Ah, poor baby. You're cold?" Kole asked.

"I'm not the baby. You're the one overreacting over a stupid name," Joshua said.

"So...my name is stupid?" Maverick asked.

"No," Joshua said. "The fact that you're getting worked up about it is stupid."

"You get worked up about things. Is that stupid, too?" Maverick asked.

"It's my religion."

"It's my name."

"No, it's not."

"My name's not Maverick?"

"It is, but I'm allowed to use that name. There are so many people in this world named Maverick. It's not *just yours*. And plus, I didn't use Maverick. I used Mav. That's just a nickname."

"For Maverick."

"It doesn't matter. It's just a name."

"Why do you keep talking?" Kole asked, butting back in.

"I..." Joshua said. "What's wrong with it?"

"For every word you say, we get to throw one warm up punch at you," Kole said.

"Augh," Joshua sighed.

"That's one," Kole said.

"But I didn't..." Joshua quickly stopped, realizing his mistake.

"That's three more! Four total!" Kole exclaimed.

But Kole didn't punch him, not yet. It was a few minutes, and Joshua still hadn't received his four punches, so Des asked, "Aren't you going to punch him?"

"Not yet. Not here," Kole said. "And don't worry, Des. I'm going to do far more than just four punches, those words won't even matter."

"Where are we going?" Reese asked, her voice shaking.

But she got no answer.

Joshua tried to break free as Kole and Maverick led the pack with him tight in their arms. Directly behind them was Des, intrigued. Patrick and Reese walked about three feet behind them. Reese had her arms crossed, and Patrick showed no emotion.

They reached the park, and they cut into it. They walked through the snow up towards the fountain. Joshua could no longer feel his feet. He had to look down at them to see if they were even still there.

And they were.

They got to the fountain. There was a hedge behind on two sides of it, so they went into the back corner. Had it been warmer, they would have been visible to the people at the park, but since it was so cold, no one was there; no one would see them unless they came closer. Kole and Maverick threw Joshua down when they got back there, and he cried out "oof!" as he hit the ground. The taste of snow: a mix of dirt and ice.

Chapter 39: Last Straw

"Would you like to do the honors?" Kole asked Maverick.

"Sure," Maverick answered, with a huge smile.

Joshua was on his feet. He stood shivering. He looked like he was going to run but wasn't able to move fast enough. Kole grabbed onto Joshua's arms, and Joshua thought he might be able to break free, but Kole squeezed him so tight that he couldn't.

"Wow, Joshua. I thought you were a swimmer. Aren't they supposed to be strong? Must be you're just not one of that kind," Maverick said, standing in front of him.

The insult wasn't enough for Joshua to regain his strength.

Maverick looked up at Kole who nodded his head. Maverick punched Joshua in the face, hitting him in the left cheek. It immediately began to throb.

"That's one. Three more," Kole said.

Joshua squirmed in Kole's arms, but it didn't do him much good. He didn't break free, and it only led Kole to hold on even tighter.

Maverick sent another blow to Joshua's face. That time, in the nose. Blood gushed out and landed in drops on the snow in front of his feet.

Everything was blurry. Joshua's headache was back, but he figured it was for a different reason.

Two more blows, and Kole let go of Joshua. He fell, and his bare arms hit the snow. Being cold enough already, the snow didn't make him feel any better. In addition, he was dizzy, so he could barely move. He flipped over so that his elbows were both in the snow. He tried to look up at Kole, and for a second, he saw two of him. That was a nightmare in itself. The two Koles formed back into one.

Joshua climbed to his knees, but he didn't make it any further because Kole kneed him in the ribs, leading him to fall back down. Joshua's hands started to bleed at the touch of the snow. Kole kicked him two more times while he was on the ground, then Joshua tried to get up again, but he couldn't. His body ached, and it froze, and it was just an awful feeling. He looked up and behind Kole he could see Patrick, Des, and Reese watching. Patrick had the same face he always did: nothing; Des's eyes had grown 10 inches; and Reese's eyes were wet. But he honestly didn't care what they thought because they were just watching, letting it happen. Joshua looked back at Kole and found some power invested in him that helped him climb to his feet.

Kole pushed Joshua, and although he stumbled, he didn't fall. Joshua tried to run, but he could hardly move. Kole grabbed onto his right arm, his dominant arm, and Joshua cried out loud, "No! Let me go! Please!"

But Kole didn't listen. He threw Joshua to the ground and kicked him. Maverick joined him. Joshua tried to crawl away, but they kept kicking him, and he lost all feeling. "Kole," he cried, but the boys didn't stop.

After a few seconds and many kicks, he was barely conscious. He heard Patrick say, "Come on, Kole! He's had enough! This is insane!"

Joshua felt a blow to his head, and everything went dark.

***

Joshua woke up on his couch, pushed up close to the fireplace under his T.V. He felt a warm pad on his forehead, and more pressed up against his arms in between the multiple blankets wrapped tightly around him. He wasn't sure if he would be able to move because they were wrapped so tightly, and he didn't know where the ends were. His whole body hurt, and despite all of the warmth, he was freezing.

Chapter 40: Pain

Joshua laid on the ground at the park, motionless. After Kole kicked him in the head, both he and Maverick stepped away. They looked at him, and Maverick pointed out, "His eyes are closed."

"I think you killed him," Des said.

Reese started crying out loud, more than just tears.

"Reese, stop crying!" Kole snapped. "He's not dead! He's still breathing! You can see his shirt going up and down!"

"We should get out of here before someone finds us," Maverick said.

"Yeah, come on! Let's get out of here," Kole agreed.

The two of them started walking away, leaving Joshua laying in the blood-covered snow. Patrick, Des, and Reese stood still and let them get a few steps away until Kole turned around and said, "Are you coming?"

Sighing, Patrick said to Des and Reese, "Come on guys, let's go."

"I'm not a guy! I'm a girl!" Reese snapped.

"Shut up, Reese!" Kole snapped. "Or we will turn you into that, too!"

Reese didn't say another word, and she walked with Patrick and Des to catch up to Kole and Maverick, leaving

Joshua in the pink snow.

Patrick, Kole, Maverick, Des, and Reese reached the sidewalk and began walking down it. They had been walking for barely five minutes when they met a group of three boys: Anderson, Gabriel, and Jeremiah.

"Hey," Kole said to them. "Don't you go to Joshua's Church?"

"Yeah," the three boys all answered at once.

"You might want to check out the fountain back at the park," Kole said.

"Okay," the boys said, confused. Kole and the others walked away, and the boys watched for a second. Then, confused and worried, they ran to the park and trekked through the snow toward the fountain.

They got there, and since it was dark, they didn't see Joshua at first. But they kept walking, following the footprints, and they found him. He was still motionless on the ground. His arms were purple, and he had blood dripping down his nose and lips and on the ground in front of him.

"Oh my gosh," Anderson cried, his eyes widening.

Gabriel and Jeremiah walked over to Joshua and picked him up. First, Gabriel felt his neck. Not knowing what happened, he wanted to make sure he didn't have any injuries there. Anderson stood watching, frozen from shock (and a little from the temperature). Gabriel and Jeremiah held Joshua over their shoulders and looked at Anderson.

The three of them began walking. He took off his glove and put his hand on Joshua's arm. "It feels like ice," he reported back.

The others didn't respond.

They got to Joshua's house. The garage light was on, showing that his family had just gotten home. The lights on inside the house showed a very distraught-looking family. They could see Mrs. Abare upstairs in Joshua's room, looking frantic. Ava looked out the window and saw the boys standing with Joshua over their shoulders. She began pointing and shouting. If this had happened about a month ago, she probably would have been screaming and crying, but she was used to the scene by now. The family all rushed to the door. Mrs. Abare was the last to get there, and the door was already open when she arrived. She got there as Anderson was saying, "We found him like this. He's cold as ice."

"Do you have a fireplace?" Gabriel asked.

"Yes, we do," Mr. Abare said, and he ran into the living room, pushing the couch towards the fireplace with Kendall's help. He then instructed the girls to go find all the blankets they could. They went to Joshua's room and ripped the blankets off his bed. Then, they went into the miscellaneous closet and pulled out some extra sheets and blankets. They ran back downstairs. Mrs. Abare went into the kitchen and grabbed some rice-filled ice packs and threw them into the microwave. Gabriel and Jeremiah laid Joshua carefully onto the couch. He didn't even stir.

His sisters came back with all of the blankets. Anderson, Gabriel, and Jeremiah helped Mr. Abare wrap Joshua in them. Kendall, Leah, and Ava watched.

Mrs. Abare came in with the ice packs that were now heated. She stuffed them into the blankets. She put two on his wrists, some on his arms, and the remaining one on his forehead.

After Joshua was all bundled up, Mrs. Abare turned to the three boys and asked, “Did you see who did this?”

“No,” Gabriel answered. “But I think we know who did it. We were walking home, and Kole came walking by with Patrick, Reese, and two other people that I don’t know. Kole asked us if we went to Joshua’s church, and we answered yes, so he told us that we should go check by the fountain at the park. We found him on the ground covered in blood, half frozen to death. I know that Joshua and Kole don’t get along very well.”

“Nope, they don’t get along very well,” Mr. Abare agreed.

“Kole...that evil jerk man,” Leah said through gritted teeth.

“Evil jerk man!” Ava exclaimed

“This has to end! I can’t bear it anymore,” Mrs. Abare cried.

“Thank you boys for bringing him home,” Mr. Abare said.

“Yes, thank you! I’m going to go make some hot tea while I contemplate over what charges I’m going to press. Would you like some?” Mrs. Abare asked. She threw in a smile at the end.

“Ah no, but thanks for the offer,” the boys said.

“Okay,” Mrs. Abare said, and she walked into the kitchen.

Mr. Abare turned to the boys and said, “What can I do to repay you?”

“Nothing,” the boys answered.

“Except...maybe give us a ride home,” Gabriel said,

smiling. "It's freezing."

"Okay, that's the least I could do," Mr. Abare said.

"But if you'd like to wait until Joshua wakes up or whatever, I understand," Gabriel said.

"No, no. It's okay. I can't bear seeing him like this. I'd rather be home when he's awake and conscious. Not like this," Mr. Abare said.

"Okay," Gabriel said.

Mr. Abare informed Mrs. Abare about where he was going, then he brought the three boys home. Kendall, Leah, and Ava stood in the living room behind the couch, silently watching as their mom sat next to Joshua trying to warm him up. She was holding a cup of hot tea, and in the other hand, she was holding a warm sack of rice on his cheek.

Mr. Abare was back after only 15 minutes. Mrs. Abare went into the kitchen to greet him and warm up some more rice packs. When she got back, Joshua's eyes were open and staring at the fire. Kendall, Leah, and Ava still stood where they were, unaware that he had woken up.

"Joshua!" Mrs. Abare exclaimed.

"It hurts," Joshua cried.

"Where?" Mrs. Abare asked.

"To breathe," Joshua answered.

"Okay," Mrs. Abare said. "Marcus, we need to bring Joshua to the ER."

"Okay."

"The *ER*?" Kendall cried.

"Yeah," Mrs. Abare said. "Leah and Ava, make sure you go potty, and Kendall you probably should too."

"Okay," the girls said.

Mr. and Mrs. Abare began unwrapping Joshua as the girls went to the bathroom. Then, it was time for the hard part: standing up. Joshua cried out loud as he tried to sit up himself. So, Mr. and Mrs. Abare picked him up as the three boys from church had. He cried the whole time, shouting, "IT HURTS! IT HURTS!"

"I know, I know," Mrs. Abare said, but Joshua couldn't refrain from crying out: he hurt too much.

The girls had come back downstairs and were watching in fear. Mr. and Mrs. Abare got to the garage door. Joshua was still crying and shouting in pain.

Once Joshua was in the car, he was still in a lot of pain, but he was in less pain. It hurt the most when Mr. Abare wrapped him back into the blankets. He did a lot of crying at that point. Afterward though, he calmed himself down, even though he was still in pain every time he breathed, talked, or made the slightest movement.

***

Joshua ended up with a concussion, mild hypothermia, and some broken ribs. The pain had subsided exponentially by the next day, even without painkillers, but it still hurt when he laid down or put extra strain on his core. His whole torso was black and blue, and so was most of his face. When he arrived like this at the hospital, his parents had to explain what happened, so it meant that Kole and Maverick were in trouble.

The incident happened Friday. Saturday, he was hardly able to make it from the *couch* to the *bathroom* without crying in immense pain. Carson came over as soon as Joshua was back from the hospital.

Joshua still could hardly move on Sunday, but Carson came over again.

Monday, New Years Eve, he felt a little bit better. He managed to get to the dinner table and sit with his family for supper. Carson came over in the morning but couldn't stay very long. The next day was the last day of break, and he was able to move around without crying in pain for most of the day, so it looked like he was probably going to have to go to school the next day.

Chapter 41: Absent

Joshua woke up the next morning in a lot of pain. Besides *feeling* awful, he *looked* awful. It had only been five days since the incident. When Joshua got out of bed, he got ready for school, but he was in a lot of pain and wasn't sure if he was going to go or not. Eventually, he decided he would, but if he was in too much pain, he could ask to come home.

After he made the decision to go to school, he stood in front of the mirror trying to convince himself that his cuts and bruises weren't that bad. This had become part of his daily morning routine, it seemed, since he met Kole. His eye was swollen, his lip was swollen, he was pretty sure his nose looked slightly off, he had a cut down the side of his face. *He was a wreck.*

Mrs. Abare drove Joshua, Kendall, and Leah to school that day, since it was in question whether or not Joshua could walk from class to class, let alone all the way to the school. They also didn't want to take any chances of running into Kole. For the second reason, Mrs. Abare offered to drive Carson and Connor as well. She parked and walked Leah to her class herself so that Joshua, Kendall, Carson, and Connor could go right to theirs.

When Joshua and Carson got inside and were

walking through the halls, people stared at Joshua. They couldn't help it, and he couldn't blame them. He looked down at the ground, walking slowly. Carson walked with him to his locker, since he was carrying his bag for him.

Sam and Aaron both arrived together after Joshua got to his locker. They greeted Joshua, then Carson. Joshua responded, but he didn't look back. They hadn't known about the fight, and he was trying to make the time they didn't know last. Carson was silent as well, other than their greeting.

When Joshua finished at his locker, he finally looked up, revealing his face to Sam and Aaron. Both boys froze, but they didn't say anything. To be honest, for them, it wasn't anything new. At the same time, these were fresh, so it meant that problems were still going on. And they were worse than they ever had been before. Still, they didn't say anything because since it wasn't their first rodeo, they knew Joshua didn't like talking about it.

They walked with Joshua to advisory in silence. Joshua, in his head, noted that Reese hadn't arrived at her locker at all when he was there. So she either hadn't gotten to school yet or was already in advisory. When he got to the Innovation Lab, he learned that it was the first one: she hadn't gotten to school yet. Nonetheless, Joshua knew that when she got there, he wasn't going to want to even look at her. He didn't sit in his normal seat in between Reese and Sam. Instead, he sat in the seat next to Aaron. If Sam and Aaron hadn't already figured out who did this (though, they *had* figured it out), they would have known by that action. This wasn't the first time Joshua had switched seats after a fight between him and Kole that

Reese had witnessed. Yet still, Sam and Aaron didn't say anything. They sat down and logged into the laptops, as Joshua was doing. But for Joshua, looking at the computer screen made his head hurt. Initially, he tried to ignore it.

After about 10 minutes, Reese had still not arrived. Joshua was dreading their first interaction, so he honestly just wanted to get it over with. But he was even more afraid of his first interaction with Patrick and Kole. His one with Patrick was coming during math class.

After 15 minutes, Reese was still not there, but that wasn't Joshua's biggest issue. He was starting to feel dizzy from looking at his laptop. He signed out and shut it, saying, "I can't do this anymore."

Mr. Hendrick heard him and asked, "Joshua, what happened?"

"I got beat up," Joshua said. "And I have a concussion, so I can't look at the screen any longer."

"Okay, I get it," Mr. Hendrick said.

Advisory ended and Reese never showed. Next, he had band. He didn't have any of *the* group in his class, but Aiden was there. He hadn't seen Aiden at all since he had come to his house that day when he was drinking a smoothie, so he certainly hadn't seen him since the fight. Joshua doubted he even knew about it.

Joshua wasn't able to play his instruments due to both his concussion and his broken ribs, but he still had to go tell Mr. Goodwell. He didn't want to sit in band either because even though it was his favorite class, he knew it would make his head hurt. He only went into the band room to tell Mr. Goodwell. The second that he stepped in and heard a trombonist blast some random sound into their instrument, sending a piercing feeling through his head, he knew he was making the right decision.

Before Joshua got to Mr. Goodwell, he was met by Aiden, who froze the second he saw him. "Oh my gosh, dude!" Aiden cried. "You look horrible!"

"Thanks," Joshua said. "I feel it, too."

"What happened?"

"What do you think?"

"Was it Kole?"

"Yeah, and Maverick."

"Wow, man. I think this is the worst they've done you in."

"It is. I spent Friday night at the ER."

"Oh, no. I'm sorry. What...what exactly?"

"Concussion, mild hypothermia, and broken ribs."

"Oh."

"Yeah. But I'd rather not talk about it."

"Okay, I get it."

"I've got to talk to Mr. Goodwell. I'm going to see if I can go sit in Mrs. Wheeling's room, since I can't play, and the noise will make my head hurt."

So, Joshua talked to Mr. Goodwell, and he let him go to Mrs. Wheeling's room during band. After that, he had to go to math, which he dreaded because of Patrick. He went to his locker first, and on his way, he met his fellow saxophonist, Teagan. Teagan had curly, light brown hair, and he always wore a light gray sweatshirt and blue jeans.

"Hey, Joshua," Teagan said to him. "I noticed you weren't in band, and now I understand why."

"Yeahhh," Joshua replied.

"It seems like this is becoming a regular occurrence."

"It is! But I just can't take it anymore. It's gone too far, and there's nothing I can do about it."

"Who is it?"

"Do you know Kole Jackson?"

"No."

"Well him, and he has an uncle here, too. He's in my next class. I'm honestly terrified."

"Oh, wow. Did the uncle do this to you as well?"

"No, not exactly. He was there, but he didn't do it."

"So Kole Jackson made you look like this alone?"

"No. He has a friend who doesn't go here. He also made me look like this."

"So, they're recruiting people from other towns to beat you up?"

"Yeah, I guess so." Joshua laughed.

"Wow, you must be pretty intimidating."

Joshua looked at Teagan narrowly. "What do you mean?"

"Why else would they gang up on you? Clearly, they fear you."

"Ha, that's funny...because I actually fear them. They don't fear me."

"Seems like they do to me."

"Do *you* think I'm scary?"

"No. But I don't beat you up, either."

"I just never really thought I was that scary." Joshua paused. "I don't think it's that. I think it's because I pushed first."

"You did?" Teagan's eyes widened.

Joshua stared at Teagan for a second, then said, "Oops, I didn't mean to say that."

"It's okay. I'm sure you had good reason. You seem like a pretty reasonable guy."

"Yeah, it seemed right in the moment. Well, no. It didn't, but it didn't seem wrong, either. I really just wasn't thinking in that moment. Well, I was, but I was mad. You know?"

"Yeah, I know. What did he do?"

Joshua sighed, then answered: "Knowing that I was religious, he said he didn't believe in it because he wasn't gullible. Basically, he was calling my religion gullible. And that was on top of many other things. Like *many*."

"Oh, I get it. It all makes sense now. I get why you pushed him, and I get why he's scared of you."

"Why? Why is he scared of me?" Joshua frowned.

"People that do this to people, you know, make your face all puffed up and black and blue, are scared of religious people."

"That's not right. There's no reason to be afraid of religious people."

"I'm not saying it's right. Usually, norms aren't right."

"Like people just can't understand why I won't swear. It's wrong, that's why, but they all think it's weird."

"Don't listen to them. You're the nicest person I know. So what if you made a mistake? We all do it."

"Yeah, but this one cost me."

"You will get through it. Pretend you're playing the saxophone." Teagan smiled before continuing, "You're good at that."

"Thanks."

At this point, the two boys parted their own separate ways. Joshua went to math, walking slowly. He was still extremely nervous, but he felt better. He walked into his math class and sat down with Sam and Sam's two friends, Drake and Mason. Mason looked at Josua's face and said, "What happened this time?"

"*This time.*" Joshua laughed.

"What?"

"It's just...weird. Like, I never used to get in fights, and now it's just a normal thing."

"So, it was a fight?"

"Yeah...I mean...if you could call it that." Joshua's voice slowly trailed off at the end.

"So...you got beat up?"

"Yeah, basically." Joshua's voice was quiet.

"You're too nice. That's why."

"No, it's not that. I mean...sure, I try to be nice, but I will fight for myself. I thought they were going to kill me. I had an awful headache, and I was in a t-shirt in zero degrees."

"That's stupid."

"I didn't have a choice. They just took me out of my house. I couldn't get a jacket or shoes, and even if I could, it was still freezing."

Joshua wanted to disappear into the floor. His explanation certainly wasn't helping him, and Mason gave him a look that said he was stupid. Honestly, he felt that way. Class began, and when he looked around, Patrick was nowhere to be seen. He realized something was going on. First Reese was gone, and now Patrick? Joshua was starting to have hope for lunch. Would Kole be gone, too?

Aiden and Daniel sat at a table alone, where they once sat with both Joshua and Patrick. Joshua and Aiden made eye contact while Mr. Henry was giving instructions.

Independent Study came later, and Reese was still not there. Recess came after that, and Kole was not out there. Joshua hung out with Carson and Camilla, but he didn't talk much. Half because he was the third wheel and half because his mind was somewhere else. He was thinking about Patrick, Kole, and Reese. *Where were they?*

They went to lunch, and Joshua sat with Carson and Camilla. He didn't talk. He just listened to them flirt while he ate.

The day went on, pain free, except for the physical result of the fight. He still hurt most of the time when he walked and got up and sometimes still when he breathed.

At the end of the day, Joshua came across Anderson, Gabriel, and Jeremiah. They asked him how he was doing. He told them he was not great, but he thanked them for bringing him home that night. He said he probably would have frozen to death had they not brought him home, and Anderson admitted that he was more of an icicle than a human being when they found him.

Even though he made it through the day, Joshua dreaded the next day because he thought that things would be different. He might have been safe for one day, but the next day was sure to bring Kole back. In addition, he felt horrible when he got home. His head was spinning, and his ribs were throbbing. Carson came over, but he mostly just listened to Joshua whine. He didn't blame him: he was in pretty rough shape and had just powered through a full day of school.

Chapter 42: Gone

Reese was missing again the next day from advisory, and Patrick was not in math either. Joshua was still wondering where they were when he walked past the guidance room on his way to the bathroom. Inside, he saw Reese standing in front of the counselor, Mrs. Finn. She had tears streaming down her cheeks. Mrs. Finn looked at her with concern and patience. Reese glanced over at Joshua as he walked by. Mrs. Finn looked over too, then she walked over to the door and shut it. Joshua quickly looked away and continued on his way to the bathroom.

Reese wasn't in advisory for the rest of the week, but Joshua still saw her once more. The next time he saw her, she was walking out of the bathroom. She didn't look at him, but he knew she knew that he was there. Joshua didn't say anything to her.

Patrick and Kole never showed up, either. Not in class, not at lunch or recess, and not in the guidance room. It was Friday at recess when Aiden, Andrew, Daniel, and Caiden came up to Joshua, who was with Carson and Camilla. Joshua's face had begun to look exponentially better...but still awful.

As soon as Aiden got to Joshua, he asked him, "Did you hear the news?"

"What news?" Joshua asked.

"About Patrick and Kole."

"What news about them?"

"I take it you haven't heard." A smile spread across Aiden's face. "They've moved."

"They what?" Joshua's face lit up.

"Yeah, they've moved."

"Where to?" A cheerfulness filled Joshua's voice.

"I don't know, but it's far enough that they won't be walking around in town anymore."

"What about Maverick?"

"He won't come bothering us without Kole."

Joshua laughed. A smile was spread across his face. "Oh my gosh! I can't believe this! I feel like someone just lifted 50 pounds off my back."

"Yeah, I know." Aiden was still smiling.

Joshua looked at Carson who didn't say anything. He didn't smile, but he seemed glad, too. Camilla didn't have an expression.

"How'd you find out? I had no idea," Joshua said.

"He told Caiden," Aiden replied.

Joshua looked at Caiden; his face turned cold. "Why'd he tell you?" Joshua asked him.

"Because he just did. I know you didn't get along, but he never did anything to me," Caiden said.

"*Didn't get along?* I thought he was going to kill me! If you continue talking to him, you will be next!" Joshua cried. "I mean...look what he did to Aiden." Joshua looked at Aiden and said, "I bet you thought you were friends, didn't you?"

"Yeah, I did," Aiden said. "But I was wrong."

"Relax, Joshua," Caiden said. "I'm not still talking to him. He just called me and told me. He didn't want anything from it. He probably just wanted us to know."

"Sorry," Joshua said.

"It's fine. I get it," Caiden replied.

"I'm just glad I don't have to worry anymore," Joshua said, his mood brightening again.

"Yeah, me too!" Aiden exclaimed.

Joshua looked at Aiden, and all he could think was, *"Aiden didn't get the worst of him. He hardly got the least of him. He doesn't know what it's like to have to constantly watch his back to make sure he didn't get beaten to the bone. He got into one singular fight, and he came out without a scratch. Sure, the police came and all, but at least he didn't almost die."* Augh! *"How could I think that way?"* Aiden was his friend. Sure, he didn't understand, but that didn't mean that what he went through wasn't hard. To be honest, Joshua didn't know what he went through. He wasn't there. But he knew that Aiden would never understand him and what he went through.

"Do you think he was forced to move?" Andrew asked after a long silence. "You know...because of all he did?"

"Maybe," Aiden said.

"No," Joshua said. "I think he did all of it because he knew he was leaving. He had acted like friends with Aiden for this whole time, but once he was leaving, he had to say goodbye without actually saying goodbye."

"And you..." Aiden said.

"It wasn't anything new with me, honestly. I did

something that stupidly made him mad, even though there was nothing wrong with what I did. So, he beat me up. But yeah, I think it was probably worse this time because he knew he wouldn't have to suffer the consequences. It's hard for me to get any help when I'm the one that pushed first. I started it, so therefore, I'm just as much the bad guy as the victim," Joshua said.

"In whose eyes?" Aiden asked, softly. "He was awful to you."

"It doesn't matter how awful he was. It doesn't change the fact that I pushed first," Joshua said.

"Will you ever forgive yourself?" Aiden asked.

Joshua was quiet before answering, in which he said under his breath, "I hope so." There was more silence, then Joshua spoke again. "I was right about one thing."

"What?" Aiden asked.

"God," Joshua said. Then, he smiled with excitement and continued, "I couldn't get Kole to leave me alone myself. Believe me, I tried! So, God had to make him move. That's what I call a Christmas miracle."

"Wow," Aiden said.

Joshua didn't say anything more. He looked at the ground, observing the snow and its marvelous sparkle under the gleam of the sun.

Recess ended, and the group of boys plus Camilla walked over to the pavement where they lined up: seventh graders on one side, eighth graders on the other side.

Joshua sat with Carson and Camilla again at lunch. Carson and Camilla didn't speak much at the beginning of the period, so Joshua said, "Camilla. Have you talked to Reese lately?"

"No," Camilla said. "She's hardly talked to me since she met Kole. Same with Zoe. I thought we were friends, but she was so quick to leave us."

"Yeah, that's what I thought, too," Joshua said.

"I can't imagine what it was like for you. Not only did she leave you in the dust, but she betrayed you with your bully. Kole never spoke to me more than three words," Camilla said.

"Yeah, it's pretty awful."

"Why were you wondering?

"I was just wondering why she's been in the guidance office this whole week."

"Are you crazy!? Isn't it obvious? It's because of what she did to you."

"Yeah," Joshua replied with his voice low.

Joshua began sitting in his normal seat again during advisory. Reese was never there, and he preferred that seat. It was the end of January—Joshua's face was almost completely back to normal; he could look at a screen without getting a headache or becoming dizzy; his ribs still hurt when he played his instruments or laid down but were fine otherwise; Independent Study was over—when Reese walked in the door part way through advisory. Her hair was half brushed, only a quick run-through. She had her hands in the pockets of the black vest she wore. Her head was facing downwards. She walked in and sat down at the table Joshua didn't sit at. She logged into a laptop and began typing. Joshua was surprised she just walked in and began working after nearly a month of absence, but he quickly learned that she wasn't actually working on the class. She was typing quickly, but it had nothing to do with the T.V. Mr. Hendrick saw her and came over to say, "Hey, Reese, glad you're back."

"Yeah," she mumbled.

Then, he told her what she could work on. She said she would, but she didn't seem too enthusiastic about it. Sam and Aaron looked at Joshua, for he was watching Reese. Sam leaned in close to him and whispered, "Do you still have a crush on her?"

"How could I?" Joshua asked. "She betrayed me."

"Good," Sam said.

"Good that she betrayed me?" Joshua asked.

"No," Sam said. "Good that you don't like her anymore."

But something inside Joshua's head kept wondering about Reese. Where had she been the past month? The guidance office, obviously. He knew that. But what was she there for? Again, obvious: the whole situation with Kole. But why? That answer was a little less obvious. Sure, what she did was wrong, but...for some reason, Joshua felt like it had more than just to do with everything that went down that night (or whole week, really). It was at least more than just being in trouble. The guidance office wasn't where people went when they were in trouble with the rules. It was where people went when they were in trouble mentally. So...that brings us back to the second question...*what was she there for?*

Chapter 43: Feelings

Joshua woke up on the 28th of January, a Monday morning, reluctantly climbing out of bed. Kole was gone, but mornings were still not his thing. He kneeled next to his bed to pray, and he was trying not to fall asleep. He went into the bathroom and took a shower. He ate breakfast, brushed his teeth, all of his morning routine.

It wasn't actually until math class when he was writing it out that he realized what the date was, and then he realized the significance of it. It had been exactly a month since the "fight" between him and Kole. Instead of doing his work, he contemplated over it. He hadn't seen Kole since...he hadn't seen Kole since seconds before a blow to his head knocked him out cold. He shivered at the thought of that.

It was Reese's fourth day back in school. She hadn't spoken to him at all during advisory, and she sat at the other table still. With Independent Study ending, they didn't have any other classes together. In the mornings, Joshua never saw her at her locker because she was always late for school. At the end of the day, Joshua's class was farther from his locker than her class, so she would hurry out of her class, open her locker, whip her bag out, then leave before Joshua could even get there. Joshua didn't try real hard to meet her, either. He wasn't sure if he wanted to or not. Sure, he once had a huge crush on her, but now, he had been betrayed. Even after a month—with no closure, no forgiveness, no verbal reason to move on—it was hard for him to get past it.

Then, on that Monday, exactly a month after the incident that broke them apart—broke Joshua, broke Reese, probably even broke Kole—Joshua was walking to his locker at the end of the day and saw Reese still there. She was looking for something, seeming panicked. Joshua figured it was probably because she knew he was coming and didn't want to still be there.

Joshua proceeded toward his locker. Ignoring Reese, he seamlessly dialed in his locker combination, grabbed what he needed, shut his locker, and turned around. Never once did he look at Reese; she didn't acknowledge him either.

So was that it? Were Joshua and Reese over? Even when she always took Kole's side, Joshua had this little feeling inside his head that wanted Reese to come to her senses and realize that she was totally betraying him. He wanted her to turn around and take his side. He wanted her to like him like he once liked her. And stupidly, he thought that day would come. Joshua thought one day Reese might see Kole for who he really was and Joshua for who he was, and not for who Kole said he was. But that day had yet to come, and at this point, Joshua didn't think it ever would. Reese ignoring him pretty much proved that.

But then he thought:

"I ignored her too, and I still can't get over it."

It was funny that even after a month, Joshua was still suffering the repercussions of Kole's constant abuse. It wasn't even just with Reese. It was more than just her. Even though Kole was gone, the fear wasn't. Everytime he turned a corner, he feared someone was going to jump out and punch him. Sometimes, all of a sudden in the middle of class, he would have this thought in his head: a thought of Kendall...or Leah. They'd be crying, hurt, and then suddenly he'd be back to reality. Even though he knew Kole was gone, sometimes his mind forgot. Joshua found himself slowly losing Carson, too. He hadn't had a *best* friend since he was in like...first grade, so he didn't know how to keep them, apparently. That made things a thousand times worse because he had no one to talk to. Sure, his family would listen, but he needed someone else, too.

Chapter 44: Let Out

March had arrived, and the snow was beginning to dry up. That helped Joshua in his healing. Everytime he stepped outside when it was below 20 degrees, or there was snow on the ground, he would have flashbacks to opening that door on December 28th. One day, he took his sisters sledding, and he totally wiped out at the bottom of a hill. He went flying into the snow and had a flashback to the fight. Hitting the cold snow made him feel like he was there again.

But now, there were only small patches of snow left on the ground. It was recess time, and Joshua sat on the swings alone. He didn't *swing*, though. He just kicked the muddy wood chips below him. He hadn't become a total loner over the past two months. Even though he and Carson weren't as close as they once were, they were still friends. In fact, he had spent the weekend at Carson's house. He was still friends with Sam and Aaron too, as well as Aiden and the others (for the most part, anyway). He still hadn't talked to Reese. She wouldn't sit with him in advisory, nor would she even look at him. Today, at recess, Joshua didn't feel like talking to any of them. He had those days sometimes. He couldn't explain it, so he just let it be, and the others just let it be, too. He sat on the swing, not looking at his surroundings, when he heard the chains on the swing next to him clink together as someone sat down.

"Hey."

It was a soft, soothing voice.

Joshua looked over and saw Reese sitting there.

"Hey," he replied, then he looked at the ground again.

"Why are you alone?"

Joshua shrugged.

"Has *everyone* turned on you?"

"No. I just...wanted space."

"Oh." Reese started to stand up and said, "I'll leave you alone, then."

"No, it's okay. It's silly. I don't know why I'm like this."

"Nah, it's not silly. I get it. People need space sometimes."

"But you don't have to leave. It's been a while."

"Yeah, and for good reason." Reese laughed a little.

"What?" Joshua sounded taken aback.

"Did he really hit you that hard?"

Joshua was silent for a moment. *Was she serious? Did she really just ask that?* Of course *he really hit him that hard! Was she* still *denying Kole's cruelty?* Then he said, "Maybe you *should* leave."

"I'm sorry, Joshua. I didn't mean it like that!" Reese quickly responded.

"It's just a tough subject. That was a horrible time in my life."

"I know, and that's why I wanted to say *I'm sorry.*

I'm sorry for everything that I did."

Joshua stopped kicking the wood chips, and he was still. *Wow! An apology!?* That was more than even Aiden had given him. Sure, Aiden had acknowledged that Kole had been a jerk to Joshua, but he never sat down with Joshua and told him he was *really* sorry.

Due to Joshua's prolonged silence, Reese said, "You don't have to say anything. In fact, *don't* think of anything to say. I don't deserve that much. I made some bad decisions, and sadly, it cost not only me but you."

"It cost you?"

"Yeah. I mean, for one, I betrayed the one person who was always nice to me, and..."

Joshua smiled, blushing a little, but he also felt a little saddened.

"...Kole ruined my life," Reese finished.

"Mine too."

"No, Joshua. He didn't *ruin* your life." Reese's voice cracked a little.

"What? You can't say that."

"It's true."

"You think getting beat up over and over again isn't bad?"

"It's bad, sure, but he didn't *ruin* your life."

"I was constantly living in fear because I didn't know when Kole was going to attack next, but I couldn't go to anyone about it because I had to live with the burden of knowing that it was all my fault."

"It *wasn't* your fault. But either way, it's over with now."

"But it doesn't *feel* over."

"Joshua, listen. I know that what he put you through was awful. I didn't realize that before. But I am telling you! He *didn't* ruin your life like he ruined mine. Maybe at the time you felt miserable, and maybe you still do, but at least you never did anything that bad."

"I pushed first, remember? The whole thing was all my fault."

"But you weren't trying to hurt anyone! You were defending your religion! You've said that so many times! As for me, I wasn't defending anything. I liked Kole, like...really liked him, and that's all I was fighting for. It's stupid because Kole wasn't very nice. And..." Reese paused. She looked at the ground. Joshua could tell she was forcing back tears. She looked back up but not at Joshua. She continued, "I can't forget that last fight you had...if you can even call it that. I just *watched* as Kole and Maverick beat you. You weren't having it. And that *was* my fault. I'm pretty sure Kole was planning on telling you goodbye some way, but I caused it to happen the way it did. It was terrifying actually. But still, I stood there. I walked with you on your way toward doom when Kole and Maverick took you to the park. I didn't get you help. I just watched. And when they punched you, I stood there watching."

Reese looked at Joshua finally. His face was horrified. He felt like he was in the moment again. He could taste the snow, the blood. He could feel the punches thrown at his face. He could feel Kole and Maverick kicking him on the ground. He could feel the final blow to his head before he was knocked out. He remembered everything going black, then he was looking at Reese again. She didn't know what was going through his head, but she could tell that he was distraught, so she said, "Sorry. I didn't mean to give a detailed description of your destruction. I might not have been the one beaten up, but I did care about you. So, watching you was traumatic to me as well. But unlike me, you were innocent. Then, to top it all off, I just walked away. I *left* you there unconscious! You were in a *t-shirt*. If we hadn't come across those guys from your Church, you probably would have frozen to death. But still, I walked away." A tear ran from Reese's eye. She closed them and said, "I just...I can't get rid of this thought. I don't know how to forgive myself for that."

Joshua was silent. He had no idea what to say. What could he say, honestly? In addition, he was still thinking about the flashback he just had.

"I had to get that out. I couldn't keep it in any longer. It was eating me alive," Reese said.

"I get it," Joshua said. He paused for a moment, then he said, "I have a question for you."

"What is it?"

"Where were you in January?" Joshua looked at her, watching her face. It went from being upset to being annoyed.

Snappily, she answered, "You know where I was. You saw me."

"But...I just need to know...did you go there yourself, or did you get sent there?"

"Why does that matter?"

"Because...it just does."

"*I* went there."

Joshua didn't say anything. He just stared back at

Reese, so she continued, "I realized that I had done something awful. Kole told me that he wasn't going back to school. He was moving. I hadn't known that until the night before. That's why I didn't go back. I was terrified. That is when I realized I had ruined my life. I had abandoned Zoe—my best friend—and Camilla. I hurt you, and I made Aiden and the others all dislike me even more than they had before. I had made a fool of myself! All for Kole. I realized that I was living for Kole, and then, he was abandoning me. I missed a day of school, but I couldn't stay home forever. My parents didn't know anything, and I couldn't tell them. I think Wendy knows some of what happened, but she doesn't know about any of the fights. Well, I don't know, she might. She hasn't told a single person anything about Kole and me. I knew I couldn't avoid school forever.

"When I went back on the second day, instead of facing Zoe, and Aiden, and...*you*...I went to the guidance counselor. It was particularly hard for me to face *you* because you looked...*awful*. With Zoe and Aiden, it was easy to forget about all I had done. They didn't have any marks on them. Though, they probably wouldn't *let* me forget. You on the other hand...you were a screaming image. So, I hid. The guidance counselor tried to help me, but I can't get help when I don't believe what she's saying. She doesn't know Kole, so she can't understand how bad it was that I had taken his side. So, even though she tried to make my life better, I couldn't believe that I deserved that. So, I stopped going, and I went back to class. But...I still wouldn't face *you*. That's why I wouldn't sit with you. Now, I'm trying to navigate through school in my life without Kole, but I can't go back to my life before Kole because I changed it. I might want it back, but Zoe has moved on, and Aiden never liked me. I was stupid to think he had," Reese said.

"We all think stupid things. Believe me, I know from experience," Joshua said.

Reese stared back at him but didn't say anything.

Students started walking toward the pavement, which meant that recess was over. Joshua and Reese looked at each other for a moment more, then they both started to walk over to the pavement. They didn't say anything to each other as they walked. When they got over there, Joshua stood behind Reese in the seventh grade line, but she didn't look back to talk to him, and he didn't try to initiate another conversation, either.

When Joshua got inside, he sat with Aiden, Andrew, Daniel, Caiden, and Carson. There were two open seats at their table now and probably forever. Joshua ate silently until Aiden said to him from across the table, "Hey, Joshua! I saw you talking to Reese at recess. What did she want?"

"Why does that matter?" Joshua asked.

"What?" Aiden asked, offended.

"We were just having a conversation alone. That's not your business."

"What did she want?" Aiden persisted. "Was she trying to seek your forgiveness?"

Joshua shrugged.

"Don't give it to her."

Joshua looked at Aiden with a glare in his eyes.

"What?"

"Why should I forgive *you* and not her?"

"Kole was just as bad to me as he was to you."

"No," Joshua replied, firmly. "He wasn't."

"You weren't there."

"No, you're right. I wasn't. But you weren't there when Kole beat me, either. And whenever you were there, you weren't with me! You were with Kole! Carson, Daniel, and Caiden are the only ones who have had my back through any of this, and there were *11* of us!"

"He called me the f-word, Joshua! That's a hate crime! That's not bad to you?"

"Yeah, it's bad. But what do you think that bullying someone for their religion is? Is that not a hate crime also?"

"That's different."

"Why!?" Joshua snapped, aggressively putting his hands on the table. "Because no one cares about religious people anymore?"

"No. That's not what I'm saying. But you're Catholic, and you just can't hate crime Catholics. Catholics rule this world."

"Not anymore they don't."

"He called the police on me, Joshua!" Aiden cried, slamming his hands on the table.

"I wish all he did was call the police on me! Instead, he constantly followed me in the halls, tortured me, teased that he would hurt my sisters, and beat me up four times in addition to the constant abuse in the halls and on the streets! The last two times that he beat me up, I could have died! And for the record, I've just barely started being able to play my instruments—one of my favorite hobbies—without being in immense pain in over two months! That whole time, where were you? WITH KOLE!" Joshua felt a tear run down from his eye, and he finished: "So *don't* tell me that he was just as bad to you as he was me because he WASN'T."

The group was silent. Andrew, Daniel, and Caiden all looked down at the table, uncomfortable. Carson looked from Joshua to Aiden. Aiden looked down at the table as well, but he didn't look uncomfortable like Andrew, Daniel, and Caiden did; he looked defeated. Joshua quickly wiped his eyes, for he couldn't cry now, or ever, but definitely not here, not in that setting. Not in the middle school cafeteria. But another tear came, and then another, and he couldn't control them anymore. Instead of sitting there, he left the cafeteria. He left his lunch box on the table, and his jacket on his seat, as he still had it from recess.

The boys still at the table all looked up at each other. Carson glared at Aiden and stood up. He grabbed Joshua's lunch box and jacket, then he went out to find him.

Aiden noticed that Reese was staring from her table. When she saw that Aiden noticed, she quickly turned around.

The table was silent for the rest of lunch.

Carson looked for Joshua in the bathroom, but he wasn't in there. He looked in the classrooms, but he wasn't in there either. He finally found him walking out the doors of the school. Carson ran over to him, shouting his name, but Joshua didn't turn around. He had his backpack on, but he was in a t-shirt.

Carson ran after Joshua who didn't run but just picked up his pace to a fast walk. Carson caught up to him and shoved the jacket and lunchbox at him, saying, "Dude, where are you going?"

"Home."

"You can't just *leave*."

"Yes, I can."

Joshua was still walking, and Carson was following.

"But school isn't even over yet."

"It's over for me. I just can't handle it. Today's been a day."

"Yes, today is a day," Carson said with a serious tone. "But at least put your jacket on."

"It's not even that cold. And plus, I've survived zero degrees without a jacket before, certainly I can survive 30."

"Augh, at least take your things! I'm not carrying them all day!" Carson snapped.

Joshua took his jacket and lunchbox, but he kept walking.

"What are you going to tell your parents when you get home?"

"My dad's at work."

"And your mom?"

Joshua was silent.

"You can't go home in the middle of the school day."

"I'll just tell her the truth. She will understand."

"Okay." But Carson didn't sound convinced.

"I just can't go back in. You don't understand."

"After *everything*, Joshua, you think I don't understand?"

Joshua was quiet again.

"You can't just run away from them. You're going to have to get used to it."

"No. I'm asking to be homeschooled."

"Are you parents going to say yes to that?"

"Of course they will."

"Oh really?"

Joshua paused before replying, "No."

"Come on, Joshua. Come back to school. If you go back right now, no one will notice that you left. If you don't want anyone to find out, then we've got to get back before lunch ends," Carson said.

"Fine," Joshua said.

They went back, but they had to go through the main office because the other door was locked.

They got back to the seventh and eighth grade hallway. People had not been dismissed from lunch yet, so Joshua went to his locker and put his things back. He had just finished when students started to come to their lockers. Joshua hurried to his next class before any of his friends could find him and approach him.

When Joshua got home from school—after school had actually finished—he collapsed onto his couch and didn't get up until his mom came to get him for swim practice.

Chapter 45: Talking

"Joshua." A girl's soft voice spoke his name. He didn't know who, for he was looking in his backpack, trying to find his pencil. He looked up to see, and there stood Wendy.

"Hey," Joshua replied.

"Um...how are you?"

"Fine. I'm trying to find my pencil."

"Oh."

"Um...how about you?"

"I'm fine, too. And, I was wondering...do you want to go to Sally's Sandwich Shop with me this weekend?"

"Uh..." Joshua stood up to be level with Wendy. "I...I can't." Joshua rubbed the back of his head. "I'm sorry."

"Okay," Wendy said, and she walked away, with her head down.

Before Joshua knew it, Reese was coming toward him and going to her locker. At first, she didn't acknowledge Joshua. They hadn't talked since the swingset, and she still didn't sit with him, Sam, and Aaron during advisory. But Joshua stood there motionless, thinking about what just went down with Wendy, the whole time that Reese was in her locker. She shut the door and looked at him.

"What did Wendy talk to you about?" Reese asked.

"It doesn't matter."

"It doesn't look like it doesn't matter."

"I mean, it does matter, but...not to you."

"So...you're still salty?"

Joshua looked at Reese and said, "It doesn't have anything to do with that."

"But it has to do with us.

"What? No, it has to do with Wendy and me."

"She asked you out. I know it. She told me she was going to do it."

"Oh. But that doesn't have anything to do with us."

"Yes, it does. I know it does."

"How so?" Joshua's cheeks were red, and he felt slightly lightheaded. *What was that supposed to mean, hahaha?*

"It's because you are going through a lot right now. You're still trying to get over what went down with Kole, with me, with your other friends. Your life is in pieces right now. You're not in any shape for a relationship. I tried to tell her, but she just didn't understand how your life is so broken. She thought that since Kole's gone, so are all of your problems. I told her that's not true, but she asked you anyway," Reese elaborated.

"Oh, that's what you meant," Joshua said, quietly. *Hahaha, oh!* "Well...now I feel bad."

"What do you mean?"

"I feel bad that I said no."

"Why?"

"Because...it seems like she really wanted to ask

me."

"Sure, but there's no reason to play with her feelings if you're just not at that point."

"You're right."

"Yeah. I'm right about a lot. I have an idea. It's probably right."

"I don't think I'd say you're right about *a lot*, but what's your idea?"

"*Wow.*" Reese raised her eyebrows. "I think *this* idea is definitely right. You should forgive me."

"What?" Joshua's face went from a little bit cheery to surprised.

"You should forgive me."

"Oh."

"Come on, Joshua. You can't stay mad at me forever."

"I'm not *mad* at you, for say. I'm just...I don't even know what...I'm just...confused, I guess...and...disappointed."

"I get it." Reese looked at the baseboard across the hallway.

"It's not that I haven't forgiven you. I just...yeah, I just don't know what I think."

"So...you *don't* hate me?"

"No!"

"Can I sit with you again during advisory?"

"Sure."

Reese smiled.

"I do have to admit, though, that I am hurt by you," Joshua continued. "But, there's no way that you can make it better if we don't ever talk."

"Do you think we will ever be like we were before?"

"I don't know, to be honest."

Reese frowned.

"I'm sorry."

"No, I get it. I broke your trust, and that was wrong. I shouldn't expect things to be the way they were."

"Thank you for understanding."

Reese nodded.

The two of them split, going to their next class.

Chapter 46: Memories

Joshua sat with Aiden and the others at lunch the same day he rejected Wendy. It had been three days since the incident where he walked out. He couldn't think of anything else to do but sit with them, so he just did. It did mostly have to do with the fact that Caiden followed him, and the others followed Caiden.

When Andrew sat down at lunch, he immediately said, "Hey. Guess what." And then everyone looked up, so Andrew continued, "Did you hear that Patrick and Kole are coming back?"

"What?" Aiden asked.

Joshua's eyes zoomed toward Andrew and locked on his eyes.

"Patrick and Kole are coming back," Andrew said again.

"No," Joshua cried, his voice shaking.

Andrew looked over at Joshua; everyone did.

"No," Joshua said again. His voice was shaking. "He can't be."

"Who said that?" Carson asked.

"Mr. Henry," Andrew said.

"How does he know?" Carson asked.

"It was on the online classroom," Andrew

explained. “Their names were back on the roster. That means they’re coming back.”

“No,” Joshua said for a third time.

Suddenly, Joshua wasn’t at the lunch table anymore. He was in the park. It was dark out, he could barely see. He was wearing a t-shirt, losing all feeling in his arms. Before he knew it, he was being thrown to the ground behind the fountain. His mouth full of snow, he spit it out then stood up, but he could barely move.

Kole was asking Maverick if he’d like to do the honors.

Maverick answered him: “Sure.” He had a huge smile spread across his face.

Kole grabbed his arms, and Joshua tried to break free, but he had no chance.

Maverick was standing in front of him and said, “Wow, Joshua. I thought you were a swimmer. Aren’t they supposed to be strong? Must be you’re just not one of that kind.”

The insult wasn’t enough for Joshua to regain his strength.

Maverick looked up at Kole, then he punched Joshua in the face. Joshua could feel the pain of his fist pressing into his skin. He wasn’t in the cafeteria, he was *in the fight*.

Three more punches. Kole let go of Joshua, sending him crashing to the ground. Joshua was dizzy, just like he had been then.

He tried to get up, but Kole kneed him in the ribs, sending him back to the ground. Then, Kole kicked him two more times. It was all too familiar.

Patrick, Des, and Reese were standing there watching. He struggled to his feet with some second wind, but it was only met by Kole pushing him. He tried to run, but he was in no shape. Kole grabbed onto him and wouldn't let him go, despite his pleas. Joshua was thrown to the ground again, only to be kicked by Kole and Maverick. At that point, even Patrick was vouching for him, until finally, he felt again that final blow to the side of his head, knocking him unconscious.

This time, Joshua didn't wake up on his cozy couch in front of the nice warm fire. He woke up on the floor in the cafeteria with not just all of his friends around him but with the whole seventh and eighth grade class around him. His friends were in front, as well as Reese and all of the staff. Joshua was breathing heavily. He sat up, but he didn't look at anyone, even though they all looked at him. He felt someone behind him put their arms under his shoulders, and they started to lift him up.

Mrs. Wheeling was marching into the cafeteria with Mrs. Finn and the nurse, Mrs. Cramer.

"Everyone out of the way!" Mrs. Wheeling shouted. Most of the students listened, but a few didn't, mostly Joshua's friends.

Carson stood behind Joshua. He was now on his feet, but he held onto Carson's arm because he was still unsure of what just happened. *He had just been at the park, seconds ago.* He had had flashbacks before, but none were quite that captivating.

Mrs. Wheeling, Mrs. Finn, and Mrs. Cramer all walked over to Joshua. They had him sit down at the table. Mrs. Wheeling began directing everyone out of the cafeteria.

"What happened?" Mrs. Cramer asked as students were exiting.

Carson was the only student who stayed. One of the lunch ladies brought Joshua a carton of chocolate milk.

"I wasn't here," Joshua said. His body and voice were shaking. "I was at the park."

"What?" Mrs. Cramer asked, confused.

"I was back in my final fight with Kole," Joshua said. "It was just like it really was."

"You had a flashback," Mrs. Finn added in.

"Yeah."

"Do you know what triggered it?"

"Yes."

"What?"

"Andrew said that Patrick and Kole are coming back."

"Wherever did he hear that?" Mrs. Wheeling butted in, annoyance filling her voice.

"Mr. Henry," Joshua told her.

"What gave him that idea?"

"They were added back onto the roster."

"No. They aren't coming back. They have not been added back to our roster."

"Oh, they aren't? They haven't?"

"No. It must have been a glitch."

"Oh, that's good," Joshua said, sounding relieved. "False alarm," he laughed, like it was all a joke, but he didn't really think that way. It wasn't a joke. He just collapsed from a flashback in front of the whole entire seventh and eighth grade; this was no joke.

"The two of them really bothered you when they were here," Mrs. Finn stated.

"Kole mostly, but yeah," Joshua answered.

"It's okay that you are struggling. My room is always open when you need it. You don't need to suffer on your own. I've helped multiple people deal with their trauma from Patrick and Kole. Now, I think we should bring the students back in here," Mrs. Finn said.

"I can't face them all," Joshua cried. "Not after what just happened."

"That's okay. I get it. You can come eat in my room," Mrs. Finn said. She looked at Carson and said, "You can come too."

"Okay, thanks," Joshua said.

Joshua and Carson followed Mrs. Finn back to her room. Mrs. Cramer went back to the nurse's office. Mrs. Wheeling brought the seventh and eighth graders back to finish their lunches.

Chapter 47: A Lot

Mrs. Abare waited until Joshua's sisters left the room before she said to him, "I heard you blacked out today at lunch."

"I did," Joshua replied.

"What happened?" Mrs. Abare asked.

Joshua sighed. He looked at the counter in front of him, then he leaned up against the one behind him. He let himself slide down it until he was sitting on the floor, then he began explaining: "Andrew said that Patrick and Kole were coming back—WHICH WAS A FALSE ALARM—but I didn't know that, and suddenly, I was reliving the moment of our final fight at the park. It was all so real like I was there again. I woke up on the floor in the cafeteria to every single person in the seventh and eighth grade standing around me. I didn't go back to school after that. I ended up spending the rest of the day in the guidance office talking about the whole situation."

"Are you okay?"

"Yeah."

"Really?"

"I guess. I've had flashbacks before, but this one was the worst." Joshua paused. "It's just..." His voice got lower. "You'd think that after all this time that he's been gone, I wouldn't be thinking about him anymore. But I am."

"It makes sense. He wasn't very nice to you, and that's a big deal. It's not something you can just move on from quickly. You're going to have to take some time to heal."

"It's like he came into my life just to dig a big hole and then leave! He was only here for four months, and in that time he ruined my friendship with Aiden, and with Reese, pretended to be my friend only to betray me twice, and managed to beat me up four times!"

"Yeah. It's going to take time to climb out of a hole that is above your head. But I'm here for you, Joshua. You can talk to me."

"Thanks."

"Is there anything else you want to say right now?"

"No. It's just like my thoughts are an endless loop always thinking about what Kole did. Not just because of him but because of that hole he left me in. All of the things in my life that have been altered, unable to go back."

"M-hm."

"I think right now I'm just going to go play the saxophone or the cornet or something. That'll take my mind off of it."

"Okay, good idea."

Joshua stood back up and went upstairs to his room. He pulled out his saxophone and started jamming.

But Joshua was mid-song when he suddenly recalled a memory from before his first fight with Kole. It was from back when he didn't realize what Kole was capable of. It was from the time where Kole was lighting the sparks that would ignite Joshua's fire that night in November. He heard Kole's voice, loud and clear: "All you ever do is play the saxophone?"

Joshua's quiet voice responded, "Yeah, I do that a lot."

"You're so boring," Kole's voice responded.

Joshua stopped playing, the notes slowly fading away. He looked back at his music, his own thoughts from now, not the past, said, "Not boring." He started playing again, but then he heard it again, *"You're so boring."*

"Augh!" Joshua cried, and he jumped up from his seat, throwing his saxophone softly onto his bed.

Joshua stormed out of his room and went downstairs, announcing to his mom, "I'm going for a walk."

"Okay," Mrs. Abare said. "Is something wrong?"

"I can't play right now," he replied.

Joshua grabbed a light jacket and went out the door. He headed down his driveway and began walking. He had another memory. That time, not of Kole, but of Aiden. The two of them were walking down the sidewalk together, silently. He remembered seeing Maverick sitting across from Reese inside Tony's Taco Bar. He remembered yelling, "I thought I could trust you!" He remembered running out of the taco bar and being stopped by the boys. He remembered Maverick's hurtful words. Joshua's stomach hurt to hear them again, even though he knew they weren't true. It was the fact Maverick had the audacity to say it that got Joshua going. He remembered Maverick asking Reese, "Who do you choose? Me...or Joshua?" Reese's answer: "You." He remembered the blows to his face and stomach, falling limp in Kole's arms, then crashing to the ground. More hurtful words, another string pulled, and finally, Joshua ran away.

Then, he was suddenly brought to the first moment he was abandoned by his friends. He had just finished his first fight with Kole. He saw Aiden again, standing in opposition to him. Reese, too. All of the others. It was all too much.

Joshua felt his heart pounding. He was alone: not at home, not even at school. Just alone. No Carson, no friends, no family. Alone. He started to cry, and he sat on the pavement, back against a shop. He cried into his hands, not caring who saw. *What was happening?*

"Hey."

Joshua felt a hand on his shoulder. He jumped, then he quickly wiped his eyes and looked up. A woman, who he had seen before but couldn't remember who she was, was standing there next to him. "Are you okay?" she asked him.

"Yeah," Joshua answered, but then he realized where he was and what he was doing, and he corrected himself: "No."

"Where are your parents?"

"At home."

"Do they know you're here?"

"Sort of."

"*Why* are you here?"

"I came for a walk, and I..." Joshua looked through his mind, trying to figure out what to say.

"It's okay," the woman said, seeing he looked distraught. "Maybe I should walk you home."

"Ah, that's okay. I'll be okay. Thank you."

"I should at least call your parents."

"No. I don't want to worry them."

"Okay. But I don't like the idea of you just being alone."

"I am a runner, so I go out here a lot on my own."

"But...you're clearly really upset about something. You don't need to tell me what, but I just think that you shouldn't be alone."

"Maybe you're right."

"I'll walk you home. I've got nowhere to be. Nowhere important, anyway."

"Okay."

The woman walked Joshua home, and it turned out she used to scrapbook with Joshua's mom when he and Kendall were little. Her name was Mellissa.

Mellissa took Joshua to the door so that she'd know his mom was home, and she said hi to her, then left. Joshua walked into the kitchen, and after Mellissa left, Mrs. Abare said to him, "What were you doing? I didn't know you remembered Mellissa."

"I didn't really," Joshua answered.

"Is everything okay?"

"No, Mom, it isn't." A tear fell from Joshua's eye.

"What happened?"

"When I was playing my saxophone, I kept hearing Kole's voice in my head, and when I went for a walk, I had memories of the incident at Tony's Taco Bar and of our first fight. I can't get Kole out of my head since the incident."

"I can see that."

"I think I'm going to just go lay down."

"Maybe you should try eating. That might help. I found most of your lunch in the fridge. You must be starving."

"No. I can't eat right now."

Mrs. Abare frowned as Joshua went upstairs to his room. On the way, he passed Kendall who didn't say anything, but she stared at him his whole walk to his room.

Joshua's saxophone was still laying on his bed. Instead of packing it up and putting it into its case, he gently set it on the floor, then he fell onto his bed. He woke up to the sound of his mom knocking on the door with a plate of food. She said that they had all finished eating. He took the plate, thanked her, and ate. Surprisingly, it made him feel a little better, but he still didn't feel great about everything.

Chapter 48: Reminders

Joshua walked into advisory the next morning, not having been in any class since he blacked out at lunch. When he walked into the Innovation Lab, all eyes were drawn to him. He tried to ignore them as he went to his seat and logged into his laptop. Sam and Aaron had glanced at him when he walked in, but they tried not to stare. Reese wasn't there yet. She came about three minutes after Joshua. Missing the stare-down, she was quick to speak to him when she arrived. She sat down and said, "Hey, Joshua."

"Hey."

"Are you okay?"

Joshua shrugged.

"I feel so guilty. It's all my fault."

Joshua was silent at first, but he said, "It was mostly Kole."

"But I am like a constant reminder of your broken life. I'm part of it."

"You think my life is *broken*?" That wasn't the first time she had implied that, either.

"Is it whole?"

Joshua shrugged, then he asked, "Am *I* a constant reminder?"

"I..." Reese said but didn't finish.

"It's okay. Yesterday was a rough day."

"Why didn't you come back after lunch? Did you go home?"

"No. I was in the guidance room."

"Oh. I know how that goes."

"Yeah."

Joshua looked over at Sam and Aaron and saw that they were staring at him and Reese. When he looked over, Aaron said, "Hold on. What is she doing here?"

"What are you talking about?" Reese asked.

"You can't sit here!" Aaron cried.

"I can do whatever I want," Reese snapped.

"Not after what you did to Joshua," Aaron said.

"He said I could sit here," Reese said.

Sam and Aaron both looked at Joshua and at the same time cried, "WHAT!?"

"I did," Joshua admitted.

"WHY!?" they both shouted.

"After all she did to you, why are you letting her come back?" Sam asked.

Joshua opened his mouth to speak, but Reese started first and said, "Joshua's the one who's been hurt, not you, so let him decide for himself."

"Joshua, how could you? You're blinded by her! I thought you had gotten over her!" Sam cried.

"Yeah, what is this?" Aaron asked.

"Stop! He's going through enough!" Reese cried.

"Yeah! Because of you!" Sam snapped.

"Fine. Maybe you're right. I should go," Reese said.

She stood up, and Joshua said, "Wait! Let *me*

explain." Reese sat back down, and Joshua continued, "It's true. Reese has hurt me. And I'm not just *forgetting* it. I *can't* forget it! Look, I'm not okay with what happened, but...it's for me to decide, not you."

"What about if Patrick and Kole come back? Reese will turn right back to them again! Then what? You will be hurting yourself all over again," Sam said.

"Patrick and Kole aren't coming back!" Joshua cried. "And...Reese..." Joshua looked at Reese who looked like she wanted to cry.

"*Joshua*," Reese said. "I'm not going to turn to them again! You don't really think that, do you?"

"To be honest, I don't know what to think anymore," Joshua admitted.

"See?" Sam and Aaron both asked.

"No, I get it," Reese said. "I deserve that."

"Then leave," Aaron snapped.

"But...I want to make it right, and I can't do that if you push me away. And...this isn't even about you! I've already said that! It's about Joshua and me," Reese persisted.

"But Joshua's our friend," Aaron said.

"Then you should want him to make amends," Reese continued.

"But he's being stupid," Aaron exclaimed.

"No, he's not," Reese said.

"Whatever," Aaron grumbled. "But this doesn't mean things are better between you and me."

"Or me," Sam agreed.

"I know," Reese said.

Joshua let out a deep breath inside his head. That

was a horrible situation to be in because he was torn between sides. Next was band, and usually, that would bring him relief, but today, for the first time ever, he was more nervous than relieved about it. He had just started playing again, but the last time he played, he kept hearing Kole's voice in his head. He tried to ignore it, and Teagan helped him with that. Teagan always had a whole lot of energy that Joshua had no idea where it came from, but he loved it.

Joshua walked into the band room after advisory. Teagan was already in there with his saxophone strapped around his neck, hanging over his light gray sweatshirt. Teagan turned around and saw him coming, so he exclaimed, "Hey, Joshua! What's up!?"

Joshua looked at Teagan and smiled, responding, "Nothing. You?"

"Not much," Teagan answered.

Joshua sat down next to Teagan and began taking out his instrument. The word *boring* ran through his head.

"Are you sure nothing's up?" Teagan asked. "It doesn't look that way."

"*Nothing* is just a default response for me," Joshua admitted.

"Oh, I get it. That's *not much* for me. Or *nm*. Is this about yesterday?"

"Partially. But, every time I pull out my saxophone, I hear Kole telling me it's boring."

"That's weird."

"Yeah, it's weird. It's stupid."

"No! That's not what I meant! I mean it's weird that Kole told you it's boring. Don't listen to him. He's probably never played the saxophone before. He doesn't know the joy it brings. It's not boring. Ask anyone here."

Joshua didn't start asking anyone, so Teagan did. He shouted to a boy in front of them and said, "Hey! Do you think the saxophone is boring?"

"No."

"See? Listen to that person," Teagan told Joshua.

Joshua still seemed expressionless, so Teagan asked another person: "Hey! Do you think the saxophone is boring?"

"Yes."

Teagan looked taken aback and asked, "Then why are you in band?"

"Because my parents forced me to."

"Aw," Teagan said to Joshua, waving that person away. "Don't listen to him. He's just salty. Take it from those of us who truly love band. But really, it doesn't matter what anyone else says, anyway. If it brings *you* joy, then it doesn't matter if Kole—or anyone—says it's boring. I bet there's so many things that he does that you find boring."

"Yeah," Joshua agreed.

"See, you get me," Teagan said.

"Yeah, and you get me." Joshua smiled. "Thanks."

"No problem, man."

"What's *not much* your default for?"

"Oh, lots of things, but that's okay because I've got you, and I've got me."

"I could..."

"No. It's okay." Teagan put his hand lightly on Joshua's shoulder and smiled.

Mr. Goodwell walked to the front of the band to start rehearsal. Joshua didn't hear Kole's voice anymore when he played the saxophone. He happily played the music he was given without the fear of Kole hanging over his shoulder.

After band, he had math class with Mr. Henry. *Mr. Henry.* He was the one who caused all of this. Well, no, not *all* of it—just the blacking-out-in-front-of-everyone part. Joshua tried not to be salty, but he was annoyed that Mr. Henry had said they were coming back when it wasn't true, even if he thought it was. It caused Joshua to blackout in front of the entire seventh and eighth grade, which was EMBARRASSING.

Joshua still often sat with Sam and his friends, Drake and Mason, during math, rather than Aiden and Daniel. Mr. Henry gave a lesson at the beginning of class, then he gave the rest of the class time to work on the homework. He put the worksheet on a stack in the front of the room and had everyone go get it. He sat at his desk, next to the stack, taking attendance. When Joshua was getting his paper, Mr. Henry said to him, "Joshua, can I talk to you for a minute."

Joshua looked at him briefly before answering, "Sure."

"In the hall," Mr. Henry added.

"Okay," Joshua said. His heart raced a little.

The two of them walked across the classroom and out into the hallway. Then, Mr. Henry said, "I've been told that what happened to you yesterday in the cafeteria was in part my fault."

"Uh..." Joshua said, his heart still racing. He might

have been slightly salty, but he wasn't going to put Mr. Henry down to his face.

"It's okay. I shouldn't have said something I didn't know was true, especially when it could have had those repercussions. All I wanted to do was say that I'm sorry I caused that for you," Mr. Henry said.

"Oh."

"Do you forgive me?"

Joshua nodded. So many people with so many apologies asking for forgiveness.

"Thank you," Mr. Henry said. He paused before continuing, "Okay, now, let's go back inside. I can't imagine leaving all those seventh graders in there alone, and I want to give you work time so that you don't have to do much, if anything, for homework."

"Okay, thanks," Joshua said. They both walked into the classroom. Joshua sat back down with Sam, Drake, and Mason.

"Why did he take you out there?" Drake asked immediately.

Joshua looked at Drake but didn't answer.

"Are you in trouble?" That was Mason.

"Ooh, Joshua's in trouble!" Sam exclaimed. "For what?"

"I'm not in trouble," Joshua told them.

"Then what was it all about?" Drake asked.

"He was just saying sorry for yesterday. That's all," Joshua said.

"Why'd he have to take you out into the hallway for that?" Mason asked.

"Because," Joshua said. "I don't know...I guess since

it's kind of embarrassing."

"Everyone knows it happened," Mason said. "So I don't see how it matters."

"Because everyone doesn't need to be reminded of it," Joshua told him.

"I'm pretty sure no one has forgotten," Mason said.

"Whatever," Joshua said, rolling his eyes. He started to work on his math homework, solving for x by putting the x on one side, the constants on the other, then dividing by the coefficient before the x. It was super easy, so he flew through it and didn't have to do any homework for math. He was glad.

Chapter 49: Laughter

Oh, math class. It once held Patrick, now it held Joshua's second worst problem in seventh grade. No wonder Joshua didn't like math much at that time in his life. Joshua, as mentioned, usually sat with Sam, Drake, and Mason. He was doing a mix of partaking in their conversation and doing his own math homework. He was at the part where he was doing his work when they suddenly all started staring at him. He looked up at them, not sure why they were all staring.

"What?" Joshua asked.

They still stared at him.

Nervously, Joshua started laughing.

"You think it's funny?" Drake asked.

"What?" Joshua asked, still laughing. *Why were they staring?*

"Why are you laughing?" Drake asked.

"Because you are all staring at me, and it's what I do when I'm uncomfortable."

"No, it's not. When you're uncomfortable, you black out. My friend just killed himself, and you're laughing!"

"What? I wasn't laughing about that!"

"Yes, you were."

"I already told you what I was laughing about! And

I didn't even know that about your friend!"

"We *literally* were just talking about it."

"I didn't hear you."

"You're a horrible liar."

"I'm *not* a liar! I'm sorry about your friend! But I *really* didn't hear you!"

"You know, Kole's right. You are everything he ever said you were."

Joshua slammed his hands on the table, looking like he was about to bounce up.

"Oh no! Watch out, Drake," Mason laughed. "He might beat you up."

"I'm not going to beat you up," Joshua said, but he wasn't sure if he was trying to convince them that or himself that.

"You sure look like it," Mason said. He looked at Drake and said, "I'd run if I were you."

"I won't run because I know Joshua's never won a fight, but people like him are exactly the types of people who would think suicide is funny," Drake said.

"Augh!" Joshua shouted, and he picked up his binder and papers and went to go sit with Aiden and Daniel.

"Hey," Aiden said when he sat down. A look of concern was spread across his face as he watched Joshua set his things down.

"Hey," Joshua replied, looking down at his things.

"What happened?" Daniel asked.

"Drake," Joshua answered.

"What did he do?" Aiden asked. Drake didn't like Aiden, so this came as no surprise to him.

"He says I think suicide is funny. But I DON'T!" Joshua cried.

"That's a horrible claim to make against someone," Aiden said.

"Yeah!" Joshua cried. "He's going to get me into so much trouble! I advocate against suicide! I don't support it, and I DEFINITELY don't think it's funny!"

"What did you do?" Daniel asked.

"They were all staring at me, so I got uncomfortable and laughed because that's just what I do! I had no idea what they said. I just saw them all staring at me. I guess they were waiting for my condolences, but I had no idea," Joshua said.

"They don't deserve your condolences anymore," Aiden said.

"Yes, they do. Losing a friend to suicide isn't something anyone should have to go through. But I can't believe they have the audacity to say I think it's funny. I DON'T think it's funny! It's a tragedy!" Joshua said.

"Yeah, it's not cool," Aiden agreed.

"But it got worse. They said that Kole was right," Joshua said.

"No, Kole was never right," Aiden said.

"I got upset, and Mason said I was about to beat Drake up."

"Were you?"

"Um..."

"You were!?"

"The thought crossed my mind, yes."

"Oh, brotha!"

Joshua blushed, then he said, "What is wrong with

me?"

"At least you didn't laugh about suicide," Aiden said. "But really, I think sometimes urges just come into our heads, and we aren't always going to act on them."

Joshua nodded slightly.

Math ended, and Joshua was off to literacy. After that, he had his choice class. He now had gym, and Reese was in there. They were currently in a soccer unit, and Joshua didn't like soccer. He was a cross country runner. The only thing good about the class was that he got put on a team with Reese and didn't usually have to wear a pinny. He was so glad about the second one, and the first one was a debatable issue sometimes. But Joshua usually talked to Reese when they weren't playing, avoiding any topic of Kole, Maverick, or any other part of the situation.

Their team started off on the sidelines. There were four teams, so not all were always playing. In the second round, the teams switched, and they were on. Joshua got put on offense because they had to run a lot, so his teammates thought he should go there. But that was still a bad idea because he couldn't kick or receive the ball.

One of his teammates passed it to him, and he totally missed it. He turned around to run for it, but the other team snatched it. Another time, he got the ball, but when he kicked it, it didn't go to his teammate like he wanted it to. Instead, it went to the other team. One time, Joshua got the chance to make a goal, but he missed. *He had such a clear shot.*

The mini game finally ended, and the shirt team got to go off. Joshua and Reese sat together on the bleachers. Reese pointed out to Joshua, "You're pretty bad at soccer."

Mrs. Carney, the gym teacher, was standing next to them, watching the game. She heard Reese and let out a laugh.

"Augh," Joshua said. "You weren't any better."

"No, but I thought you were supposed to be athletic," Reese said.

"I am! I'm just not a soccer player! I would rather go running for 50 minutes than play soccer even for just one minute," Joshua said.

"Believe me," Mrs. Carney said, adding to their conversation. "If I could, I would let you go running during this time instead, but I can't do that."

"Ah," Joshua said.

"It's okay. I know you try," Mrs. Carney said, then she looked at Reese.

"Don't look at me like that!" Reese laughed.

Mrs. Carney laughed, but then she had to turn around to snap at someone for fouling.

Gym class didn't get any better, even with Mrs. Carney's sympathy, but like all bad things do, it ended.

Joshua left class with Reese, and she asked him, "Do you think suicide is funny?"

"No!" Joshua snapped.

"Drake says you do."

"He's twisting my words...or more like my laughter. I *didn't* laugh about suicide. Never! You know me, Reese, don't you?"

"Yeah, I do, but he was saying that you do. That's all."

"I can't believe that he was saying that behind my back."

"Yeah. Do you think abortion is funny?"

"Um..." Joshua said, nervously, accompanied by a nervous laugh.

"What? You do?"

"I don't know what that is."

"What!?"

Joshua repeated himself.

"Oh my gosh." Reese shook her head. "Kole's right, you *do* live under a rock."

"Hey! Never say those words again! I will NEVER talk to you again!"

"Sorry."

"Instead of ridiculing me about it, how about you just tell me what it is."

"It's this thing where women kill their unborn babies then call it reproductive liberty and women's rights."

"What?" Joshua's eyes widened.

"People think that by calling it a liberty and a right, it makes it okay. Liberties and rights sound good, right?"

"No."

"If you didn't know the context, it would. If I asked you if you supported women's rights, but you didn't know about abortion, you'd probably say yes, but you wouldn't know I actually meant to ask if you supported killing babies."

"Wow. That's horrible."

"Welcome to the real world. You know, the one that's not under a rock."

Joshua crossed his arms. Then, he said, "That's not funny, and neither is abortion, and neither is suicide."

They walked together, past Drake and Mason, along with almost all of his other classmates who had lockers near his, plus a few other people who were waiting with their friends. As they passed, Drake shouted, "Joshua thinks suicide is funny!"

"No, I don't!" Joshua snapped.

A bunch of people looked over at Joshua. One person had the audacity to say, "Wow, Joshua, that surprises me."

"I *don't* think it's funny!" Joshua cried.

"You laughed at it," Drake said. "That means you think it's funny."

"No!" Joshua snapped. "I didn't laugh at it!"

Joshua stood in front of Drake and stared him in the eyes. Oh, how he wanted to push him in that moment, but he refrained...for a time, anyway.

The next day at recess, he didn't so easily refrain. Well, actually, he didn't refrain at all.

Joshua was talking with Sam, who was near Drake. Joshua overheard Drake say that Mr. Goodwell was awful, and being that Mr. Goodwell was his beloved band teacher, Joshua stepped in snappily and said, "I love Mr. Goodwell!"

"Yeah, that doesn't surprise me, considering you think suicide is funny," Drake said.

Joshua pushed Drake, losing it.

"Woah!" all of the people there exclaimed (which was Sam, Aaron, Mason, and a boy named Adam).

Drake pushed him back.

"What do you mean?" Joshua asked, trying to act like he *didn't* just push Drake.

"What are you talking about?" Drake asked.

"About Mr. Goodwell."

"He's having us sing a song about suicide in chorus."

"What does that mean?"

"It means he's for it."

"No, it doesn't. A lot of songs are sad. That doesn't mean that he's for it. You take things the wrong way."

"No, I don't."

"Joshua, if I were you, I'd walk away," Adam said, chiming in. Adam was best friends with Drake, but he was once really close with Joshua, and he still liked him. "You're going to do something you will regret."

"I agree," Sam said.

Joshua let out a breath, then he listened. He walked away, crossing his arms.

Drake once had respect for Joshua, but Joshua knew that was no longer the case. Drake no longer liked him, and it was all a misunderstanding. Well, to be honest, Joshua wasn't sure if it was really about that. He was taking it too far. Guess a lot of seventh graders just took things too far. Joshua walked aimlessly until he spotted Teagan's curly hair from a distance, and he decided to go see him.

"Hey, Joshua!" Teagan exclaimed with his same usual energy.

"Hey," Joshua said, dully.

"What's up, my man!?"

"You know, the usual."

"'Nothing?'" Teagan winked and made pretend quotations with both of his hands.

"Yeah." Joshua smiled.

"I've heard some rumors about you in the past couple of days. They're not true, are they?"

"Are they from Drake?"

Teagan nodded.

"They're not true in the least."

"Good. Is that why *nothing*'s up?"

"Yes. It is."

"Tell me."

Joshua let out a sigh, then he began: "I've been sitting with him in math because he's friends with Sam. And he said that his friend killed themself, but I didn't know that he said that because I wasn't listening. So anyway, they all started staring at me, and I laughed because I was uncomfortable. And he took it out of context. And now, everyone's thinking that I think suicide is funny. But I don't! And this is extremely bad because suicide isn't funny. And I'm afraid that it's going to trigger someone. If someone's truly suicidal, and they hear these rumors, what are they going to think? They're going to think that I support it, and that might lead them to..." Joshua trailed off and paused. After a moment, he continued, "I couldn't live with that. People who are suicidal shouldn't be hearing that it's funny, or that someone thinks it's funny. They should be hearing that they matter. They should be hearing that there are people out there that care about them, not that there are people who think it's all a joke. It's not a joke. They matter!" Joshua covered his face and said, "I can't do anything right. Everyone just wants to make me look bad. It's just like with Kole."

"I think you need to hear something."

Joshua uncovered his face and looked at Teagan.

"You matter."

Joshua wiped a tear that had slipped from his eyes, and in response to that tear, he said, "Gosh."

Teagan continued, "What Drake is saying is awful. You're right. People need to hear they matter. *You* need to hear that you matter. These people are being awful. And just know that their actions are not a reflection of you but of them. I don't know about Kole, but I know that Drake is only saying these things because he is upset. He lost a friend, and that must be hard. He likely doesn't realize the repercussions of what he's saying, but there's nothing you can do about him. But what you can do is show people that you don't think it's funny. Show that you believe every life matters. You know what it's like to struggle, so show others who are struggling that you hear them, and that they matter."

"Wow, Teagan. Thanks."

"No problem." Teagan smiled.

"You matter."

"Thanks." Then, Teagan looked at his other friends and said, "We're just talking...about stuff."

"Stuff, huh?"

"Yup."

"What kind of stuff?"

"All kinds of stuff."

"Okay," Joshua said, tentatively but with a smile on his face.

"You can join us."

"Okay."

The rest of recess went well, and so did lunch. After that, Joshua had humanities. It was okay. He didn't mind humanities because he did pretty well. It was world stuff, so he got to learn about different countries, which was pretty fun.

Chapter 50: More Laughter

After humanities, Joshua had science class. As it was beginning to get warmer outside, they were starting to go outdoors more often. Today, they were going to look at leaves. They had done this before, and it was extremely boring because it didn't make sense to Joshua. None of science really made sense that year. That's why Joshua wasn't doing so well grade-wise in the class. But he didn't realize it because he didn't have his report card in front of him, nor did he really understand it anyway. Vermont had just switched over to "proficiency-based grading," so it was all new. It would have made sense to Joshua if he cared to figure out how it worked, but the new system had such a bad rep that he didn't even try to understand. Plus, seventh grade was not his year, which meant that trying to decipher the proficiency-based grading was not on his priority list.

They finished looking at leaves early, so the teacher, Mr. Kreisten, let them have a little bit of an extra recess, which was like...10 minutes, but still, enough time for Joshua to get into a fight...

I mean...

What?

Joshua was hanging out on the swings with Sam

and Caiden who were both in his class. They were discussing an apparently very controversial topic, even though one answer should have been obvious. Yet, the *other* answer was deemed obvious by many people.

"Lying is not okay in any case," Joshua was saying to Caiden.

"I am willing to lie," Caiden said back.

"It's wrong!"

"If I ever had to lie for my family, I would."

"Why would you have to lie for your family?"

"If it would protect them."

"Why would you need to lie to protect them? Did something happen?"

"No. I'm speaking hypothetically."

"But why would you even dream that up?"

"Because I'm just thinking realistically here."

"No, you're not. I am!"

"Augh! Kole's right! Everything has to be your way or no way! I don't get it!"

Joshua pushed Caiden, and he fell right off the swing. Caiden jumped up and snapped at him, "Hey!"

"DON'T say that!" Joshua snapped, and he pushed Caiden again.

Caiden pushed him back a lot harder than he imagined he would. Joshua nearly fell, but he didn't. The two boys kept pushing each other until Caiden got fed up with the fact that nothing was happening, and he punched Joshua in the face. It didn't hurt as badly as when Kole and Maverick punched him, but it did still hurt. Sam pushed Caiden now, and this time, he fell to the ground again.

"HEY!" another voice shouted.

The three boys turned around to see Mr. Kreisten hurrying over.

"What's going on!?" Mr. Kreisten asked.

All three boys stopped and looked at Mr. Kreisten.

"Separate, now!" Mr. Kreisten snapped.

Joshua started laughing, instinctively and nervously.

"Joshua! This isn't funny!" Caiden cried.

"I don't think it is," Joshua said, but he was still laughing.

"Then *why* are you laughing!?" Caiden cried.

"Because it's just a thing that I do when I'm nervous," Joshua said.

"Joshua, separate, *please*," Mr. Kreisten said.

"Okay," Joshua said softly, looking at the ground. He walked away, Sam following him, leaving Caiden alone on the swing.

Joshua and Sam stayed together though, and Mr. Kreisten didn't tell them otherwise. They walked over to the side of the hill, and Joshua sat down. "What am I doing wrong?" he cried. "Pretty soon, I'm not going to have any friends left. I'm honestly surprised you pushed Caiden for me and followed me over here. I wasn't sure how much you liked me right now."

"Eh," Sam shrugged. "Why do you always fight with people?"

"Because...they're *wrong*."

"Do you think people *like* being told they're wrong?"

"No. Probably not."

"Then don't tell them. You're not helping anything."

"But I can't just stand there and let people say and do awful things."

"You simply can't change everyone...or even anyone."

"But I *can't* just stand there. Don't you get it?"

"No, I don't."

"People used to trust me. I used to be that quiet person in the class who didn't try to cause harm. Now, I'm a fighting idiot who can't shut up or stop laughing."

"True."

Joshua laughed.

"It's funny?" Sam crossed his arms.

Joshua stopped laughing. "Sorry. Look! There I go, doing it again!"

Sam laughed now. "I'm kidding! It's funny!"

Joshua smiled, and then he laughed. They both laughed together for a minute, but then Joshua sighed and said, "But I just can't stop. How can I not defend my beliefs?"

Sam shrugged.

"I don't know what to do." Joshua pulled his knees up to his chest and buried his head between them.

"I don't either, but it seems like whatever you're doing now isn't working, so I would try something else."

"Thanks a lot." Joshua unburied his face just to cross his arms.

Mr. Kreisten started calling everyone to go inside. Joshua stood up and walked in. On his walk home (Mrs. Abare started to let Joshua, Kendall, and Leah walk home again when Kole was gone. They actually only ended up getting a ride for the week that they didn't know he was gone), Joshua told his sisters, "I've gotten myself into a lot of trouble today."

"Oh no, what did you do?" Kendall asked.

"If you have detention, then who will walk us home? Will Mom have to come pick us up?" Leah asked.

"No, no. I don't have detention. See? I'm here. I didn't get in trouble with school. I got in trouble with classmates," Joshua said.

"What did you do?" Kendall asked.

"I laughed, and then Drake said I was laughing about his friend killing himself and told what seems like the whole school that I think suicide is funny. Well, actually, that happened the other day, but I'm still not getting a break from it. And for the record, I *don't* think suicide is funny. I'm an advocate against it! Teagan told me I should show people that I hear them, but I just keep messing it all up because today, Caiden and I were arguing about lying...and...I laughed again!" Joshua said.

"Arguing about lying?" Kendall asked.

"Yeah. You know, whether it's right or wrong," Joshua said.

"But there wasn't any violence, right?" Kendall asked.

Joshua looked at the ground but didn't say anything.

"Joshua!" both Kendall and Leah snapped at the same time.

Joshua shrugged.

"But I don't see any marks," Kendall said.

"It was mostly just pushing around. I only got

punched once, and it was by Caiden. He doesn't punch quite like Kole and Maverick, and...I think my face has toughened up a little bit, so I don't get bruised as much anymore," Joshua explained.

"Ah," Kendall said.

"Joshua, why do you get in so many fights?" Leah asked.

Joshua shrugged. Then, he said, "I don't try to."

"It sure seems like it," Leah said.

"You should become a boxer," Kendall said, smiling.

"Then people would literally be able to beat me up without getting in trouble for it," Joshua said.

"They don't get in trouble for it anyway," Kendall said.

"True," Joshua said. "But still...no."

"You know, you'd think that by now you'd be able to win a fight," Kendall said.

"But I can't," Joshua said. "I don't *like* getting into fights."

"Yeah, I don't get you. You don't like fights, and I don't either, but you always seem to get into them," Kendall said.

"Yeah," Joshua said. "But does *anyone* like them?"

They reached their house, and the second they got inside, Kendall announced to Ava and Mrs. Abare that Joshua got into a fight. Mrs. Abare got all concerned, fearing that what happened with Kole was going to happen all over again.

Joshua explained all that happened: Drake's rumor, the argument about lying, and then Mrs. Abare gave Joshua another inspirational speech kind of like Teagan's, but she continued with, "Don't feel like what Drake said means you need to carry so much weight on your shoulders. Just because you messed up with Caiden doesn't mean that you've let people believe you don't hear them. We all make mistakes. And you matter, Joshua! Please, be easy on yourself! I'm worried about you."

"I know," Joshua said.

"I love you," Mrs. Abare said.

"I love you, too," Joshua said.

They hugged.

The brokenness between Joshua and Drake didn't heal overnight, and it didn't appear that it would anytime soon, especially since Drake soon announced that he was moving to Florida.

Caiden tended to act like nothing happened, but Joshua couldn't get past the fact that he supported lying. It just wasn't right, so Joshua had a hard time being friends with him after that.

One day, Joshua was having another dispute with Caiden. This one wasn't nearly as bad as what happened at recess. In fact, it was pretty minor, it just annoyed Joshua a little bit. Caiden took his book and was hiding it in his desk, which was the only one to have a small shelf under it. Caiden only meant fun and games, but it really got Joshua going (mostly because it wasn't his book; he was borrowing it). He was in the middle of trying to get it back when he felt a sensation that caused him to turn around, and he saw that girl named Isabella holding her tablet up in the air like she was going to hit him with it. She didn't say anything, but she lowered it. Joshua knew that Isabella had a crush on Caiden, but Joshua didn't realize it had gotten that extreme. Then again, he remembered his encounter with her in the hallway that day a long time ago when Kole was still there. He turned around to find Isabella about to hit him over the head with her water bottle, or so it appeared that way.

Chapter 51: Wrapping Up

Seventh grade was coming to an end with less than a month left of school to go. Joshua was so glad for this horrible year to be over. It was—he considered—the worst school year of his life so far. But as the year ended, he thought about what would happen in eighth grade. Right now, his situation was miserable, but all of the good things about it would be gone in eighth grade. The main thing was Teagan. He would be gone because he was graduating. And he wouldn't have Reese's locker next to his anymore. Despite all of their ups and downs throughout the year, Joshua liked that his locker was next to hers. The weight of all his broken friendships would still be very present. Kole and all of them might be a thing of last year come eighth grade, but their effects would not be any different. Mends were never made between Joshua and his friends. The school year was ending, and he was already dreading the beginning of eighth grade.

The last day of school came. Teagan was gone. The eighth graders got out of school a day early, a luxury Joshua had been waiting for since he was Leah's age.

There were so many luxuries coming in eighth grade that Joshua was looking forward to, but they wouldn't come until the end of the year, so he would still have to make it through the torment of being at school with his broken relationships first.

Joshua was glad for summer vacation to come, but he never wanted it to end. Reese had told him about this T.V. show, and the third season was coming out that summer, so Joshua was excited. And with summer came swim team: Joshua's favorite sport.

Joshua celebrated the last day of school when he got home by going for an hour-long run. It felt good. With every step he took, he felt like he was leaving behind the pain of seventh grade. He got home, and sweating, he walked right through the house and took a shower.

When he was done with his shower, he went into his room to play his instruments. Now, he didn't just have his saxophone and cornet. Somehow, he convinced his parents to let him rent a tenor saxophone, and in addition, his grandmother's cousin gave him her old but extremely nice clarinet. He had *four* instruments! But not only that, he had his uncle's old keyboard, the recorder he got in fourth grade, and sometimes, Kendall would let him play her flute.

With the tenor sax and clarinet being new, Joshua chose to play those. He was in the middle of putting the five different pieces of clarinet together when he heard a knock on his door.

"Who is it?" he asked.

"Ava."

"Ava," Joshua repeated. "Come in."

The door opened, and Ava skipped in. She ran over to Joshua and said, "Can I play one?"

"Um...sure."

"Yay!"

"How about you play the keyboard."

"Okay!"

Joshua put the clarinet down, and he went into his closet whose floor was covered in all of his instruments. He took the keyboard out and set it up next to the outlet and plugged it in.

"Can I have a book, too?" Ava asked.

"Sure."

He grabbed one out of his pile of instrument books that once were sorted by instrument but not anymore. He handed it to Ava, even though she didn't actually read it.

"Thank you," Ava said. She went over to the keyboard and set the book down. Joshua sat back in his chair and finished putting together the clarinet. He placed the reed onto the mouthpiece, which was much smaller than the saxophone. He was about to put the clarinet in his mouth when he heard, at full volume, a mixture of low E, F sharp, and G all at the same time. Then, he heard Ava's laughter.

He spun around, laughed, and said, "How about you turn down the volume. Not past three."

"Okay," Ava said, frowning, but she listened.

Joshua opened up the clarinet book and began playing, entering a whole new world.

Chapter 52: Summer

So, summer began.

For Joshua, it was filled with a lot of swimming, running, and writing. He had been planning to play his instruments all summer also, but then he didn't.

Eighth grade was coming right around the corner for Joshua, and he was still dreading it.

Poor eighth grade, Joshua disliked it before he even gave it a chance. He wanted it to be over before it began. It was his last year at the school where he met Kole, was betrayed by his friends, got into fights, was falsely accused, and lost friends over beliefs. He was ready to leave that behind him when he headed off to high school where most of them wouldn't follow him. They had high school choice, which meant that only some of Joshua's classmates were going to the same high school as him. Joshua knew most of his *friends* weren't going to the same one as him.

Just one more year.

Chapter 53: Eighth Grade

The first day of school came, and as Joshua got ready that morning, he told himself that he was going to make new friends. He hadn't talked to any of his school friends at all over the summer, not even Carson or Sam. He was hoping to make friends with one of the new kids; they always had new kids, and they were rarely as bad as Kole.

As Joshua and Kendall walked toward the middle school together that morning, Kendall assured Joshua that it was going to be better than he thought. As much as he wanted to believe it, he had doubt in his mind, so he just had to hope.

Kendall quickly found some of her friends, leaving Joshua to stand alone while they waited to go inside. He knew he was supposed to find out from Mrs. Wheeling what class to go to first, but he could see that she had a large crowd of students around her already, so he waited because he wasn't ready to socialize with his classmates yet.

As he stood alone, a tall lady with red hair walked over to him and introduced herself as Mrs. Carlton, the new principal, and she stuck her hand out to greet him. He shook it and said, "Hi, I'm Joshua."

"Hi, Joshua," she said. She was holding a piece of

paper, and she looked at it. He realized it was the same paper that Mrs. Wheeling had. After a moment, she said, "Joshua Abare?"

He nodded.

"Great. You're right on top. You've got Mr. Kreisten," Mrs. Carlton said.

"Cool, thanks," Joshua said. Joshua had Mr. Kreisten last year for science, and he was looking forward to having him again—even though that class had been a little traumatic for him, and he didn't get good grades in it because it didn't make sense.

After Mrs. Carlton walked away, Joshua found himself standing alone again, and he didn't go looking for anyone to stand with either. He glanced over at Kendall, who was talking with so much excitement to her friends. He looked over at Mrs. Carlton who was looking over at him, but when he looked at her, she looked away.

Finally, it was time to go inside the school. Joshua walked inside alone, for a time, until he heard someone behind him say his name. He turned around to see a boy named Miles, who was friends with Sam and those guys. They had talked before, having known each other since preschool. They had their ups and downs—mostly downs—but they never got physical...well, never a real bad fight, anyway.

"Hey," Joshua replied.

"What are you wearing?" Miles asked him, grabbing the sleeve of his t-shirt.

"What?" Joshua asked, annoyed.

"This shirt looks like it's two sizes too big for you."

Joshua's face turned bright red.

"It's the first day of school. You should be wearing something nice."

"I don't really care. You shouldn't judge what people wear, either."

"I know you have nicer clothes; I've seen you wear them before."

"I don't care what I wear. Last year, on the first day of school, I wore something a bit nicer than my usual, but it ended up being a horrible year. So I really couldn't care less."

"You should because now you look like you just rolled out of bed."

Joshua looked up at the sky, which was turning into the ceiling as he walked through the front doors.

"You could be something; you could have someone better than Reese if you would just dress a little nicer," Miles continued.

"Augh, I don't *have* Reese."

"Oh, really?" Miles asked, crossing his arms.

"I haven't spoken to Reese almost all summer, so yes really."

Changing the subject, Miles asked, "Who's your core one teacher?"

"Mr. Kreisten. Who's yours?"

"Mrs. Greenwood."

At that point, they departed. Joshua was one of the first people to arrive to Mr. Kreisten's classroom. He walked in and was immediately greeted with excitement by Mr. Kreisten: "Hey, Joshua!"

"Hey," Joshua said back. It was surprising he showed him so much enthusiasm. Joshua guessed that even though he didn't do well and got into lots of fights, Mr. Kreisten still liked him. Apart from those *minor* setbacks, Joshua was a pretty good student. Before seventh grade, Joshua was one of the smartest and most well-behaved students.

Joshua sat down and waited for class to begin. For the time being, the room was silent.

More students arrived after not very long. One of the next people to walk in was Daniel. He saw Joshua sitting, still alone, and he came and sat down next to him. I'm not going to describe exactly how Joshua felt in that moment, but just remember how he wanted to make new friends. As Daniel greeted him, he reminded himself that Daniel had always been nice to him and never did anything wrong to him. Plus, Daniel was joining cross country that year.

Another person to walk in shortly after was Reese. She walked into the classroom and stared her seat down until she got to it. She did not look up at anyone; she didn't even acknowledge Joshua. He could tell she wanted to be there just as much as he did...which was not at all.

Finally, it was time to start class, and not a single *un*familiar face walked in through the door. Joshua knew *everyone*. That meant there weren't *any* new kids! Not a single one! Throughout the day, he learned that there weren't any new kids in any of the other classes, either. When he asked his friends about it, especially Aiden, they seemed glad because they thought they might just get another Kole.

Joshua's humanities teacher, Mr. St. Paul, was a former swimmer, and his kids now swam. They were younger than him, being that they were Leah and Ava's age. As the year would progress, he would become Joshua's favorite teacher for many reasons, apart from him being a swimmer. He was an amazing teacher.

Joshua had Mrs. Greenwood for literacy, and he had Mr. Henry for math again.

Cross country didn't start until Thursday, so when Joshua got home, he went for a run on his own. He had been running all summer, and really all year—except during the super cold months where he gave his body a break, or when he was avoiding Kole—so he was feeling really good about the upcoming season. It was good because it meant he at least had one thing to look forward to besides graduation.

After Joshua had showered from his run, he sat in the living room and watched T.V. Kendall came in and asked him: "How was it? Was it as bad as you thought?" Their walk home was filled with Leah telling them about her day, from eating breakfast to walking out of the school, so they didn't have time to talk at all, and Joshua left as soon as he got home.

"Pretty much," Joshua answered in reply.

"Aw," Kendall said, annoyed.

"There weren't any new kids, so I just had to hang out with the same people."

"That's not *bad*."

"I want new friends: ones that haven't betrayed me, fought with me, don't support lying, you know?"

"I get it...mostly. But...they aren't *all* bad."

"Some of them are okay, but they're still friends with the traitors, instigators, and liars."

Kendall shrugged, unsure of what to say. She couldn't keep track of every detail and problem in Joshua's life. She had her own life to think about, especially when Joshua simply wasn't going to change his mind about this, no matter how hard she tried.

"Whatever, enough about my day. How was yours?" Joshua asked.

"Good," Kendall said. She sat down and grabbed the remote, saying, "I don't want to watch this."

Joshua opened his mouth to argue, but he didn't say anything. He didn't really care, to be honest. He got up and went to his room where he wrote until supper. He'd rather write than watch T.V. anyway.

Chapter 54: Point Proven

With Aiden and Daniel being on the cross country team, and Joshua spending a lot of time with them through that, he began to feel bad for wanting to make new friends. But today, as he sat alone at a table in the cafeteria, he suddenly didn't feel so bad. He wasn't completely alone, but at the same time, he basically was. There was another person across the table who was on the cross country team and talked to him sometimes. She didn't seem to have any friends, so Joshua tried to become friends with her once, but when he tried to talk to her, she just said "sksksk" and turned around. Still, he now found himself sitting at her table, but he sat on the opposite side, and they didn't talk.

Why wasn't he sitting with his friends? You know: Aiden, Daniel, and the others. It was because there wasn't any room with them. It wasn't even because he was acting stuck up or anything. It was just that he didn't have a space anywhere. Not even Carson would come sit with him, and believe me, Joshua tried to get him to. Carson just said sorry and sat at a full table with Sam and six other people. Miles took his seat at the table with Aiden and Daniel. Of course he did, am I right? That morning, Miles was ridiculing Joshua because his backpack was too big. But why did that matter to Miles?

There were also three other new members of the table group. Apparently, Patrick and Kole's seats at the table *had* been taken, not left empty.

Joshua couldn't stand being alone, despite his loner episodes he frequently had last year. He had a fear of it because it made him more vulnerable. But he couldn't really blame his friends for not leaving him space to sit, since he didn't talk to them all summer, and he secretly was planning on making new ones anyway.

It was already the middle of September by now, and Joshua still hadn't found a good resolution for his seventh grade problems. He shouldn't have been dragging them around anymore. He should have left them in seventh grade, but he messed that up with his *attitude* on the first day of school.

Reese was sitting with her old friend Zoe again. There was plenty of room at her table, but Joshua didn't try asking her to sit there. She was finishing her lunch, and she brought her tray into the back room. On her way back, she went and sat down next to Joshua who felt like he wanted to cry. No, not cry. He wanted to stand in front of a punching bag and just have at it. Violence was no answer...*when it came to people*. But he could punch a punching bag all he wanted and no one would get hurt.

Joshua looked at her, feeling embarrassed because he was alone.

"Why are you sitting by yourself?" Reese asked him.

Joshua looked toward the opposite side of the cafeteria where both of his friend groups sat at full tables, with no room for him. Then, he looked back at Reese and said, "No room for me."

"Oh." Reese looked down at the table.

"It's okay. You don't have to feel bad."

"Well, I do. You're my friend, and you don't deserve to sit alone. I'll stay here for the rest of lunch."

"Aw, thanks. But, you don't..."

"Joshua, it's cool. Things have been kind of weird between me and Zoe and the others ever since I was friends with Kole. I mean, I don't blame them. I was kind of a jerk when he was here. You could agree, couldn't you?"

"Mm...yeah." Joshua smiled.

"I know things have been kind of weird between us too, but you're alone, so you could use someone."

"Okay." Joshua had to admit it *did* feel better having Reese there opposed to being completely alone.

The two of them talked for the rest of lunch. As Joshua left the cafeteria, he thought to himself: *"I was right all along. I* do *need new friends. But what about Reese? Is she different now? Can we be friends? Maybe I really don't need a new friend. Maybe I have Reese. We have shared trauma."*

But that quickly ended. Joshua and Reese were in the same gym class. Zoe was also in that class, so they weren't usually partners. Reese usually partnered with Zoe, and Joshua was partnered with a guy named Brenden. But later in the week, Zoe was absent one day, and instead of being Joshua's partner, Reese partnered with Brenden! That left Joshua partnerless.

"Nope," Joshua thought to himself. *"Reese is* not *all I need. I really do need a new friend."* Then his thoughts continued to say, *"And what was I thinking!? Reese and I*

don't have shared trauma! We are each other's trauma!"

After seeing his partner with Reese, Joshua walked up to Mrs. Carney and said, "I don't have a partner. Can I please just go for a run?"

"You know what? Sure. We are going to go outside after we warm up, and when we do, I will allow you to run around the path," Mrs. Carney told him.

"Ah! Thank you!" Joshua exclaimed, with a huge smile.

"No problem," Mrs. Carney said, smiling back.

So, Joshua suffered through the torment of warm-ups, then they went outside, and he went running. He had cross country practice later too, so he was going to be tired by the time he got home, but that beat his other option.

It wasn't long before Reese and Brenden were *dating*. Joshua couldn't believe it, to be honest.

Chapter 55: Kolby

“Hey!” Joshua found himself yelling, as he came across a fight during recess. He had no idea what it was about, so it probably wasn’t worth the pain of getting involved. But instinctively, he had to do *something*. He didn’t even think of the possibility of getting a teacher or something harmless until it was too late.

Joshua didn’t simply just shout hey, he stepped into the middle of the fight. Both boys were covered in blood, one more so than the other. The one covered in less blood looked at Joshua and pushed him.

Suddenly, Joshua saw Kole standing in front of him. But he was no longer at school. He was in the park behind the fountain. It was no longer a warm September day, but it was a freezing cold December night. He hit the snow, beaten and battered, covered in blood himself.

Kole and Maverick were kicking him, and he suffered the final blow to his head, knocking him unconscious.

Then, he was back at school, trying to break up a fight.

“Why get into the middle of a fight if you’re just going to stand there after?” the boy who pushed him asked.

Joshua had no idea what was going on. Why was he *there* again? Why was he here now? He was so confused.

A teacher had finally caught onto the fight, and they came over, scolding all three boys, even Joshua, who was totally confused. They got brought inside, and as they walked, Joshua realized what happened. But he stayed silent. They were sent to Mrs. Wheeling's office. Joshua didn't say a word. Thankfully, the one who didn't push him said that he was only trying to break up the fight, so Joshua got mostly off the hook. Mrs. Wheeling just told him that he should have gotten a teacher instead of trying to break it up himself. The boy who pushed him rolled his eyes.

"Sorry," Joshua told Mrs. Wheeling.

"It's okay," she replied, surprisingly gently. Then, she let Joshua go. He didn't tell her about the flashback.

When Joshua left, the seventh and eighth graders were just barely coming back in from recess, going to lunch. Joshua had to fight against the current to get back to the small hall full of graduated handprints to get his lunch box and water bottle. The last person to come in was a girl named Lorelei.

"Hey, Joshua," she said.

"Hey," Joshua said back.

"Where are you coming from? How come you weren't outside?" she asked.

"I was in Mrs. Wheeling's room."

"Why?"

"There was a fight, but I wasn't in it this time, so I got to leave."

"This time? Have you been in fights before?"

Joshua looked at Lorelei. She hadn't come until February last year, he remembered, so she had never been there when Kole was there.

"Yeah," Joshua said sadly, wishing that he had left out "this time."

"Wow, that's surprising. You don't seem like the fighting type. You're pretty quiet. And...from what I've seen, you've always appeared to be pretty nice," Lorelei said.

"Yeah, that's what a lot of people thought, until it happened."

"I think a lot of people actually still think that. But who was it with?" They began walking toward the cafeteria. "Was it Drake? Is that why he moved to Florida?"

"No. I mean, yeah, Drake and I had our differences, but this was someone else."

"Who?"

"Ah, you wouldn't know him. He left, too. Before you got here."

"Oh. He started it?"

"Um..." Joshua said for about five seconds straight. "No."

"*You* did?"

Joshua nodded.

"Wow." Lorelei raised her eyebrows. "But you *weren't* in the fight this time?"

"No. I was trying to break it up."

"Guess you're just sick of fights."

"Yeah. Guess so."

They split when they entered the cafeteria. Lorelei

went to the lunch line, leaving Joshua stranded at the entrance, trying to find who to sit with. As he stood there, he looked around, and he saw the back of a boy's head. Wait...what? Curly, light brown hair. Light gray sweatshirt. Blue jeans. Was that...Teagan?

Teagan?

Teagan, what are you doing here?

The boy turned around, revealing his face. Joshua sighed. Not Teagan. Silly him. Teagan wasn't there. He was in high school. He graduated! *Remember!?*

Joshua found himself sitting next to Kolby: one of the five new kids from last year; they had spoken a little bit over the school year since they were in band together. Every other Friday, they got "free sit" in band, and Joshua sat next to him once. Kolby was cool; he was nice.

Kolby sat at a table with the jocks, though Kolby didn't play any sports. Joshua's friends had always been the opposite of jocks, but Anderson and Jeremiah, his Church classmates, the ones who brought him home after the final fight, sat at Kolby's table. They were nice, and so were about 90 percent of the people at the table, Joshua believed.

Joshua was mostly quiet the whole time, but Kolby talked to him a little bit at the end of lunch. Kolby was even quieter than Joshua, but the two of them seemed to have more to talk about with each other than with anyone else, so it seemed good.

Joshua talked to Kolby the next day at recess. He was friends with a boy named Sawyer, who Joshua had talked to before and who was in his math class. When they went inside, Sawyer sat with Sam and all their guys, but

Joshua sat with Kolby at the table they did the day before.

As October came, sitting with Kolby had become a regular occurrence. They didn't always sit at the same table as the first day. After a little while, the fifth new kid from the previous year, named Jayden, started to sit with them, after his own friends betrayed him. Joshua wasn't sure what happened, but he heard Kolby tell him, "Wow, that's awful" after he got done explaining it to him. Joshua hadn't heard what Jayden said. With the three of them, there wasn't enough room for them all at Kolby's original table.

So Joshua, Kolby, and Jayden sat at a different table with three other boys. One of them was named Isaac, and Isaac had a friend named Malachi. And the third boy was...Miles. (Miles switched around friends, too.) That was Joshua's only downside since it didn't seem like Miles had a filter. Miles would often insult Joshua's clothes or lunch choices, but unlike Joshua's old friends, the other boys at the table would always stick up for Joshua. Usually, it was Malachi that would stand up for him.

Malachi was in Joshua's gym class, and one time, this girl got partnered with Joshua and asked Malachi who he was. Malachi looked over at Joshua and said, "That's Joshua. He's really nice." Joshua smiled in his mind, thinking, *"Wow, someone who hardly knows me sees* beyond *my fights and still believes that I am nice. They don't shame me for what I did."*

Joshua had been acquaintances with Malachi for a long time. They played basketball together when they were young, but Joshua switched to winter swim team and stopped playing. Well, actually, it was more like he just didn't like basketball, so he was going to stop anyway, but then he started doing swim team in addition to stopping.

None of Joshua's old friends ever approached him wondering where he was, which told him that he was better off with Kolby. That was until one day, but he still didn't go back. Caiden came to him, as if he didn't remember what happened last year, as if he didn't remember that day when Joshua wasn't at the table but sitting alone, and said, "Why don't you sit with us anymore?"

Joshua stood there staring at Caiden, remembering his past, but he didn't mention any of that. After a long silence, he finally answered, "Because."

"Because why?" Caiden asked.

Joshua scrounged for an answer. He couldn't just say why because Caiden didn't seem to understand, so he said part of why: "I want to sit with Kolby."

"Oh," Caiden said.

The two of them parted.

Chapter 56: Lorelei

Joshua walked out of the school and started walking along the front to meet his sisters on the other side of the school, as he usually did. He was one of the last people to leave the school, right after Lorelei. She walked out a little bit ahead of him, but she slowed her pace to wait for him. Joshua didn't know why, but he noticed that he hadn't sped up at all and was catching up to her. They had only talked twice before. Once that year, after the fight Joshua tried to break up, and once last year during humanities. Lorelei had randomly asked him from a different table how many siblings he had.

"Hey, Joshua," she said when he caught up to her.

"Hey," Joshua replied.

"What bus do you ride?"

"I don't ride one."

"Oh, so you get picked up?"

"No."

"Do you walk, then?"

"Yeah."

"Same."

"Cool."

"How far away is your house?"

"Five minutes."

"That's not bad. Mine's about five minutes, too."

They reached Kendall and Leah, and Lorelei asked, "They are your sisters?"

"Yeah," Joshua answered.

"Hi," Lorelei said to them both.

Kendall shyly replied, but Leah just stared at her. The four of them started walking, and Lorelei whispered to Joshua so that Kendall and Leah wouldn't hear, "Wow, they're even quieter than you."

Joshua's face turned red.

Lorelei lived on a road that was about a two-minute walk from Joshua's house. She turned down it, saying goodbye to him and his sisters, then Joshua walked with Kendall and Leah the remaining two minutes.

"Who's that?" Kendall asked Joshua after a few seconds, so Lorelei wasn't within earshot anymore.

"A girl from my class," Joshua answered.

"What's her name?" Kendall asked.

"Lorelei," Joshua answered.

"Oh," Kendall said.

"She's weird," Leah said.

Joshua laughed.

"Are you dating?" Leah asked.

"No," Joshua answered.

"Then why was she talking to you?" Leah asked.

"Because Lorelei's hobby is talking," Joshua answered. "And plus, just because I talk to a girl doesn't mean I'm dating her. I talked to Reese all last year, but we weren't dating."

"But you liked her!" Leah exclaimed, teasingly.

"Sometimes," Joshua said. "But we weren't dating."

"Whatever happened to you and Reese? Are you still friends?" Kendall asked.

"I don't know," Joshua admitted.

"Do you still have a crush on her?" Kendall asked.

"Mm...I'm not really sure. I think *she's* moved on, but I guess it's not like she ever really liked me to begin with. But lately, she's moved on from even being friends with me. She started dating this guy named Brenden, and they've been talking nonstop. I'm really not interested in getting in between her and her man again," Joshua said.

"Ah," Kendall said. "It all makes sense."

"I was starting to think we were all right, even after last year, but I guess I will just never be her number one," Joshua said. "But it's whatever. I'm starting to like her less anyway...less as a crush."

"Really? Why is that?" Kendall asked. "Because I mean, if Kole couldn't stop your feelings toward her, I can't think of who would."

"I..." Joshua started to say.

"Have *you* moved on?" Kendall asked.

"Uh...yeah, I guess," Joshua said.

"With who!?" Kendall asked, raising her voice.

"Does it *have* to be with a person?" Joshua asked.

"Is it not?" Kendall asked.

Joshua was quiet. They had reached their driveway and stopped. Their feet faced their house, but they looked at each other.

"Have you found someone new?" Kendall asked.

"Possibly."

"Who?"

Joshua still didn't answer.

Kendall gasped. "It *is* Lorelei!"

Joshua shrugged.

Leah let out an excited shriek.

"Does she know you like her!? Is that why she walked with you!?" Kendall exclaimed.

"No, she has no idea. I haven't told a single person until now."

"So...she just talks to you...*because*?"

"Yeah. I told you she really likes to talk."

"Apparently."

They started walking again, and as they stepped onto the front steps, Kendall said, "Does this mean that you like school now?"

"No way," Joshua said. "I still want school to be over."

"Okay," Kendall said, smiling.

They opened the door. Mrs. Abare was in the kitchen, fixing Ava a snack.

"Hey," she said as Joshua, Kendall, and Leah all walked in.

"Hey," Joshua and Kendall said.

"Hey, Mommy," Leah said, setting her bag on the floor gracefully. "Joshua's in love!"

"No!" Joshua snapped.

"You just said you were!" Leah whined.

"I'm not *in love* just because I said I *like* someone," Joshua said.

"Fine, you're *in like*," Leah said.

"You like someone?" Mrs. Abare asked, looking at Joshua. She had a smile on her face in response to Leah's statement.

"A little," Joshua answered.

"They left school together!" Leah exclaimed.

"Not Reese?" Mrs. Abare asked.

"No, not Reese," Joshua said.

Mrs. Abare let out a small sigh of relief, but Joshua barely noticed, as she quickly asked, "Who?"

"Lorelei," Joshua answered.

"Oh, she was new last year, right?" Mrs. Abare asked.

"Yeah," Joshua answered.

"You've told me about her a few times," Mrs. Abare stated. "So...you walked home together?"

"No, no. She lives on Spruce Street," Joshua said. "So, she only walked with us for a few minutes."

"But you still left together?" Mrs. Abare asked.

"Yeah," Joshua said. "It doesn't mean anything, though. We only left together because we were some of the last people to leave the school, and we both walk. So what else were we supposed to do?"

"I don't know," Mrs. Abare replied.

Then, Joshua smiled and said, "Ah, well...she *did* slow down to wait for me."

"Ooh!!!" Kendall and Leah both exclaimed, then Ava saw their excitement and copied them with a huge smile on her face.

Chapter 57: Two Weeks

Mrs. Greenwood assigned new seats every two weeks, and the coming exchange was on Kendall's birthday. This didn't affect Kendall, however, only Joshua. When he would arrive at class, each desk would have a popsicle stick on it, and he would have to find the one with his name. Joshua walked in and looked for his own name. He found it. No one was sitting at his desk group yet. He sat down and looked to see who else he was sitting with. He looked across from him and read the name just as the person came and sat down.

Lorelei.

Joshua's eyes widened. He looked up at her, then quickly looked away. Then, he looked at the other two desks in his four-desk table group. The one next to him said Albert, who was a boy that was friends with Sam. Back in sixth grade, when Joshua would sit with those boys every day at lunch, Albert would always say something that was *mean* (usually about Reese), then Joshua would tell him, "That's mean." Eventually, it led Albert not to like Joshua anymore. The person across from Albert was named Delilah. He hadn't heard much from her in a long time. He used to have a crush on her in second grade, but things got a little nasty between them when

Delilah found out. Now, Joshua usually tried to steer clear of her. That wouldn't be so easy sitting at the same table. This was the only class Joshua had with her.

Last year, Delilah got Lorelei in trouble by looking something inappropriate up on Lorelei's tablet and leaving the tab open. Joshua didn't quite understand it all. Something was found on Lorelei's iPad, and everyone claimed it to be Delilah, but Lorelei wouldn't say it was. She just stood there frozen up against the classroom counter. But Joshua was certain Delilah did it because she thanked Lorelei and hugged her. They had a sub that day, one that was well-liked. Joshua wasn't sure whatever happened after. Delilah did end up in Mrs. Wheeling's room for a while, but at the same time, she might have been in trouble for something else.

Albert and Delilah arrived shortly after Lorelei, and class began. The students had just got done writing an essay, and Mrs. Greenwood sat them strategically this time with people whose essays were similar. That was unlike the way she usually did it, where she pulled random popsicle sticks out of a cup and set them down. She said that she would come around and talk to each group separately about ways they could improve their essay.

Initially, when Joshua heard this, he thought, *"Oh, cool. Now I know something about Lorelei's work. It's similar to mine!"*

But then Mrs. Greenwood came over to their table first and said to Joshua, "Your essay was unlike anyone else's so I just had to sit you here. I will talk to you first, then I will talk to the rest of you." She looked at Lorelei, Delilah, and Albert when she said "the rest of you."

Joshua's face was red; he could feel it.

Mrs. Greenwood told him that they would go sit on the couch: a luxury that students would sometimes get to sit on during reading time or other select times.

Joshua walked over there, and they sat down to talk about his essay. Overall, he was on track. His essay was pretty good. See? Being a writer paid off! She told him he could sit there for the rest of class, as she would be talking to the rest of his table group.

When there was about five minutes left, Joshua went back to his table group. He began putting his things together when Delilah said to him, "Hey, Joshua."

Joshua looked at her.

"Lorelei has a crush on you," Delilah said.

Joshua was silent.

"No, I don't," Lorelei said.

"Yes, she does," Delilah insisted.

"No!" Lorelei snapped.

Joshua still didn't say anything.

"Girl," Lorelei pleaded to Delilah.

Joshua was still silent. He felt slightly lightheaded. Class got done, saving him from the situation.

Joshua went to the bathroom after, still feeling lightheaded. He did his business, washed his hands, then left. When he walked out, he felt a little better than he did when he walked in. He went to his locker and got his lunch box. When he closed the door, Kolby was standing behind it, silently and ominously.

"Woah," Joshua said, jumping.

"Haha!" Kolby laughed.

"Gosh, Kolby, you scared me," Joshua said, but he

smiled.

"You know, I've always wanted to stand in the shadows and scare people," Kolby said.

"Consider yourself successful," Joshua said.

They walked outside. Joshua dropped his lunch box and water bottle off in the hallway. When they got outdoors, they found Sawyer and Jayden standing at the top of the hill waiting for them. They walked to the top and greeted them. Joshua didn't tell them about literacy. He hadn't even told them about Lorelei. When he had a crush on Reese, everyone knew. He told every single person who talked to him, it seemed. He wasn't like that anymore. He was more secretive now. He didn't want his crush to get out, especially with what Delilah said. He didn't believe her. He believed that she was lying to him, and that would make the fact he liked Lorelei even worse.

Joshua frowned when he remembered that he was stuck in that seating arrangement for the next two weeks. He had been excited to see Lorelei sit down across from him, but now, he dreaded literacy.

The next day, he arrived before any of the others, as he had before. He sat down in his seat, and he was joined by the others quickly. Lorelei was first, but she still didn't talk to him.

Today was different from the first day. Mrs. Greenwood didn't talk about essays, so Joshua stayed at the table all of class. She started off by telling everyone what to work on, then she sent them to do it. Their assignment was to work on editing their essays. It was going to be a pretty laid-back class, especially for Joshua.

But as they began to work, Delilah said quietly,

"Joshua."

Joshua ignored her at first, but she said his name again, so he looked over.

"Do you like Lorelei?" Delilah asked.

Joshua didn't answer. He just stared at her. He wasn't going to tell her, but he was not a liar. It didn't matter if it was just a little white lie. He wasn't a liar in any case. You know that! And so does Caiden! So, he stared at her hoping his shyness would get by as an excuse for why he didn't answer.

And it did.

Lorelei turned to Delilah and said quietly, "Joshua's pretty quiet. How many words do you think he says in a day?"

"I don't know. He's sitting right there. Why don't you ask him?" Delilah snapped, despite the fact that Joshua had just ignored her completely.

Lorelei looked at Joshua and said, "How many words do you say in a day?"

"What?" Joshua laughed, in disbelief that she really had the audacity to ask him that.

Lorelei repeated herself: "How many words do you say in a day? Uh...you know...about?"

"I don't know," Joshua said.

"That's four!" Lorelei exclaimed.

Joshua smiled. Delilah shook her head. Albert laughed.

"So...would you say about four maybe?" Lorelei asked.

"No! I say more than that!" Joshua exclaimed.

That was the second time Lorelei had asked this

question about Joshua. Last time, Joshua had been walking with Carson, and Carson complained that he had all of his classes with Lorelei, but so did Joshua, both this year and last year when Lorelei came. He didn't think it was all that bad. Lorelei asked Carson that day how many words he thought Joshua said in a day. Carson didn't answer, but of course, his answer would have been much higher than four, since they used to be best friends at one point, a while ago, before Lorelei ever came to that school.

Throughout the next two weeks, Delilah gave up on the claim that Lorelei liked Joshua. He wasn't sure if that meant it was untrue or if it just meant that he was sick of teasing. However, one day at lunch, one of Delilah's friends approached Joshua and said that this girl liked him. Joshua knew it was a lie because she got a boyfriend only a couple of days later.

More incidents continued to happen. Other than the one at lunch, it was always Delilah. She always told Joshua that some different girl liked him, but it wasn't true! Joshua just knew it wasn't.

Joshua couldn't stand it. He couldn't stand these humiliating lies, and what he couldn't stand even more was the reasoning behind them. Why did they have the boldness to spread these lies to him? It wasn't even just to him. It was to many people. Joshua was sitting with Malachi when Delilah's friend told some girl that Malachi liked her, but it wasn't true. This added to Joshua's feeling of wanting school to be over. He wanted somehow for school to just end. He didn't know how exactly, but he just wanted it to end. He wanted it to go away. He couldn't wait for summer vacation. He couldn't rely on week-long breaks to set him free of this misery, either. He wanted it to end then. Right then. He didn't want to go back anymore. Winter swimming was starting in about a week. Maybe his life could just be swimming. If he swam all day instead of going to school, then maybe he could become good enough to do it professionally. Then, he wouldn't need an education because he could just swim for life...*right?*

Even when they got new seats, Delilah was still telling Joshua that people liked him. The next seating arrangement, Joshua escaped her, but the next one after that, he was put with her again. Not just her, but Albert, too. It was just the three of them. No Lorelei this time.

Albert was slightly intimidating, too. Albert used to threaten to fight Joshua. Though he never did, Joshua didn't want to be around him. He was trying to put his fighting self behind him: leave it in the dust. And even if he wasn't, someone who threatened to fight him wasn't an ideal table mate.

Joshua didn't look mad as he thought about how much he didn't want to be at that table, though. Instead, he looked nervous. He was avoiding eye contact with both Delilah and Albert.

But Delilah didn't care that he looked nervous and said, "Joshua."

Joshua rolled his eyes privately, then looked over at Delilah.

"Josephine likes you," Delilah said.

"No, she doesn't," Joshua said.

"Yeah, she does," Delilah insisted.

"No," Joshua said, sternly. "She doesn't."

"Delilah likes you," Albert said, chiming in.

"Yeah," Delilah said, smiling.

"No, you don't," Joshua said.

"She just wants to get into your pants," Albert said.

"Ew," Joshua said, his voice cracking, and his cheeks turning red.

Delilah smiled

Thankfully, Mrs. Greenwood started class, forcing them to stop talking. Joshua looked away again.

Only one more week left until Thanksgiving break. After that, only three weeks until Christmas break. After that, seven and a half weeks until February break. Following that, six and a half weeks until April break. After April break, school would just fly by. They'd be having all of their fun eighth grade activities like their field trip, beach party, graduation, last day of school before everyone else, you know, all the good stuff. But even so, after April break, only four weeks until Memorial Day when they'd get a day off from school. After that, Joshua would only have to make it through three more weeks of school. Then, summer vacation would be there: back to swimming, goodbye to old reputations, hello to new beginnings, no more school, no more dealing with...everything. While going through his daily countdown in his head, Joshua completely missed instructions, but he didn't care because he was too glad about the end of the year. He was glad...that was...until he had to ask Delilah and Albert what they were doing.

"Wait...what are we doing?" Joshua asked.

"Were you not listening? She just said it," Albert said.

"Mm...no. I wasn't listening."
"Why? Were you thinking about *Delilah*?"
"No."
"Then what *were* you thinking about?"
Joshua sighed. Then, he said, "It doesn't matter. Can't you please just tell me what we're doing?"
Delilah and Albert gave in and told him.

***

The next day, Delilah wasn't in class, so Joshua and Albert sat alone. Looking at Delilah's empty chair, Albert said to Joshua, "Whoo, Joshua. You must be really glad that Delilah isn't here."
"Why?"
Ignoring him, Albert went on, "I am. I hope that she's sick and doesn't come back for the rest of the school year. Don't you?"
"No."
"Why not? You couldn't seriously like her, could you? You know, she's so *mean* to you?"
"Yeah, but she's still...I don't know...*human*."
"But she's *mean*, so does that matter?"
"Yeah."
"Right. That's *mean* of me. You think I'm *mean*, so you probably want me gone, too."
"No, and I never said I wanted Delilah gone, either."
"So...you like this table arrangement, then?"
"No."

"Wow, *that's* mean."

"Sorry...I mean..."

"No, it's fine. I don't like it either."

Joshua was silent. Thankfully, after that day, there were only three more days until Thanksgiving break.

But at the same time, Thanksgiving break wasn't going to be a break mentally for Joshua.

Chapter 58: One Year

Thanksgiving break would mark one year since it all began. One year since Joshua's first fight with Kole. One year since Joshua told Kole about the chastity talk. One year since Joshua pushed first. One year since Patrick, Kole, Maverick, Aiden, and *Reese* all stood in opposition to him. One year since things would never be the same again. One year since Joshua and Kole headed down a rocky road on opposite sides of the path. One year since last Thanksgiving break. One year.

At first, Joshua had forgotten about the relevance of the time because he was just glad to be on break. That was until he went for a run Saturday morning. It wasn't a year to the date, but it was a year to the break. He stepped out his front door and immediately had a flashback to him sitting on his front porch, writing. He never sat out on his front porch to write anymore. He'd always write inside his house. He used to write outside a lot.

Kole had seen him sitting out there and came to talk. He should have kept walking, but he didn't.

Kole told Joshua writing sounded boring.

Joshua could clearly remember Kole saying, "I came by earlier, and you weren't home. Where have you been?"

It echoed in his head.

"Where have you been?"

"Where have you been?"

"Where have you been?"

Soon, Joshua was back in their first fight. Kole said to him, "I'm just not buying it."

Joshua asked him, "Why not?"

Eventually, the conversation progressed to Kole saying, "Because I'm not gullible.*"*

Every word pierced through Joshua's brain. It hurt. Those words. They hurt.

"Because I'm not gullible.*"*

"Because I'm not gullible.*"*

"BECAUSE I'M NOT GULLIBLE*!"*

Joshua found himself pushing Kole as he said firmly, "I'm not *gullible."*

And so there it was.

But the flashback wasn't over. Joshua continued the fight, and soon, he was on the ground, looking at the four boys and Reese *standing in opposition to him.*

Joshua gasped, suddenly back to reality. He was no longer on his feet but laying on the porch. He heard the door open behind his head, and his mom cried, "Joshua!"

Mrs. Abare put her arms under his arms and pulled him to his feet. He was shaking, so she sat him down on the outdoor couch.

"What happened?" Mrs. Abare asked him.

"I...I..." Joshua stuttered. "I was there...again...I had...I had a flashback."

"To your last fight with Kole?"

"No." Joshua looked at the grass in front of his house, where it happened a year ago. "Here."

"Your first fight?"

Joshua nodded.

"Oh."

There was a small silence, then Mrs. Abare said, "That was exactly a year ago, wasn't it?"

Joshua nodded again. He was still shaking.

"Maybe it would be best if you took today off," Mrs. Abare said.

Joshua nodded, and that's what led Mrs. Abare to realize how upset he really was. They went inside, and Joshua sat down on the couch.

Chapter 59: Ending

Joshua continued to get sat with Delilah and Albert during literacy every other time they got new seats, and 12 weeks into the school year when he started Algebra I—which Delilah was also in, and the teacher was also Mrs. Greenwood—Joshua started getting sat with her every other two weeks there, also. If he didn't get sat with her in literacy, he was most likely going to get sat with her in Algebra I. She continued to tease him, but he usually just ignored it, reminding himself that he was almost done with middle school.

On the flip side, whenever Joshua didn't get sat with Delilah in literacy, he often got sat with Lorelei.

But after a while, Lorelei stopped talking to him. It went from them talking once or twice a week to suddenly not talking at all. They used to walk out of the school together a few times, but as time had gone on, Joshua hardly ever walked out at the same time as her. Around Christmastime, a boy asked Lorelei if she wanted to go to a hockey game with her. Of course, Lorelei really liked hockey, but Joshua was pretty sure this boy was trying to get her to go on a date. Lorelei didn't seem as enthusiastic about it as the boy, but Joshua was still pretty sure this had to do with the reason they weren't talking as much.

Joshua had been sitting next to Lorelei in literacy when this boy asked her out.

Oh well, Joshua was stuck in school, so every day he went, he would see how it would play out. He wanted it to end somehow, someway, but it just wouldn't. It couldn't. How would school end? They *had* to go. That's what Joshua believed. But after February break, as March was beginning, Joshua started having second thoughts on that whole idea.

It was Friday March 13, 2020. Joshua was sitting in Algebra I, doing his work, which didn't make any sense. He couldn't stand algebra. He was always trying to find out what *y* equaled, but it didn't equal anything; it just equaled a reduced equation full of *x*s. He wanted a definite answer. He didn't like the wishy-washy answer he always got. He wanted a number that seemed real, like it made sense.

Then, they were introduced to graphing. That was a whole new level of horrible.

Half the time, Joshua got the wrong answer, and that was pretty bad.

The only thing that could save him from this was his saxophone lesson once a week. One day, they were going around the classroom putting their answers on the board. Joshua got called on to go one minute before he had to leave, so he said, "Oh, I've got to go to my saxophone lesson." At that point, he was the only one still going to his lesson.

The music room was just a few feet away, and the class could hear Mr. Goodwell jamming on the piano, so Mrs. Greenwood responded, "It sounds like Mr.

Goodwell's not in a hurry, so you can do the problem first."

Joshua sighed, but he listened. It was horrible because he also had to explain how he got the answer. He went to the front of the room with his paper and began teaching the class. He heard some people talking and laughing, and he knew it wasn't in his head because Mrs. Greenwood had to tell them off.

After Joshua got the problem done, he hurried off to his lesson, relieved that he could leave.

But on Friday March 13, 2020, Joshua didn't have an instrument lesson, so he was stuck in class, fighting through his algebra work, coming up with wishy-washy answers that didn't make sense, and creating graphs that were completely unnecessary in his mind.

Delilah wasn't at his table but at the table over, and Joshua could hear her talking, saying, "A lot of schools are shutting down for two weeks. We could do the same."

Shut down? Two weeks? That sounded almost perfect to Joshua. A two-week break. Aw, how nice. That was a pretty long time, for it seemed like eternity when Joshua spent two weeks sitting at a table with Delilah. Though the reasoning wasn't that nice. There was a virus spreading across the country (and the whole world), and it was coming fast and furious. It was called the coronavirus. Joshua hadn't quite wrapped his head around the fact that it was a virus that killed people, and he just thought about how an unexpected break would be nice.

Joshua looked up. Delilah was in his line of vision, but he wasn't trying to look at her. Yet, she immediately saw and said to her friends who she was talking to, "Girls, look. Joshua's staring at me."

Joshua quickly looked back down at his algebra work, the endless handwritten numbers, symbols, *xs*, *ys*, and lines. *"No, I wasn't,"* he thought, and it was true. All he did was *look up*. Delilah didn't say anything more in regard to Joshua, so he just thought about what she said. Shut down? Shut down!? *Shut down!?*

Joshua had swim team that night, and on the ride home, he was texting his best friend from another school. Ironically, his friend was named Cole, but with a C. They had known each other for a long time because of the swim team. Cole told him that his school was shutting down for three weeks, which gave Joshua the clue that it was true. Schools *were* shutting down. The night went on, and there still had not been any news from the Abares' school.

Nothing happened Saturday or for most of Sunday, but Sunday night when the Abares were eating supper, the phone began to ring. Mr. Abare answered. He said *hello*, but then he was silent. The rest of the Abares watched him.

After the call was over, Mr. Abare set down the phone and looked at the table, all eyes on him, and he said, "School is shutting down through April 3rd, a Friday. Tomorrow and Tuesday there is optional school to go back and get your things."

"Are we gonna go?" Joshua asked.

Mr. Abare looked at Mrs. Abare. "You should probably at least go Monday, but...Tuesday, we can talk about it."

"Yeah," Mrs. Abare agreed.

"I want to go both days," Joshua said.

"What? Wacko!" Leah exclaimed.

"I do too," Kendall said.

"WEIRDOS!" Leah exclaimed.

"But Joshua...I thought you couldn't stand school," Kendall said.

"Doesn't change the fact that I'm trying to get perfect attendance," Joshua said. "I haven't missed a day yet all year."

"You confuse me. You dread every day that you have to go to school, yet you want perfect attendance. I thought the kind of people who got perfect attendance were the people who *liked* school," Kendall said.

"I guess you thought wrong," Joshua said. "And plus, it's only two extra days. I need to pick up the slack for all the school I missed last year, and that means making sacrifices this year."

Kendall shook her head.

"I've actually got perfect attendance this year! I'm not going to let some virus ruin that," Joshua said.

"Actually, it won't affect your attendance whether or not you go," Mr. Abare said.

"Do you still want to go?" Kendall asked Joshua.

"Yeah," Joshua said. "Because I don't believe that."

"They said it," Mr. Abare said.

"But people sometimes say one thing and do another. I'm going. What harm will it do, even if it's true?" Joshua asked.

Mr. Abare shrugged, then he said, "Do you guys have any questions about the coronavirus?"

"What's the coronavirus?" Leah asked.

"Where have you been the past week?" Joshua thought in his head, but he didn't say that out loud.

"It's a sickness that's spreading across the world, and it's the reason that schools are shutting down," Mr. Abare explained.

"Why are schools shutting down for it? I thought the flu was a virus, and we don't shut down for that," Leah said.

"The thing with the coronavirus is that it's new. We've never had it in the U.S. before, and there have been some serious ones in the past. We don't know what we are up against, so our government is shutting down schools in hopes to stop the spread of it."

"What about you?" Joshua asked.

"*What* about me?" Mr. Abare asked.

"Are you going to work?" Joshua asked.

"No," Mr. Abare answered. "I will be working from home."

"Wow, so we're all just going to be home together for three weeks?" Joshua asked.

Mr. Abare nodded.

The Abares went to school on both Monday and Tuesday. Even Leah went both days. Then, school was out for two and a half weeks.

The last two days of school were very empty. On Monday, about 59 percent of the student body was there. On Tuesday, that percentage dropped down to about 18.

Joshua was glad he went to school both days because the teachers *did* in fact take attendance. Somehow, Joshua just knew they would.

It was March 17, 2020: St. Patrick's Day.

Their teachers told them to take their things all out of their lockers because they were unsure about the future of the whole situation.

At the end of the day, Joshua had humanities. Everyone was together, as there were only 13 people there from his whole grade. Kolby was there, and Joshua sat with him. Sawyer and Jayden weren't there because Sawyer simply just didn't want to and Jayden's mom worked at a nursing home and thought it would be best if he didn't go to school.

Joshua's class played a game to help them study for their U.S. Constitution test that was supposed to be coming soon in Mr. St. Paul's class. They were probably going to have it over the shut down, which meant that Mr. St. Paul was forced to allow it to be open book. He said, "I am going to make it open-book because I know that if you are at home, no one is stopping you from looking at your notes. I know some of you are honest, but there are many of you who wouldn't think twice before pulling out your notes. So, instead of having you go behind my back, I am going to say that you all, honest or not, can take the test open-book." But still, they studied.

They finished their game with about five minutes left in the day, so Mr. St. Paul gave a speech that was so heartfelt Joshua nearly cried, but to avoid crying at school, he laughed a little. Ah, laughter, how dirty it had done him, yet how much happiness it had brought him in times of trouble.

At the end of the day, Joshua walked out of the school with no idea of what was going to happen next. Though, he pretended like he knew. He had always done that. He had always *pretended* like he knew what was going to happen next. He walked across the sidewalk in front of the school until he met Kendall and Leah who were waiting for him at the playground. They walked home together. When they walked in the door, their mom made them take their clothes off and throw them right into the washer without touching anything. Joshua took a shower.

So it began: the fear, the newfound germaphobeness, the sorrow, the loss.

***

It was just over a week later, the day before Leah's birthday. She and Ava had already gone to bed. Joshua, Kendall, Mr., and Mrs. Abare were all in the living room when Mrs. Abare made the announcement that school was shut down not merely until April 3rd but for the rest of the school year.

"What!?" Joshua cried at that announcement, tears spilling out of his eyes uncontrollably. "No, it can't be over." He quickly wiped his eyes, embarrassed, but it was no use.

"I don't get it," Kendall said. "I thought you wanted the school year to *just end.*"

"Huh?" Joshua cried.

"You kept saying you wanted it to just be over," Kendall said.

"Yeah, but I didn't think it would ever happen. I'm not ready for high school! I never got to say goodbye. I never got my trip, my party, my graduation, my last day of school before everyone else. I'm not ready," Joshua cried.

"Wow, I didn't think of that," Kendall said. A small, single tear ran from her eye. "I'm not ready for *seventh grade*."

"*Seventh grade*. Seventh grade is the reason this is all happening," Joshua said.

"What? How?" Kendall asked, crossing her arms.

"Because of seventh grade, I wished away eighth grade, and now, I've gotten what I asked for. Guess I should have never taken it for granted because now it's gone, and I don't know what I'm going to do," Joshua said. His face was red.

The room was silent for a minute, then Kendall said to her mom, "How do you know?"

"Because it's on the school's page," Mrs. Abare said.

"I don't want to go into high school...I mean, I do...but not yet. I'm not ready. I need proper closure," Joshua said.

Chapter 60: The Bible

Mr. and Mrs. Abare broke the news to Leah and Ava the next morning, even though it was Leah's birthday. They were worried that it would upset her, and they didn't want that on her birthday, but she took it to be a wonderful birthday present. They told her because even though they had nowhere to go, they were doing online swim practices with their swim team. It was mostly dryland workouts, which Leah would scream about every time she had to go on, but still, her parents made her log on and work out every day. They didn't want her to find out from her teammates, so they told her ahead of time.

The next day was Ava's birthday.

After her birthday, March was practically over. April came, and with it, Easter. By Easter, the whole shutdown thing should have been over, but school was still shut down, and so was the whole world. That meant that the Abares weren't going to see their grandparents, they weren't going to go to Church (in person, anyway, but on T.V. for sure), they weren't going to see their cousins, and they weren't going to have any of their Easter traditions.

They were.

Stuck.

At.

Home.

They managed to have a good Easter, but it was nothing like their usual Easter.

That night, Joshua was getting ready to go to bed, when he remembered something that Patrick once said. It wasn't that *Patrick* said it that caused Joshua to remember it. It was the *words* that reminded Joshua of it.

It was the day that Aiden told the "friend" group that he was gay. What was Patrick's reply? What did he say? He said, "The Bible says gay people go to hell."

That was a famous claim, and it caused so many people to automatically believe that all Christians are homophobic. But that's not true. God calls us to love, not hate. A priest once said that God doesn't love us because of what we do...he loves us because of who we are. But how was Joshua supposed to know any of this? He hadn't ever *read* the Bible. Sure, he went to Church and all, but they only read certain scriptures. There aren't nearly enough Sundays in each Mass cycle to cover every topic the Bible holds in its wonderfully told words.

Kole had always tried to argue Joshua's religion, and half the time, Joshua didn't know what to say. That's probably what started the whole fight. The first push. Joshua didn't know what to *say*, so he *pushed*. He needed to read the Bible. He needed to know for himself whether the Bible really said that gay people go to hell. He needed to know if all the claims—claims made by atheists and other non-religious types—were true. He was done being told what his religion said by those who could care less about pleasing God. He didn't know what Patrick thought, only Kole, but he knew that Patrick's comment was one shared by the types of people previously mentioned. It was time for him to find out for himself. What better time to start than *Easter*? It was time for him to pick up the Bible and read it!

Wait...

Pick it up.

But he didn't even have a Bible.

Then, he remembered. His *parents* had a Bible.

Joshua finished getting ready for bed, then he went to his parents' room. The door was open, for they always kept it open at night. He stepped in, and his parents were still not in bed yet. They were still getting ready.

"Hey, Joshua," his dad said, as he was the first one to see him. "What's up? Are there monsters under your bed?"

"What?" Joshua laughed.

"Just kidding," Mr. Abare said. "Last night, in the middle of the night, I woke up to Ava standing in our doorway crying. She told me there were monsters under her bed."

"Oh," Joshua said. "Now you've got me thinking, but no. I was wondering if you still had the Bible you let me borrow for my retreat. I mean...obviously, you still have it. Can I...borrow it...or like...have it?"

"Sure," Mr. Abare said. "You going to read it?"

"Um...yeah," Joshua said. The "um" was long and drawn out while Joshua tried to figure out an answer, but the "yeah" was positive and confident as if he knew the answer all along (because he did).

"Okay. Did Mr. Landon assign you some homework or something?"

"No."

"Oh." He went into his nightstand and pulled out the Bible. It was the *Good News Bible*.

"Good news," Mr. Abare said. "I found it."

Joshua smiled as his dad handed him the Bible.

"So...you're just doing this all on your own?" Mr. Abare asked.

"What? Reading the Bible?"

"Yeah."

"Yeah."

"I'm proud of you."

"Thanks...I mean...I'm doing it on my own, but it's because it's what I feel like I have to do. I want to *see* what God wants. I don't want to be *told* what He wants."

"Ah, smart. Because people will say some crazy things. You'll see."

"Oh, I've seen." Joshua looked at the Bible in his hands, then he looked back at his dad and said, "Thank you."

"No problem."

Joshua walked out of his parents' room and went to his own room. He laid on his bed and opened up to the table of contents. There were a lot of books in the Bible. Joshua decided to begin in the beginning with page one, chapter one, book one: Genesis. "In the beginning, when God created the universe, the earth was formless and desolate" (*Good News Bible,* Genesis 1.1-2).

Joshua read for 15 minutes, and he learned what God did in the first seven days of the earth's life.

Joshua read the Bible the next day, only for 15 minutes again. But he knew he wouldn't finish the Bible that day even if he sat down to read it until he was finished. The Bible was long. He started off his journey by reading it for 15 minutes each day, then he decided he would instead read three chapters each day. That quickly became a habit. Joshua decided to find time in each day to read three chapters of the Bible. On Sunday, he would read double.

He finished Genesis, finding Joseph's (the son of Jacob's) story to be very compelling. But that was only the beginning of it. He hadn't even gotten to when Jesus was born yet. He finished Genesis and went on to Exodus.

Chapter 61: High School

April went on, and there was still no sign of school reopening as May began. Before Joshua knew it, it was June 11, and he was leaving middle school behind him. He had the most informal ending to eighth grade he could have imagined. All of the eighth graders drove up to the front of the school where they would wait in a line of cars to get out just long enough to receive their diploma and get a picture with the principal. He had to wear a mask, which he took off for the picture. But when he got home, his grandparents were over for supper.

With the end of school, summer officially came, and it was the swim season. That year was going to look much different than any other year, but the Abares were more than happy to at least get into the pool. The worst part was that there was no State meet.

After the swim season, school was right around the corner. They were going to go back but in a much different way than before. They were going to wear masks and only go two days a week in-person. The rest of the days were at home, and for Joshua, that meant that he had to attend online meetings for every class at the start of class, and he had to stay on them as long as the teacher pleased.

Joshua also joined the high school cross country

team, and although there technically was no varsity and JV at the meets due to the COVID protocols put in place, Joshua would have been on varsity. He also got to go to the State meet, which was only for varsity because of COVID.

When Joshua went back out into the world after the shut down, he learned that most people didn't call the sickness the coronavirus; they called it COVID, short for COVID-19.

Chapter 62: Religious Conflicts

Joshua learned he and Kole weren't the only ones in the world to have conflicts that stemmed from religion. He was in his global citizenship class when he realized that there were a lot of conflicts that had something to do with religion. He learned about the Jews and Muslims fighting over Israel/Palestine, and he also learned about the Catholics and Protestants who fought over Ireland.

Before that class, Joshua didn't know much about Muslims, but his teacher explained that the Muslim religion began when God showed Himself to the prophet Muhammad. Muhammad was a descendant of Abraham, who was also the ancestor of the Jews. Joshua knew about the Jews because the Old Testament in the Bible was all about Jews. The Jews were descended from Isaac, and Joshua learned that the Muslims were descended from Abraham's son Ishmael. Isaac and Ishmael were half-brothers.

After World War II, Britain promised Israel/Palestine to both the Jews and the Muslims, and that led them to fight over who actually got to live there. But that fight really didn't start with Britain. It started a long time ago.

The fight between Catholics and Protestants in

Ireland was a fight between government ruling. Their neighbors in England used to fight over Catholic and Protestant reign. The Catholics wanted a Catholic king or queen, and the Protestants wanted a Protestant king or queen.

In both cases, all four different religions—Judaism, Islam, Catholicism, and Protestantism—often had conflicts with each other in areas besides Israel/Palestine and Ireland. They seemed to be fighting over who was right. Of course, Joshua was Catholic, so he believed Catholicism to be right. But Protestants, and all other Christians, believed in the same God and in Jesus Christ. They were all basically the same religion, but with different ways of practicing it. Joshua didn't see that as any reason to fight.

Jews and Muslims prayed to the same God as Joshua and each other, and something about that made him realize that there wasn't any reason they couldn't all live together in unison without fighting. In addition, Jesus was Jewish.

Chapter 63: New Sports

There wasn't any swim team that winter, so Joshua decided to try out Nordic skiing. About 90 percent of the team was on the cross country team, but all of the friends Joshua made were not. He made friends with two freshmen boys and a junior boy—the four of them were all beginners. The freshmen were named Arthur and Landon, and Joshua went on to become great friends with them. The junior was named Alex, and Joshua was good friends with him in Nordic, but likely due to the difference in grade, they did not become as close.

Joshua had a rough start to his Nordic season. He was the most clumsy skier on the team. He would fall every few feet when he first started. It was normal to fall, especially as a beginner, but he fell far more than any of the other beginners. It was quite discouraging. To make matters worse, when he had a particularly bad fall, he would have a flashback to his fights with Kole. Joshua had less flashbacks in high school than in middle school, likely due to the fact that he was in a new place, but usually, the winter air, no matter where he was, brought him back to seventh grade.

As the season went on, Joshua got better. By the last meet, he only fell once, and he felt like it could have been avoided if it weren't for the fact that he was being crowded on an uphill.

After the Nordic season, Joshua joined the Track & Field team. He started out trying to be a jumper like his mom, but he ended up getting directed toward throwing, which was a better match. Arthur also did Track and threw javelin after initially trying out sprinting and pole vault.

With that, Joshua's freshmen year came to an end. That summer, swim team was back to a more *normal* form, and Joshua helped coach the younger swimmers. That was certainly an *experience.*

Chapter 64: Like It Never Happened

It was Joshua's first day of sophomore year. Everyone still had to wear masks to school, but they were going to go five days a week instead of two. Joshua was waiting outside the school for a bus to bring his class to the sports complex for a class pep rally. He was standing with Arthur and Arthur's friends, Avery and Max. While they were waiting, they were talking and catching up, and a boy walked over to them and said, "Hey."

"Hi," the boys replied.

The boy looked at Arthur and said, "Do you remember me from last year in band? I was the one who always told you I liked your sweatshirt."

"Yeah," Arthur said.

"What's my name?"

"Uh..." Arthur laughed, embarrassed, and said, "I'm so bad with names!"

"I'm Simon."

"Oh, okay."

Simon looked at Joshua and said, "Hey."

"Hey," Joshua said back.

"What's your name?" Simon asked.

"Joshua."

"Hi, nice to meet you."

"You too."

The boys started talking with Simon. They were still talking when two *other* boys walked over. Joshua knew one of them, and the other one he didn't know.

"Hey," the two boys said.

The one who Joshua knew peered over at him but then quickly looked away. Joshua felt tension in his stomach. The boy whom Joshua didn't know looked at him and said, "Hi, I'm Sean."

"Hi," Joshua said, his voice shaking.

The other boy, who he knew, looked at him, and they locked eyes. "Hi, I'm Maverick."

Joshua was silent and stared.

"What's your name?" Maverick asked him, not breaking eye contact.

Right then and there, Joshua and Maverick made a silent agreement to not bring up their past, like it never happened.

"I'm Joshua," he finally said, his voice firmer than it had been before but still nervous.

"Nice to meet you," Maverick said.

A weak sound came out of Joshua's throat, like a nervous laugh.

Kole's voice rang in Joshua's head: "Would you like to do the honors?"

A huge smile spread across Maverick's face as he answered: "Sure." Maverick's harsh words as Kole held him like a prisoner: "Wow, Joshua. I thought you were a swimmer. Aren't they supposed to be strong? Must be you're just not one of that kind."

Joshua finally took his eyes away from the present Maverick and looked at the other boys who didn't seem to notice the tension between the two boys' eyes. Perhaps what felt like minutes to Joshua and Maverick was only milliseconds to the rest of the boys.

"You will never guess what I did last night," Maverick said, trying to distract himself from Joshua.

"What'd you do?" the other boys asked.

"I taught Harley how to get going. To *really* get going," Maverick said. He looked over at Joshua who looked like he might pass out and said, "Sorry. That's personal. I get it."

Finally, the bus arrived. When they reached the sports center, they all went to the gym and sat with their advisories for the pep rally. Each advisory was like a team, but a group of jocks did most of the work. Joshua wasn't a fan of pep rallies. He didn't like cheering and making a show of himself in front of the whole school—or in this case, simply just his whole class.

The pep rally ended, and there was still a little while before the bus was going to come back to pick them up. It wouldn't come for them until it was ready to bring the freshmen to the sports' center. Joshua wandered around the gym between friends. Mostly just between Arthur and Landon, his two Nordic friends. Joshua saw Maverick one time, but he didn't say anything to him. Whenever Joshua looked at Maverick, he could feel the chill of that cold December night.

After school that evening, Joshua had cross country practice. Unlike last year, they had a preseason, so it wasn't their first practice. In fact, they already had two meets. One of them was a two-person relay, and the other one was a 5k. Joshua hadn't come in top seven at either of the meets, so he was bumped down to JV—a great disappointment after the last year when he thought that maybe he could make varsity all four years in cross country. But he didn't beat himself up too much. His times weren't any worse than his freshman year, and he was still within reach of the two people ahead of him.

Mrs. Abare came to pick Joshua up after practice. He was exhausted and nearly fell into the seat when he opened the door.

"How was practice?" his mom asked him as they began to drive.

"Hard. We did intervals, and today was the first day of school, so it was extra hard."

"Oh. How was school, then?"

"Fine."

"Any of your friends in your classes?"

"Yeah," Joshua answered. There was a silence before he continued on, "You'll never guess who I saw today."

"Oh yeah? By the tone of your voice, I wouldn't guess them to be your friend."

"Ha! That's an understatement!"

"Who'd you see?"

Joshua was quiet for a second, then he answered, "Maverick."

"Maverick!? You mean...*the* Maverick?"

"Uh-huh."

"Did he...do anything?"

"No. He pretended like he didn't know me."

"And how about you? What did you do?"

"I just went along with it. There was no reason to stir up trouble that we finished three years ago. Neither of us want that. I can tell. And plus, he wasn't the real problem. Kole was."

"But wasn't Maverick there that night at the park? Wasn't he at Tony's Taco Bar? Wasn't he..."

"Sure, he was there. Sure, he was part of the problem. He was mean, but it wasn't on his own terms. It was on Kole's. This just proves it. But...you don't have to worry about it. I just wanted to let you know."

"Oh, I'm going to worry about it."

Joshua crossed his arms and thought to himself, *"Why did I tell her that?"* But the sound of Maverick's voice in his head reminded him: "You think this is Kole's doing? Let's ask Reese."

Reese. Joshua hadn't spoken to her in a long time.

Chapter 65: Memory

It was August *2020. The swim season was over, and Joshua's head was filled with a mix of emotions between trying to get over losing eighth grade and beginning his freshman year. It was a rainy afternoon, and Joshua was in his bedroom. With five months out of school, he was trying to find something to do other than write. He hadn't played his instruments in ages and honestly didn't have any interest in doing so, even though he was still enrolled in band for the upcoming school year. He settled on painting, which wasn't something he had done in a while. It was messy and his artistic skills weren't the best, but lately, he had been getting into drawing, so he thought why not add some colors to his work?*

His painting supplies were on a measly shelf in his closet that wasn't used much, and it had loads of things piled on top that he had just tossed aside once they weren't being used anymore. Some of it had slipped down on top of his box of paints through the small space between the shelf and the wall behind it.

Joshua picked up his paints and looked inside at the fallen items. The first thing he picked from the top was a picture from the first seventh grade dance he had been to. It was of him and Reese. They were both smiling at the camera, though they made no physical contact. They didn't look like a couple. They looked like two friends. At the time, Joshua thought maybe they could become more than that, but this picture proved that they never were going to be, with or without Kole's involvement.

Joshua set down his paints and stopped thinking about adding color to his drawings. Instead, he thought about Reese. After Kole left, they had their differences, for sure, but they started to make up, and Reese talked to Joshua about things that she had never told anyone else, and if she had told other people, those people were close to her. That meant he was close to her. *In eighth grade, Reese found a boyfriend and nearly forgot about Joshua, or maybe he forgot about her. He wasn't sure. He seemed to move on from a lot of his friends...or they moved on from him...he wasn't sure about that, either. But he sat there, holding that picture and thought,* "I miss Reese. I miss talking to her. I miss her talking to me." *It wasn't that he still had* feelings *for her, not as a crush. He just missed her, as a friend.*

He set the picture down, ignoring his thoughts, and he took out the rest of the things in his paint box. He brought it over to his desk and began painting. He finished one drawing and decided that painting was not his thing. Some spots had too much paint, some spots had too little. His paint brushes were too big to color in the small eyes. Augh. *What had he done? He should have put his drawing through the copier before he ruined it with paint.*

Still, he left it out on his desk to dry because he

wasn't going to throw it away, since it was pretty good before *he painted it. Maybe he could trace it, he thought. But he put the paints back onto their shelf to collect dust, and he went back to his desk and pushed his paper aside. He pulled out his laptop to write, but he began to think about Reese again.*

When Mrs. Abare came up to Joshua's room to tell him it was time for supper, he realized that he hadn't done any writing. He went downstairs and ate supper with his family. Afterward, while his parents were putting Ava to bed, he went into the kitchen and picked up the telephone. He dialed in a number that was once so familiar that he still had it memorized, and he waited as it rang.

"Hello."

"Hi. Reese?"

"Joshua?"

"Yeah."

"It's been a while."

"Yeah. How have you been?"

"Fine. I'm lovin' the break from school."

"Ha. I know it's been a long time, but I miss hanging out with you. Do you want to get together sometime before school starts again? You know, social-distanced."

"Um...listen, Joshua..."

"As friends," Joshua quickly added.

"Oh...sure."

"Great, cool."

"When were you thinking?"

"Maybe tomorrow?"

"Okay. I'm free. I'm literally free every day."

"Same. Nothing to do when the world is shut down."

"Yeah. We can't really go anywhere because everything's closed."

"We could go to the park and hang out."

"Okay."

The next day, Joshua went to the park to meet Reese. He brought a mask with him, and when he arrived at the park, he put it on. He found Reese already there. She didn't have a mask on, nor did she appear to have one, but Joshua decided to ignore that, and he continued on over to her.

Reese was wearing a black skirt and a maroon-colored shirt with flowers. Joshua, meanwhile, wore sweatpants and a loose t-shirt, absolutely nothing out of the ordinary.

They greeted each other, and the two of them started to talk, mostly about high school. They were going to different ones, and they were sad about that. They talked for about an hour. While they were talking, Kendall and Leah walked past the park. They had gone on a walk together, it appeared.

Eventually, Joshua and Reese had run out of things to talk about, but as they were about to leave, Reese said, "When you called me out of the blue to hang out, I was kind of confused and surprised, but I'm glad we hung out. It's nice to have a friend like you. We should hang out again before school starts."

"Yeah, I agree," Joshua said.

So, they did. They hung out again the following

week. And after school began, they hung out again, and that day, they had a lot to talk about. It was a Sunday, since that was the only day that Joshua had free.

"How's high school been for you?" Joshua asked her that day. She had joined his attire. He still wore sweatpants and a loose t-shirt, and now, she wore either sweatpants or leggings and either a plain t-shirt or sweatshirt.

"Not great, to be honest," Reese replied, monotony.

"Oh. That's too bad. What's the matter?"

"I'm...quiet."

"What? Reese? Quiet? I can't imagine that." Joshua smiled.

"Yeah. I know. It's pretty crazy. I thought that going back to my old school would be good. It was awful here for me, and all I wanted to do was go back to my home. Now, I am home, but I feel even lonelier than I did here."

"Oh," Joshua said, unable to give an adequate response.

"How about you? How's high school been for you?"

"Fine. I'm on the cross country team, and I have become friends with one boy. But while I am at school, I don't talk to anyone."

"Maybe that's my problem. Maybe I should join cross country and make some friends that way." She was silent for a moment as her and Joshua locked eyes, then she started laughing. "Just kidding! I would rather be friendless than run a 5k every weekend!"

"Hm," Joshua said, nervously.

"But maybe some other sport like volleyball or golf.

They seem easy enough."

"I don't know. They might not be running, but I've tried them a couple of times, and I wasn't too great."

"I'd rather be bad at something than have to run...and then still be bad."

"Okay," Joshua replied, smiling.

They continued their conversation, steering away from sports, since they clearly had a different opinion on them.

The two of them continued to meet up once in a while. In fact, they eventually stopped scheduling their hangout and just showed up. Every other Sunday afternoon, they showed up, even as winter began. But one day, for no particular reason, Joshua arrived at the park and Reese wasn't there. He waited a little while, and she still never showed up. He wasn't sure why. It wasn't that it was cold, for it was a mild temperature, warmer than many days they had endured already. After giving up, saddened, Joshua left the park. He went back to his house. His three sisters were in the kitchen making hot chocolate, and curious as to why he looked upset, they asked him. He told them the situation only in a couple of words. They suggested he call her, so he did. All he got was ringing.

The next day, when Joshua walked into advisory, he made a big gulp, then walked over to Wendy. She went to his high school, even though Reese didn't. She was sitting at her lone desk in the corner with headphones on, watching some show, totally oblivious to the world outside her. Joshua was afraid to speak to her since he wasn't really sure how good of terms they were on. She used to like him, and he used to like her cousin. AND NOW HE WAS ABOUT TO ASK HER ABOUT HER COUSIN*! But he still walked up to her.*

When Joshua approached her, she didn't look up from the video she was watching. Joshua took a deep breath, then he said, "Wendy."

His voice was quiet, so she didn't hear him.

"Wendy," he said again, that time a little louder, but she still didn't hear him. So, he said again, even louder, "Wendy!"

Suddenly, Wendy looked over at him. She took her headphones off and set them on her shoulders. She looked up at Joshua and said, "What?"

"Um..." Joshua said, nervously. Was *Reese* the best topic for him to ask her about after not talking to her in about two years? *Well, what choice did he have now? He had already caught her attention. He continued on and said, "Is...is Reese okay?"*

"Yeah," Wendy said, unaware of why Joshua would ask such a question.

"Is she sick or something?"

"No."

"Busy?"

"No."

"What? Then what has she been up to!?"

"I don't know. I just know she hasn't been sick or busy. She's always on her phone or computer or something."

"Hm." Joshua crossed his arms. "Do you talk at all?"

"Not much lately."

“Lately? *Like, within the past couple of weeks...or what?”*

“I don’t know. It’s not really your business.”

“Sorry. You’re right.” Joshua paused, thinking. “I just...” he started to say, but when he looked back, Wendy already had her headphones on again and was back to her video. Joshua sighed and walked away.

That night, when he got home from Nordic and had taken a nice warm shower, he called Reese again, but she still didn’t answer.

The following Sunday, Joshua went to the park, even though it wasn’t one of the Sundays that the two of them usually met up on. Reese never came. He tried again the next Sunday, and she still wasn’t there, so at that point, he stopped trying.

Winter ended, and Joshua didn’t talk to Reese at all. In fact, he simply just didn’t think about her. He began Track & Field, and one day, he was staying late after practice trying to figure out the high jump when he saw Reese walking on the path. She was walking with her older sister, who was a year older than them. Joshua looked up at Reese, and the two of them made eye contact. Reese wanted to keep walking, but Joshua ran over to her. Her sister kept walking, but Reese stopped when Joshua reached her.

“Hey,” Joshua said. “What’s up?”

“Nothing,” Reese said, looking at the ground and wiggling her toes into the cement under her feet. “What is that you’re doing? It’s funny looking.”

“High jump. I’m not very good at it. That’s probably why it’s funny looking.”

Reese shrugged.

"Where have you been?" Joshua asked, his tone darkening.

"What do you mean?"

"You just stopped showing up at the park, and you wouldn't answer any of my calls."

"That was a long time ago."

"Only...like...two months ago. But I haven't seen you since then, and right now, you don't seem like you want to talk to me. But it's not like I'm going to just forget about it. I thought we were friends."

"Oh."

"Why did you start ignoring me?"

"It's not you." Reese looked at Joshua who simply wasn't buying it. She continued: "I just want to forget about middle school...completely. It was an awful time for me."

"But what did I *do to you? Why do you want to forget about* me*?"*

"You are part of it."

"So? What's that matter? I'm not your bad experience, am I?"

"You kind of were."

"What did I do to you*?"*

"Nothing, but you just remind me of it all."

"That's not fair."

"Listen, Joshua. Middle school was really rough for me, and I just want to forget about it. I'm sorry. But I couldn't be that important to you after all I've done."

"Actually...you are," Joshua said, quietly.

Reese didn't respond. Her sister came back over,

interrupting the silence, but separating the two of them.

Upset, Joshua sprinted back over to the high jump, but instead of stopping, he turned and jumped over the bar. He made it over—a height that he hadn't been able to jump over after a whole week of trying. He laid on the mat, which was extremely comfortable, and he stayed there thinking until someone walked over to him and asked him if he was okay. He told them he was, at least...he wasn't physically injured. Only his heart was, but he didn't tell them that.

So, that was it. Joshua never talked to Reese again. And now, he was faced with one of the very things that tore Reese away from him. *Maverick.*

Though, Maverick wasn't in any of his classes, so it wasn't likely that he would see him too often. High school was different from middle school. Joshua didn't see people that much if they didn't have classes with him.

Chapter 66: Re-meeting

Wednesdays were the tough lunch days. Every other day of the week, Joshua sat with Landon at lunch, but he did not on Wednesdays. He struggled to fit in with his table group on Wednesdays because he was sitting with friends of his friends.

He was sitting with Avery and his friends, but they didn't pay much attention to him. Sometimes, they would ask him if he wanted a chair. They sat at a tall table that only had three seats, but Joshua always said he was fine—it was at a height where he could comfortably stand. But that was about all the attention they paid him.

There was one Wednesday though when Joshua felt more lonely than he ever had before. They had a guest sitting with them, and that guest was nowhere near inviting. The guest mostly just ignored Joshua, but Joshua couldn't ignore him.

"*I* taught Julia Thornburger to kiss! So, when people say that she's such a good kisser, *I* am the one who made her that way! She used to be so bad at it, but then *I* taught her how to do it right! During biology, in the room behind the stage, we were at it, and *I* showed her how it was done," Maverick said.

Joshua's stomach tightened. What was this? And

why was he sitting (or standing, really) at the same table as Maverick? He didn't have anywhere else to go, so he stayed there.

"Do you guys know Ari Shwizer?" one of the other boys asked them all.

"Oh yeah, I know her! I've had sex with her! She's the only freshman that I've done it with," Maverick said.

Joshua had nearly lost his appetite. He had just barely plopped a tater tot in his mouth, and then he chewed it and chewed it, unable to swallow it. The boys talked about Ari, but Joshua wasn't paying attention because he was just trying to swallow his tater tot without throwing it back up.

He had just gotten it down when Maverick said, "Oh yeah, I know her, too. We had quite the summer. I taught her well, too." Joshua hadn't heard the name, only Maverick's comment. They talked about the girl, and then one of the boys showed Maverick a picture of a different girl without saying her name. Joshua didn't see who they were showing. The one who showed Maverick the picture said, "Do you know *her*?"

"Oh, yes," Maverick said. "She's in my geometry class. She's so beautiful, but I'm afraid to talk to her because she's a virgin."

"I kind of like her," the boy said to Maverick. "So hands off."

Joshua picked up his trash and brought it to the garbage. But afterward, instead of going back to his table, he left the room. He had had enough of Maverick. He wasn't sure what made him more uncomfortable, Maverick or what he was talking about.

There were still 10 more minutes left of lunch, so Joshua didn't go back to class. He went into the bathroom and washed his hands (for 10 minutes). He didn't know why he was washing them, but he just did. He was drying his hands off when the bathroom door opened. He didn't think much of it, for he didn't own the bathroom and expected people to come in and out, so he didn't look up to see who was there. Not at first, anyway, but when they stood in the entrance and said his name sternly, he looked up.

"You look like you're going to be sick," Maverick said to him.

Joshua didn't respond. He looked back at the paper towel in his hands.

"Did I make you uncomfortable?" Maverick asked. "I know you're Christian and all, so you must be a virgin and probably have never kissed a girl. So...I'm sorry. That was inappropriate for me to say with you sitting there. I'll try to mind my audience. But may I ask...why did it take you so long to leave?"

Joshua was silent, overwhelmed with Maverick's speech.

"Joshua?" Maverick asked. He stepped closer to Joshua.

"I...I didn't have anywhere to go," Joshua finally answered.

"Yeah, I get it. You can't hide out in the bathroom all of lunch."

"No, I guess not."

"I guess maybe you could. I mean...I once spent the whole lunch period in the bathroom with...ah...you know what...never mind."

Joshua's face was redder than when he mistook a habanero pepper for a bell pepper (when he was five).

"I'll leave," Maverick said. And so he did. Joshua stood where he was for a moment. Beneath one of the stall doors, he could see a pair of gray sneakers that had red laces, then he heard the owner of those shoes flush the toilet, so he decided it was time to leave before they came out.

Chapter 67: Herman

Interviewing random people in the hallways was the last thing that Joshua wanted to be doing, yet still, he found himself stuck doing it. He wanted to be the cameraman or sound checker, but nope. He had to try something new. So, he stood in front of the camera, holding a microphone in his hand. The camerawoman, a senior girl named Brittany, said to him, "Just throw yourself out there."

"Why don't you be the interviewer?" Joshua asked. "You like it more than I do."

"Because you haven't been it yet, and we're all supposed to get a chance," Brittany replied.

Joshua sighed.

"Here, ask him," one of his other classmates, the sound checker named Kade, said, pointing at a boy who Joshua didn't recognize.

"Okay," Joshua said. He stuck the microphone out at the person walking by and said, "Hey, do you want to be interviewed."

"No," they said, going around him.

"No, no," Brittany said. "You've got to be more assertive. You can't let them think that they have a choice."

Joshua sighed again. He stuck the microphone at

another person and said, “Please, come get interviewed.”

“Okay,” they said.

Joshua didn’t recognize them, either.

Brittany looked into the camera and shifted it. Joshua looked at her, and she gave him a thumbs up. Joshua held the microphone up to his mouth and said, “Hi, this is Joshua Abare, and I’m here with...”

He held the microphone to the boy’s mouth, and the boy said into it, “Herman.”

“Herman,” Joshua repeated, putting the microphone back under his mouth. “I have a question for you. How many stars are there in the sky?”

“I don’t know,” Herman answered.

“Just...um...I don’t know...guess,” Joshua said.

“Uh...do *you* know the answer?” Herman asked.

“A lot.”

“Hey...what is this? Digital media?”

“Yeah.”

“Are you on camera a lot? Your name sounds familiar...and your voice.”

Joshua looked at the camera, confused. Then, he looked back at Herman. “No, I’ve never ever been on screen. Joshua’s a pretty popular name.”

Herman looked down at Joshua’s shoes and gasped. Then, he looked up at Joshua’s chest. Joshua had a cross necklace dangling from his neck. “Likely story,” Herman said, squinting his eyes.

“What?” Joshua cried.

“Should I stop rolling?” Brittany asked.

“No, keep it going,” Kade said, adjusting his headphones.

"You're a judgmental hypocrite!" Herman snapped at Joshua, pushing him, causing the microphone to fall to the ground and Kade to cringe.

"Woah, woah, what was that about?" Brittany asked.

"Butt out of this!" Herman snapped.

Joshua stood pressed up against the wall, Herman's hand on his shoulder.

"I don't even know you," Joshua said, his face red.

"You're right, you're right. I'm sorry. My bad," Herman said, and he walked away.

As Herman walked away, Joshua looked from his light brown hair down to his sneakers, and he realized that he had seen them once before. They were very unique to Joshua, being that they were gray sneakers with red laces, and the one time he had seen them before, they were the only part of the person he had seen. Herman was the one in the bathroom when Joshua was talking to Maverick.

Joshua looked at the camera, which had a red flashing light on it. "Were you recording that?"

"Yes," Brittany replied.

"Augh! I'm done! This is all so stupid!" Joshua cried.

"Is that why you're dropping out?" Brittany asked him.

Joshua was quiet.

"You think we wouldn't hear?" Brittany asked.

"You can't give me a hard time. I hear...and see...the way you talk," Joshua said.

"But we're not doing anything about it," Brittany said.

"Look, I have classes I need to take, and this class just isn't working out for me. It's two periods long. That's too much commitment for something that I don't..." Joshua stopped. "Are you still recording?"

Brittany pressed a button on the camera and said, "No."

"Augh," Joshua said, and he walked away.

Joshua didn't go back to class. He walked around, not really sure where he was heading. The bell went off, but his class wasn't over (because it was two periods long). He decided that he should probably go back to class so that he didn't get in trouble, though he wondered if he would get in trouble, considering what happened. He figured he might because he kind of blew up *on camera*.

But much to his dismay, when Joshua got back to class, his crewmates were showing their teacher the video. After they finished, Joshua's teacher wanted to talk to him, and Joshua almost broke down. Though he made it through, and his teacher told him that he would never have to be the interviewer again. That wasn't too hard to say because, after Christmas break (which was in a week), Joshua would only be in the class for two more weeks. They honestly probably would only have one more day of interviewing because they only had one more "episode" before then.

Chapter 68: Psychology II

Christmas came, and then it went. Two weeks went by, then it was Martin Luther King, Jr. Day. Joshua's high school had the day off, and so did his sisters' school, but when Joshua went there, they did *not* get the day off. Joshua wondered if the high school had it off before when his school didn't. The day after, Joshua got a second day off because of in-service, but his sisters did not. The next day they went back was the start of the second semester. With that, he was done digital media and had two classes to fill in his empty spots. For period two, he had Psychology II. For period three, he had gym class.

Teagan, from band in seventh grade, was going to be in his psychology class. Teagan went to Joshua's high school when he was a freshman, and Joshua was excited that they'd be together again after eighth grade. But when Joshua was in eighth grade and picking classes out for his freshman year, he messaged Teagan and learned that he was switching to a different high school. Joshua had a quiet meltdown. Joshua's geometry class freshman year, he learned that Teagan was supposed to be in his class, but since he switched, he wasn't. Joshua was pretty upset about that. But last spring, Joshua was at Leah's softball game. Teagan had a sister Leah's age, and they were playing against each other because there were two teams, and their sisters were on different ones. Joshua and Teagan hardly recognized each other at first, but Joshua decided to message Teagan and ask if that was him. Teagan said it was. Joshua should have recognized his uniquely curly hair and his usual light gray sweatshirt and blue jeans, but it had been a while. So, Joshua went over to him, and they talked. Teagan told Joshua that he was coming back to his high school. Joshua was excited. But Teagan told him not to tell anyone because he hadn't told very many people that yet. Though they originally didn't have any classes together, after Joshua switched to psychology, they were going to be in a class together. Teagan had stopped doing band after his freshman year.

After period one, it was time for Psychology II. When Joshua got to class, Teagan was already there with his friend, Aldin. Teagan was still wearing his gray sweatshirt and blue jeans that he wore when Joshua was in seventh grade, and his hair was still just as curly. There was an open seat next to Teagan, so Joshua went and sat down in it.

"Hey, Joshua! What's up!?" Teagan exclaimed.

"Nothing," Joshua said. "You?"

"Not much," Teagan replied. He looked over at his friend and said, "This is Aldin. Have you met before?"

"Yeah," Joshua and Aldin both said.

"Sweet!" Teagan exclaimed.

"Did you both take Psychology I?" Joshua asked.

"Aldin didn't."

"Okay, good. Have most of the people in this room taken it?"

"Around half."

"So there's a good amount of people who haven't?"

"Yeah."

"Okay, good. I was nervous I'd be the only one."

"Ah, nah."

The bell went off, meaning that it was time for class to start. The teacher, Mr. Castellon, walked into the room. His desk was behind the class, and he began to do attendance. Joshua could immediately tell who had been in Psychology I because they did not turn around as Mr. Castellon started attendance. Joshua, on the other hand, did turn around, and so did all of the other people who had not been in Psychology I.

Mr. Castellon began going through the list, starting with...

"Joshua Abare."

Of course.

"Here," Joshua said, raising his hand.

"Hello," Mr. Castellon said. He called the next name, and the next name, and so on. He had called about half the class when one of the two classroom doors swung open. There stood a boy who Joshua knew slightly, but of what he did know, he didn't want him to be in that class.

"Hey, Mr. Castellon, sorry I'm late," Herman said, walking across the room. But he pronounced Castellon as Castleton.

"It's okay, Herman," Mr. Castellon said, sounding annoyed. "We all have our reasons." Then, he added, "And it's Castellon, not Castleton. That's a college down near Rutland."

"Right. Sorry," Herman said.

Herman's eyes began scanning the classroom and found one of the few empty seats. It was in front of Joshua. He walked over to it and sat down. He turned around and looked at Joshua, raising his eyebrows to acknowledge him. Joshua just looked back, without showing any emotion. Herman was the very last person in the alphabet, so Joshua had no warning of his arrival.

Mr. Castellon talked for most of the class, giving a brief overview of the course. He talked about masks, too. He was very adamant about wearing them...and wearing them *properly*. For that, he went to the front of the room so that everyone didn't have to crane their necks to look at him, as they did when he took attendance. He left the last five minutes of class for people to take out their phones. The second he started walking to the back of the room, Herman turned around to Joshua and said, "Hm...Joshua...in psychology? What brings you here? I thought you had digital media right now."

"No," Joshua said, quietly. "I switched out."

"You mean...you quit?" Herman asked.

"I wouldn't..."

"It's okay. I get it. We can't all be perfect. So anyway...what makes you want to do psychology?"

"Uh...I don't know." Joshua's voice shook.

"I'm just curious. My goodness. Don't act so victimized. It's an interesting topic."

"Oh. I guess I agree. It's an interesting topic, and that's why."

"Hm, okay. Some people believe psychology can make you read minds."

"They do? Mm...I don't think so. I think that's more

figurative than literal."

"Good." Herman squinted his eyes. "Because I don't want you to have another reason to think you're better than everyone else."

Teagan butted in: "What's that supposed to mean?"

"Is he your friend?" Herman asked.

"Yeah, of course!" Teagan exclaimed.

"I'd watch out if I were you. Joshua likes to think he's better than everyone else," Herman said.

Joshua crossed his arms and said, "You don't even know me."

"But I know enough," Herman said, and he looked at the cross hanging from Joshua's neck.

The bell went off.

Joshua got up from his seat and left the room. Teagan and Aldin followed right behind him, and when they got out of the classroom they took him aside and said, "Who is he?"

"Honestly...I don't even know him," Joshua said.

"Then why is he getting so uptight with you?" Teagan asked.

"I don't know. I was doing some interviewing for digital media, and he just came up to me and said he recognized me. Then, he called me a judgmental hypocrite. But I don't even know what I did," Joshua explained.

"Is that why you quit...I mean...switched out of digital media?" Teagan asked.

"No," Joshua said. "I made that decision before that incident."

"Oh," Teagan said.

Then, Joshua was off to gym class.

Chapter 69: COVID's Gone

Joshua's Nordic season as a whole was a lot better than the last year. By the end of the season, he was on varsity and went to States. He rarely fell in any skate meets anymore, though he'd still sometimes fall once or twice in the classic meets. That was a great step forward from where he was before. For reference, there were two types of Nordic skiing, and they were skate and classic. Skate is like skating on skis, and classic is like running on skis.

As Nordic ended, so did COVID. Coming back from February break, all mask mandates were dropped—except for in hospitals, doctors' offices, dentist offices, and other places where germs were either high or easily spread. The Abares no longer had to wear them to school or to work. After a couple of weeks, people hardly thought about COVID anymore. There were some people who still wore their masks, but it seemed like someone had flipped a switch and COVID was suddenly gone.

Shortly after, it was time for Track & Field again. Of the three sports Joshua did through school, this was by far his favorite. He was extremely excited. He began the year just throwing, but after a few weeks, he decided to try jumping again. That year, he successfully did long jump in a meet, which was not something he had done the previous year because something about it just didn't click in his head. But he still did all of his throwing events, and he was improving a lot, particularly in discus.

Chapter 70: Blog Post

Mr. Castellon's psychology students didn't show their learning with a big, long unit test like in most classes. In his class, they showed what *they* learned, not what their teacher *wondered* if they learned. They showed what they learned by writing out a blog post about a topic from that unit. Basically, it was an essay with a fun name. Of course, throughout each unit, there was a small little vocabulary test, but it wasn't anything too strenuous. After writing the blog post, they would read two other people's blogs. Mr. Castellon had a list of everyone's names in alphabetical order on a spreadsheet. Their names had two columns for each unit next to it where they would write down who they were supposed to review. Usually, they would count a certain number of people and edit whoever they counted to. If that person's blog wasn't done, they'd go to the next person. They could never edit someone more than once.

Joshua was at the very top of the list, of course. After they were done reading the blog post, they would say two things that were good, two things that could be improved on, and two questions. Joshua wasn't a fan of that part because he took it really seriously, so he always struggled with it.

It was peer review day, and they were to pick the

person one and two after them. Joshua looked to see who was after him, and it was someone he did not know because Mr. Castellon put both of his psychology classes on the spreadsheet. It didn't matter, though. Joshua could still read their blog post, even if he didn't know who they were. The assignment was still the same. He had gotten through only a sentence when Herman turned around and said, "Hey, Joshua! I get to read *your* blog post!"

Joshua frowned.

"Isn't that pretty cool?" Herman asked.

Joshua didn't respond.

"What!? I didn't hear you!" Herman exclaimed.

"Herman," Mr. Castellon said. "Turn around and do your work."

"But Mr. Castellon, I'm reading his blog post. That's all," Herman said.

"Okay, but that does not require you to talk. You need to be quiet to read," Mr. Castellon said.

"Right. My bad, my bad," Herman said, turning around.

After Herman had turned around, Joshua rolled his eyes.

Joshua didn't finish his peer reviews within the class, so during advisory, which was right after for only 10 minutes, he tried to quickly finish. In addition, he went and approved his comments so that the people who read his could get credit. Herman had already posted his comment, so he read it:

1 thing yo did good was u used youre own experience to talk about ptsd but at the same time you could be a little less self centered. No one cares about ur experience, they just want to know what is ptsd. u dont have to be so self centered. i thought that Christians were supposed to be humble, not high and mighty on themselves. Another thing u could do is actually include a proper link to ur work cited. What? R u trying to not give credit where credit is do? That doesn't sound very Christianlike. Oh...another thing you did well was that you gave other examples other than just you. That's good. Shows that other people matter. A question I have is how old were you when the stuff happened that caused you to have flashbacks? Since you brought it up, im curious now. Another question I have is why u think that your better then everyone else? I kinda got that general vibe from your blog.

"Joshua, are you okay?"

Joshua looked up, and his advisor, Ms. Daye, was looking at him.

"Huh?" Joshua asked.

"Are you okay?" Ms. Daye asked again.

"Oh...yeah...I'm okay."

"Your cheeks just got really red."

"Oh. Yeah, I just...I was reading something...um...*interesting*. That's all."

"Okay."

"Thanks, though."

"Yup."

Joshua approved the comment and moved on with his day, but for the record, he had only written three sentences about his own experience, nothing too boastful, and even if he had written more, it wasn't something he was necessarily proud of, anyway.

Chapter 71: "Sick and Twisted"

Joshua was at a home Track meet. He began the afternoon at long jump, then he went to shot put, then discus. He ended the meet after about four hours with javelin. Joshua's teammates had hurried away as soon as they finished, leaving him to walk back alone because he wanted to change his shoes first. He walked across a long field over to the equipment shed holding a javelin in his hand.

By the time Joshua got near the equipment shed, his teammates were already leaving. He walked over to the entrance when a boy in a red shirt and ripped jeans walked out from behind it.

"*Joshua*, Track & Field, huh?"

"Herman?" Joshua asked, surprised and nervous. "What are you doing here?"

Herman stepped beyond the shed, revealing two other boys who were with him. They were in his gym class, but he didn't know their names yet because he hadn't known them before. "Me and my buddies..." Herman continued, "...came to shoot some hoops." Herman nodded his head toward the basketball hoop that was at the edge of the parking lot near where the team threw javelin during practice. "But there were so many cars here that we weren't able to."

"Oh," Joshua said, quietly.

"You throw spears...for fun?" Herman asked.

"We call it javelin," Joshua explained, still, his voice was quiet.

"That's sick and twisted," Herman said. "These are weapons." Herman yanked the javelin out of Joshua's hand and looked at it. "But I've always gotten the impression that you were a bit sick and twisted."

Herman's eyes were drawn to the cross necklace hanging from Joshua's neck, and Joshua knew immediately what this was all about. A wave of anger filled him. He had a flashback, a less vivid one, closer to a memory this time, of him pushing Kole that very first time. The word gullible floated through his mind, but that word seemed like nothing compared to "sick and twisted."

"What? Are you going to just stand there? Aren't you going to say something?" Herman asked.

But Joshua didn't know what to say. He didn't think javelin was sick and twisted obviously, and it wasn't, not the way they did it. But Herman didn't care to hear his opinion. The only thing Joshua could think to do was push him, but he wasn't going to do that, so instead, he said, "Give me the javelin back...please."

"Oh, sorry, my bad," Herman said, handing it back to him, but his smile showed mockery. Joshua took the javelin back, but he didn't move. He just stood in the same spot. He waited for Herman to leave, and he did.

As the three boys walked away, Joshua heard one of Herman's friends ask him, "Who's that, and what's that all about?"

"He's a Christian," Herman said.

"How do you know?"

"Because I heard him talking in the bathroom, and I see that he wears a cross," Herman explained.

Joshua, hearing that, looked down at his chest, where the silver-colored cross hung. Herman was out of earshot now, so he walked in and put his javelin away. Then, he walked over to the high jump where his mom was. She was volunteering at it. He stood at the edge of the track, watching the last few high jumpers execute their jumps. Though, he wasn't thinking about what he was seeing. He was thinking about Herman. The words "sick and twisted" were moving through his head. He said to himself in his head: *"I am* not *sick and twisted."*

Chapter 72: Coughing

Joshua woke up one morning feeling horrible. His throat hurt, and his nose was stuffy. Kendall had been sick, and last night, he had been developing a sore throat. Despite his symptoms, he still got up and took a shower like he did every morning.

When Joshua got out of his shower, as he was getting dressed, he completely forgot that he had woken up sick...because he simply didn't feel sick anymore. It wasn't until he was walking out the door that he realized the revolution his symptoms went through. He honestly couldn't believe it, but it meant that he would be going to school.

When he got there, it was enrichment (aka study hall). He went to his enrichment room and checked in, then he went off to the band room. Teagan had enrichment there, so Joshua went there and met with him to teach him how to play the trumpet. They had been doing this for a couple of weeks now.

Joshua got to the band room, and Teagan was sitting with some of his other friends, including Aldin and a boy who had been in Joshua's digital media class. Joshua walked over to them, and Teagan greeted him. Then, the two of them went into one of the rooms that were on the side of the band room and set up shop.

"Just a warning..." Joshua said as they were taking out their books and putting their mouthpieces onto their instruments, "...I woke up this morning feeling sick, but when I took a shower, I suddenly felt better. That's why I still came, but I just thought I would let you know."

"Ah, I don't mind. Listen to me," Teagan said. He breathed in through his nose, and the air rattled through. "I'm not 100 percent, either."

"Oh," Joshua said. "Okay."

So, they played anyway.

The next day, the same thing happened to Joshua. He woke up feeling horrible, took a shower, then felt completely normal. In fact, the same thing happened all week.

Partway through the week, Kendall and Leah tested positive for *COVID*, proving it hadn't ended. Ava was sick, but when she tested, she tested negative, so she still went to school. She tested everyday and kept testing negative, even though she was sick. But since she was negative, she was still allowed to go to school. Joshua didn't test.

The weekend came, and Joshua continued to take a shower in the morning because it made his symptoms go away. He didn't have a Track meet that weekend.

But one day, Joshua's symptoms were different when he woke up, and when they became different, they didn't go away after taking a shower. His symptoms went from sore throat and stuffy nose to this horrible cough where he would have hard phlegm that was impossible to cough out. In addition to that, he had a runny nose. But he didn't take a day off. He wasn't in middle school anymore.

He didn't have time for a day off anymore. Was that the right decision? Probably not. But did it happen anyway? Yes.

School was manageable, but once he got to practice, things were different. It started out with his warm-up lap. As he ran it, he breathed heavily, and due to his sickness, his chest rattled and he could hear the air catching on the phlegm. He only ran one lap around the track, a quarter of a mile, and then he decided that he would not run again until his sickness was better. Then, he headed over to discus because that was the only event he had left. Sometimes, he practiced jumping still just for the fun of it.

Joshua arrived at discus, and there was no one else there. So, he stepped right into the circle and threw. He did the full spin, which was something that he had been getting better at that year. His freshman year, he never did it because he would never throw as far with it. In his sophomore year (this year), his coach had been encouraging him to try it more whether or not he was good, and that led him to improve because he was actually practicing it.

Joshua watched his discus fly through the air. It was fine. It went through the middle, but it wasn't exceptionally far. He went and retrieved it, and he walked back to the circle. But when he got back, he didn't go back in to throw because he started coughing. And once he started, he didn't think he was ever going to stop. He kept coughing and coughing, and once he thought he had caught his breath, he quickly learned he hadn't, and he kept coughing again.

After multiple minutes, he was able to regain

himself and go back into the ring. Never once did he think that maybe he should have called it *quits* and gone home. No. He kept throwing, and after every throw, the same thing that just happened would happen again. Coughing fits. He got a couple of breaks between throws where he didn't cough his lungs out, but for the most part, he was coughing up a storm everytime.

Some girls came over at the end, and Joshua was still having a coughing fit. But they didn't say anything. He wasn't sure if they cared or not, but they at least didn't say anything.

Joshua decided the next day he would do two things differently: (1) he wouldn't do his warm up lap at all, and (2) he would bring water with him when he went to throw discus.

He felt a little bad about skipping the warm up lap, but if one of the coaches said something to him, he had a *valid* reason for not doing it. And he was pretty sure that they would trust its validity, especially due to his sincerity towards it in the past. Then, he went over to discus, and he brought his water bottle.

This time, though, when he got to discus, there was someone already there.

He was nervous. The person who was there was a senior girl, named Carley. She had taught him to throw shot put when he was a freshman, but he hadn't talked to her much since then. Joshua always got nervous around people he didn't know that well, especially if they were of the opposite gender.

To make him even more nervous, he didn't think that she was expecting anyone to come over. She had her phone laying on the circle playing music. He was pretty sure that she wouldn't put that there if she was expecting someone to come. In addition, her throw as he arrived went very out of bounds. She let out a little cry of frustration, then she went out and got it. Joshua didn't think that she had seen him yet.

He had seen her throwing when he started walking over, but he knew that he had to go to discus anyway because that was what he needed to practice. Since it was the only event he had left, it would have been immature and antisocial to go to one of the other events just because someone was already there.

Carley picked up her discus and turned around, and then Joshua knew he had been seen.

"Oh," she said with a nervous laugh. "Did you see that?"

"Yeah," Joshua replied.

"Ah, okay. We don't need to repeat it to anyone," Carley said.

"Okay," Joshua said.

Carley went back into the ring and threw again. That time was better, much better, and she said it so: "That's better." Then, she continued and said, "Here, you can go." She stepped out of the circle and let Joshua go.

So, Joshua did go. He stepped into the circle and made a throw. It wasn't his farthest, but he made it in bounds. They both went and retrieved their disci. When they came back, Carley went again, meanwhile Joshua started to cough. When the coughing came, he went and got his water, but that didn't help him in the least.

Carley finished her throw, and she stepped out of

the circle. She looked at Joshua who was still coughing, so she went out and got her discus. He was still coughing, so she threw again. But he was still coughing after, so she said, "Are you okay?"

"Yeah," Joshua said, in between coughing.

Finally, Joshua finished coughing, and Carley was still standing there. She didn't come super close.

"Are you sure?" Carley asked.

"Yeah," Joshua insisted.

"Okay," Carley said. "You can go throw now."

So, he did. And then they both got their disci. Joshua started coughing again when they got back. This time, Carley just ignored him the whole time, until he was done and waiting for his next throw.

"Maybe you shouldn't throw...if it's making you cough that much," Carley said.

Joshua shrugged.

Carley looked at the grass, then she looked back at Joshua and said, "If you really want to keep throwing, then you can go ahead."

So, Joshua did. Then they got their disci *again*, but Joshua didn't cough. Carley threw, and Joshua still hadn't coughed again, so as he stepped into the circle, he said, "Look! I didn't have a coughing fit that time!"

"Congratulations," Carley said, seeming unimpressed.

Joshua threw again, and he still didn't have a coughing fit.

Carley threw a couple of more times, and Joshua went in between, then she left. Unlike Joshua, she had more than just discus left to do, so she wanted to practice all of them. The very next throw after she left, Joshua had another coughing fit. He desperately drank his water, but it didn't do a single thing for him. He kept coughing and coughing. But once he finished, sure enough, he went back into the circle and threw again. He wanted to get better at throwing. He didn't care about his cough at that moment. He didn't have *time* to sit around and wait for it to go away.

So, he threw again and had another fit. Then, he had a few breaks, and during that break, two junior girls came over. He had talked to one of them a little bit last year, as teammates, and the other one he had never really talked to before, but she had gone to middle school with him. One of Joshua's friends thought she was pretty.

Joshua threw a couple more times, taking turns with the two girls. The girl who did not go to middle school with Joshua complemented some of his throws, including asking him: "How do you get it to always go straight?"

Joshua shrugged, sheepishly. Then, they continued to throw.

The two girls were still over there when Joshua had his next coughing fit. They did not say anything to him about it like Carley did, but Joshua didn't mind that. He didn't want to bring attention to it. Pretty soon, his water was gone because despite the fact that it wasn't helping him, he still drank it like he thought it would. He was sad because he still wanted it.

Chapter 73: PR

Saturday was the meet that Joshua had been practicing discus for. It was a relay meet, but that didn't mean much for throwers. They would get ribbons based on their team scores, but mostly, it was still individual for them. They could still get a PR, and that's what Joshua was looking to do. The only difference for throwers was that only the top three in each event were able to go. That was why Joshua was only throwing discus. It felt relieving to only be doing one event. He only had to worry about being in one place rather than the usual *four*. He wouldn't have to worry about whether or not he'd have multiple events at a time or not. Discus wasn't for a little while, so he didn't have to rush at the start of the meet like usual.

It was an extremely hot day outside. It was so hot that the sky was pure blue, and the air had a hue to it. Joshua had never been in a sauna before, but he had to imagine that was probably what it felt like. Except, here, the sun was beating down on him, and he had to move around.

And you know what? He neglected to pack sunscreen. He never thought about sunscreen because he never wore it. He never used to be the outdoors type, and that was going to cost him.

He was still sick—still coughing like crazy.

Joshua had a long time before his event, so he wandered around between friends. The middle school coach, who had a daughter that went to school with him, let him try high jump, since she had seen him trying it. But he didn't make it over the bar. Arthur also persistently told him to put on some sunscreen, but he didn't listen, so his skin started to turn red.

After a while, it was time for discus to begin. Joshua had already put his throwing shoes on, so he was ready. He went over with his new friend Jonah, and they met their third teammate, Iggy. They all did a few warm up throws before beginning.

Joshua's turn to throw came partway through the lineup, and he walked up to the circle. He had been practicing that event so much lately, so he was feeling confident. He went to the back of the circle and faced the net, his back facing the throwing area. He leaned to one side, then suddenly he was spinning, moving so fast that he didn't even know what he was doing until suddenly he was standing with his left leg facing the throwing area, and his discus soaring through the air. He stood in the circle, making sure to come to a complete stop before exiting. Then, he walked out the back of the circle.

He walked out to retrieve his discus, then he listened for his distance.

"25.60."

It was in meters.

Joshua walked over to his teammates, and Iggy quickly typed into his phone a conversion, since Joshua only knew his PR in feet, not meters. His PR in feet was 81 going into the meet.

"84," Iggy said.

Joshua smiled.

"Is that a PR?" Iggy asked.

Joshua nodded.

"Nice!" Iggy exclaimed. Then, it was his turn to go. He went to the circle and threw. He threw farther than Joshua, but that was no surprise because he usually did, and it *wasn't* by much.

Soon, it came to be Joshua's turn again, and he stepped into the circle and did the same thing over again. That time, his distance was even farther, 27.13 meters, and again, Iggy put it into the conversion because Joshua didn't care about the meters, only the feet.

"Wow," Iggy said, looking at his phone, before he read out the number. Then he reported: "*89* feet."

"Wow," Joshua said, still smiling.

That time, his throw was farther than Iggy's was. Though, Iggy hadn't done his second throw yet. *And,* they got a third throw. Next throw, Iggy outdid Joshua's throw, but Joshua didn't mind too much, still.

It became Joshua's turn again. After he threw, Iggy told him his final result: 92 feet (28.04 meters).

"What was your PR before?" Iggy asked.

"81," Joshua answered.

"Wow!" Iggy exclaimed. "So, you just increased by 11 feet!"

"Yeah," Joshua said, happily. Then, he had a coughing fit.

Iggy walked off to throw during it, and when he got back, Joshua was *still* coughing. After Joshua finished,

Iggy said to him, "You good?"

Joshua nodded.

"That's quite the cough you've got."

"I know."

"Haven't you had it for a few days?"

Joshua nodded, then he said, "About a week."

"Wow."

Then, the two of them walked back to the shed with Jonah. When they had put their disci away, Joshua and Jonah went to the bleachers because Joshua had become friends with Jonah. Even though they were all done throwing, the meet was *far* from over. There were still a lot of running events left.

Joshua and Jonah sat down next to a boy who didn't do track but was there because his girlfriend was on the team. Joshua had seen them around, but he didn't know him that well, so Joshua sat in silence, watching his teammates as they ran past. Jonah talked to the boy.

While Joshua was watching his teammates, he heard a group of boys sit down behind him, but he didn't look back until he heard them talking and recognized their voices.

"Roe v. Wade's going to be overturned."

"I hope not," another voice said. That voice was much more recognizable to Joshua. "If it is overturned, my girlfriend will probably break up with me."

Joshua looked back, and there sat Herman. He was with his two closest friends: Bryan and Tucker. Joshua had only recently learned their names, but they were the same boys who came to play basketball with him the night Joshua was putting away the javelin after his meet.

Herman looked down at him, and Joshua quickly turned around, his cheeks turning red. Jonah hadn't noticed Joshua looking back.

Herman leaned forward and put his hand on Joshua's shoulder. "Hey, *Joshua*," Herman said. "Didn't see you there."

Joshua didn't respond. Now, Jonah had looked over at him, and so did his friend.

"What do *you* think about abortion, Joshua?" Herman asked, patting his shoulder twice.

"Because I'm not gullible*."* Kole's voice pierced through Joshua's head.

"Joshua?" Herman asked. Joshua was frozen, and Herman said, "Is it what I said?"

Joshua was still quiet. Kole's voice kept ringing in his ears. *"Because I'm not* gullible...*I'm not* gullible...gullible*."*

"Answer me, Joshua," Herman said.

"What?" Joshua asked. His voice was shaky because he was stuck in the middle of reality and the past.

"Wow," Herman said, unimpressed. "I asked you what you think about abortion."

"Oh," Joshua said. "Abortion is wrong because it kills an innocent child."

"Is that why you looked back at us?" Herman asked.

"I was just...confused."

"About abortion?"

"No, no. I'm not confused about abortion."

"Confused about what, then? I wasn't even talking to you."

"But I heard you because you're sitting right behind

me, and instinctively, I turned around. I don't know why."

"Yeah, I don't know why either, you eavesdropper."

"Herman," Jonah chimed in. "What's the deal?"

"Mind your own business, Jonah. I'm talking to Joshua. Are you eavesdropping, too?" Herman asked.

"Come on, Herman," Jonah said.

"It's just a simple question. It shouldn't be that hard. Joshua, what's your problem?" Herman asked, looking back at Joshua.

"I...I just was confused because I didn't understand why your girlfriend would break up with you just because Roe v. Wade was overturned," Joshua said.

"Why do you think?" Herman asked.

Joshua's jaw dropped, then he quickly said, "That's not right!"

"What? It's our choice. We have the right to choose," Herman said.

"It's not up for you to decide," Joshua answered.

"You're right," Herman said. "It's not up to *me*. It's up to *her*. She's the one that's going to get pregnant, not me, and not *you*. It's her body, her choice."

"No, it's *not* her body. It's *not* her choice," Joshua said.

"Oh yeah? How about you tell *her* that? See what *she* says," Herman said.

Joshua didn't respond.

"What? Are you not *man* enough? *I* will tell her and see what she says," Herman said.

Joshua wanted to turn around and show him how he really felt, but he was overtaken by a vivid memory.

"I'm not *gullible," Joshua snapped, and he pushed Kole.*

Kole pushed him back, and Joshua wasn't expecting it, so he fell to the ground. Kole laughed.

"Would you like to do the honors?" Kole asked Maverick.

"Sure," Maverick answered, with a huge smile.

Joshua felt a shiver, everything went black for a moment, then he was back on the bleachers at the track. He had to get out of there, so he stood up and walked away.

"Chicken!" Herman exclaimed.

Joshua kept walking, and Jonah followed him. Jonah's friend remained seated. When Jonah caught up to him, he said to Joshua, "What was that all about?"

"Herman's anti-Christian or something, and...I'm Christian, and he knows it," Joshua said.

"Oh," Jonah said.

Joshua stopped walking and looked at Jonah. He looked him in the eyes and asked, "What do *you* think about Christians?"

"I'm okay with them," Jonah answered.

"Good," Joshua said. He continued walking, and he continued to walk until they had reached some of their teammates, who were standing inside the track, watching and cheering. Joshua cheered with them, but other than that, he was quiet. Jonah was the same.

Chapter 74: Rowan

A petite girl with smooth brown hair, a blue skirt, and a white tank top was storming at Joshua with her fists clenched. When she reached him, she opened her right hand and slapped his left cheek. It hurt really bad because his face was burnt from the meet two days earlier.

Joshua was about to leave his locker when the situation occurred. He looked at her with a frown and said, "Who are you, and what was that for?"

"I'm Rowan, and Herman told me what you said!" she snapped. *Oh, so this was Herman's girlfriend.* "You think you know what you're talking about! But you're just a boy, so you don't know anything about a woman's body!"

"Actually," Joshua said. "I *do* know what I'm talking about, and it's not a woman's body that I'm talking about."

"Yes, it is!" Rowan snapped, and she slapped him again.

"Stop slapping me! We've hardly even met! I just learned your name five seconds ago!" Joshua snapped. Then, he asked, "Do you even know how pregnancy works!?"

"Yes, I do! Idiot!"

"Then why are you arguing with me about this?"

"Because you're trying to tell me what I can and

can't do with my body!"

"No, I'm not. Because it's simply not your body. During pregnancy, a real live baby is growing *inside* a woman's..."

"You will never get pregnant, so you can't tell *me* how pregnancy works!"

"Just because I can't get pregnant doesn't mean I don't know how it works."

"But you can't tell me what to do."

Joshua wanted to argue again that he wasn't, but instead, he decided to ask, "Have you ever been pregnant before?"

"No. But that's none of your..."

Joshua interrupted her and said, "I know that one day you will know what it is like to be pregnant better than me, and when that happens, you will see that what I'm saying is true. A baby is a baby, even in the womb."

"You are the biggest jerk I've ever met! Herman's right! You *are* an idiot!"

"What?"

"How *dare* you talk to me like this! It's men like you that are the reason we *need*..."

Joshua didn't care to listen to the rest of what she was saying. He politely shut his locker and walked away to his next class: Psychology II, *with Herman.*

As he walked away, he whispered to himself, "Yeah, I did *not* handle that well."

Joshua entered his psychology class and sat down. Herman, somehow, had beat him. Probably because he came in early to make sure that Joshua got his lecture from Rowan. Herman turned around to Joshua as Mr.

Castellon entered the room and went to his laptop.

"Your cheek looks a little red, Joshua," Herman said. "Did something happen?"

"I have a pretty bad sunburn," Joshua answered.

"You know what I'm talking about," Herman said, smirking. He winked.

Joshua rolled his eyes.

***

Joshua still had one more meet. He was only going to do discus in it again, and it was his last chance to qualify for States. Being that he still had his horrible cough, he had stopped jumping as much after practice because sports made him tired. But he still practiced discus and usually did a couple high jumps at the end of practice if his friends were there.

Joshua walked up to the equipment shed to get a discus at one of his practices, and as he went around the corner walking in, a javelin was suddenly thrusted at his stomach. He jumped, his heart stopping, and he looked up at the holder of the javelin.

"Hahaha," Arthur laughed.

"Arthur! That's not funny! You could have shish kabobbed me!" Joshua cried.

"Haha. No, I couldn't have. This is the non-pointy side."

"I've stuck that side into the ground before, so I think you should think otherwise."

“Relax. I wasn’t *actually* going to hit you. It’s obvious you’ve never been in a fight before.”

“I was just kidding. I didn’t actually think you were going to shish kabob me. But actually, I have been in a fight before.”

“Getting taunted by Herman and slapped around by his girlfriend doesn’t count.”

Joshua’s jaw dropped.

“What? You think I didn’t know?”

Joshua shrugged, looking at the ground.

“Yeah,” Arthur said, long and drawn out.

Joshua looked up at him and said, “I wasn’t talking about that.”

“Fine. So you *have* been in a fight before. But have you ever *won* a fight?”

“No,” Joshua said quietly, looking back at the ground again.

“Yeah, I didn’t think so,” Arthur said, and he walked away.

Joshua walked into the shed and took out a discus.

Chapter 75: Disc Golf

It had been just over three weeks since Joshua's symptoms changed from nothing to a horrible cough, so it was four weeks since he had gotten sick to begin with. Somedays, he felt better or worse than others, though his cough still remained, and it was horrible. He didn't go to Track practice anymore. He didn't have any more meets because he didn't qualify for States. At his last meet, the "Last Chance (to Qualify for States)" Meet, he didn't PR, but he did better than his original PR. He really wanted to go to States, but he didn't make it. Maybe for the better. He needed rest. Last year, he kept going to practice even after he was done with meets, since he really liked Track, but this year, he was burnt out from being sick.

The first week of June was already upon him. The school year was quickly coming to an end. Joshua's high school was going longer into the summer than almost any other school in the state, including his sisters' school, because the state said that snowdays and other school cancellations didn't need to be made up, but Joshua's school was going to make them up anyway. His sisters' was not.

Kendall was graduating.

But for now, there was still school left for both

schools. It was a Tuesday, so it was actually the four-week anniversary from when Joshua got sick at the beginning. *And*, it was the day before his dad's birthday.

Joshua had gym class first thing in the morning, and he was playing disc golf at the place where the new pool was in the process of being built. At the beginning of the unit, he was pretty bad at it. He played in middle school and was pretty bad back then, too. He thought being a thrower might help, and although it did a little bit compared to in middle school, throwing a disc for disc golf was a little bit different than throwing a discus. He soon learned to adjust to the lightweight disc. In all of his throwing events, not just discus, he was always taught to form an arc in the air, which meant throwing upward slightly, but when he did that with the disc, it would catch the wind and fall to the ground. By now, he was getting used to throwing the disc flat across the ground, but still, it was a work in progress. He certainly wasn't the best.

During class, Joshua got into a group to go through the course with a boy from the cross country team, named Calvin; a girl from all of his sports minus swimming, who played disc golf on her own, and who lived a couple of houses away from him, named Suzy; and one of Suzy's friends, named Jessie. Joshua was the youngest in the group, as Calvin and Suzy were seniors, and Jessie was a junior.

They went around the holes and continued at a fairly steady pace because they had the only experienced person on their team. Though, that didn't continue when Jessie accidentally threw her disc on top of a rock ledge next to them. Joshua and Calvin offered to go get it for her, but she insisted that she would get it on her own.

So, the other three waited and watched her climb up the rocky ledge as she went to retrieve her disc.

They were waiting when a disc flew past Joshua's face, right in between him and Calvin. Both of them jumped and looked at each other, then all four of the group members looked back to see who threw it.

"Oops." It was Bryan, and he was with Tucker. "*Heads.*"

Joshua looked away quickly. Bryan walked in between him and Calvin to get his disc, and when he walked past Joshua, he pushed him. Joshua stumbled a little bit, as it was unexpected. Bryan walked over to his disc, and when he walked back by, he pushed Joshua again. This time, he pushed harder, and this time, Joshua fell into the rocks beside the trail. His butt was in instant pain. "Clumsy," Bryan said.

Joshua tried to get back onto his feet, but he was barely standing up yet when Bryan pushed him again. This time, he stuck his hand behind him to catch himself and sliced it on a rock. It started to bleed.

"Hey," Suzy said. "Leave him alone. That was completely uncalled for."

"He's going to try and rule your life," Bryan said to Suzy. "He thinks he knows better than you."

"Joshua? Really? I don't think so," Suzy said.

"You don't know him that well, then," Bryan said.

"I'm his neighbor," Suzy said. "And I'm on three sports teams with him. So, I think I'd know."

"I thought my neighbor was cool until I saw the police with their blue lights pulling into his driveway,"

Bryan said. "They took him away in handcuffs."

Suzy's eyes widened, and she found herself speechless.

"I'm not trying to rule anyone's life," Joshua said. He was back to his feet now, and Bryan pushed him again. That time, Joshua didn't fall, but he knew that he wasn't going to keep his balance any longer.

Joshua felt the urge to push him back, but he was overcome by a vivid memory, pulling him away from reality for a few seconds as he relived a moment in his past.

"I'm not *gullible," Joshua snapped, and he pushed Kole.*

Kole pushed him back, and Joshua wasn't expecting it, so he fell to the ground. Kole laughed.

"Would you like to do the honors?" Kole asked Maverick.

"Sure," Maverick answered, with a huge smile.

Joshua started to walk away, but Bryan walked up behind him, and pushed Joshua again. He nearly fell to his knees, so he could scrape them up too, but he didn't quite hit the ground. Joshua started running. He hadn't run at all in four weeks, so he was pretty out of shape. He tripped over a root right as he was about to exit the woods, and this time, he did hit the ground and scrape his knees. And he cut up his hand even worse. But he didn't get back up because he started to cough. He coughed so hard and couldn't stop. He heard footsteps behind him, and he was being pulled to his feet. He thought it was Bryan...or maybe Tucker...and he would have tried to pull away if it weren't for the fact that he was coughing. But shortly, he realized it was Calvin, Suzy, and Jessie, who held him as he continued to cough. The three of them sat him down on a large rock and let him continue coughing. When he finished, which was at least a solid minute later, they could tell he was feeling weak, and Jessie put Joshua's arms over Calvin and Suzy's shoulders, and they started to carry him to the teacher.

When they got to the teacher, Joshua had begun coughing again and was out of control, so the teacher, Mr. Cassidy, took Joshua inside the lodge to get some water to drink. Joshua was embarrassed because he had been in the lodge the night before for WSI training. He was recently hired to work at the pool as a swim instructor. Joshua drank some water, but it didn't help him stop coughing. He knew it wouldn't. It just soothed his throat. Joshua kept coughing and coughing, and finally, he finished, and then he sat down in a chair.

"Wow, Joshua." That wasn't Mr. Cassidy, but his new boss.

"What happened?" Mr. Cassidy asked this time, seeing the blood on Joshua's hands and knees.

"I fell," Joshua said.

Calvin, Suzy, and Jessie were standing in the entrance, and Calvin butted in to say, "Actually, he was pushed."

"I *did* fall," Joshua said.

"And then he was running away, and he tripped," Calvin said.

"Oh," Mr. Cassidy said. "From who?"

"Bryan," Calvin answered.

Joshua's boss cleaned out the cuts and then bandaged them. *Then*, she took out a binder, and she told Joshua to write down his injury in the book. She had him do it so that he would know what to do that summer if he had to clean up someone else's wounds. After that, gym class was over, and everyone got on the bus to go back to school.

***

Joshua woke up the next day feeling worse than he had yet. In fact, he felt like he was going to die. He wasn't sure if that was actually what it felt like to be near death, since he hadn't ever actually been so sick that he was going to die. Nonetheless, he stayed home from school. That night, Leah had a softball game, which Joshua did not go to. It was Mr. Abare's birthday, but he really liked softball, so he didn't mind going to a game.

The next day, Joshua felt good enough to go to school, but he didn't really feel spectacular, so Mrs. Abare called the doctor. He didn't get to go in until the next week, and he found out that he had a sinus infection.

Chapter 76: Indifference

Joshua walked in the school doors and passed a group of students who were talking to each other. Joshua could hear that they were talking about Roe v. Wade. They said that they believed abortion should be a choice, not a privilege. Well, Joshua didn't think it should be either of those: not a choice, not a privilege. Hearing them talk was different than hearing Herman and his friends talk. When he heard Herman talk, he felt mad. Herman was a jerk, so it didn't surprise him. Just like when Kole said *he wasn't* gullible, it made Joshua mad. But when Joshua heard these other people it instead made him *sad...disappointed.* This group of people were, what Joshua thought to be, *nice*. In fact, he was even friends with a few of them. It was like when Aiden and all of them betrayed him to Kole, even when they were friends. That made him *sad* and *disappointed*, but it hadn't made him *mad*. He never wanted to push any of these people. He didn't really want to push Kole or Herman either, but with these other people, he didn't even get the urge to. It was different because he had always known Kole and Herman to be jerks, but these other people had never acted like a jerk to him.

As Joshua continued walking, he heard *yet another*

group of people talking about Roe v. Wade. And they were saying the same thing as all the others Joshua had heard talk about it! They were *in support of* abortion! Joshua was bewildered. He couldn't understand. He couldn't be the only one who thought what he thought...*could he?*

"If I'm in the minority..." Joshua thought to himself. *"Does that mean I'm wrong? I mean...if* everyone *else believes it to be good...then...is it?"* He paused for a moment, then his inner voice snapped, *"No! That's absolutely not what it means! Never* ever *let yourself believe that those who support murder are right! But...they* say *it's not murder. What about that? Don't listen to what they* say*! They just don't want to believe it's murder because they don't want to believe it's wrong. Being in the minority doesn't mean you're wrong."*

Joshua had reached his class, which was band.

A voice in Joshua's head told him: "Never *be guilty for being against murder."*

Joshua set his bags down, and he got himself a chair and stand. Then, he began to assemble his instruments (both the alto saxophone and the cornet).

Pretty soon, the school year was over. Finally, Joshua wasn't sick anymore.

Chapter 77: Busy Summer

Even though school was over, working and getting up early was *far* from over. *In fact,* getting up for school was like sleeping in compared to Joshua's summer schedule. The same was for Kendall. A new pool had been built—which, don't get me wrong, was awesome—but not only was the pool now farther away, so they had to be driven instead of being able to walk, practice was starting half an hour earlier: at SEVEN in the morning, all summer long. Then, after practice, Joshua was coaching, then teaching swim lessons. He only had to work until 12, but he had to like...swim...hard...in between then. *And,* he was going to be out in the sun the whole time. *And,* it started at seven in the morning, while he was not a morning person in the least. *And* he had to like...teach.

Joshua had a pretty funny-looking tan. Wherever his track uniform covered, it was white, but his arms and face were tanned. His legs were mostly tan, except for a small line of white above his knees where his shorts covered what his bathing suit didn't. His feet and ankles were white from his socks. He had found that pretty comical, for the time being.

Joshua's best friend, Cole, wasn't swimming that summer. He had told Joshua that, but Joshua had a hope that he would end up doing it. Cole had told Joshua many summers that he wasn't swimming again, but this time, it was real. Even though he hoped it wouldn't be true, he knew this time was different because last year, Cole told all of the coaches, and everyone cried, and there was cake.

Besides the fact that swim team was at a new pool, and that it was now at seven in the morning, and that Cole was no longer on the team, the swim season was going to be completely back to normal the way it was before COVID. Even though a lot was changing, and Joshua was deeply devastated, especially about Cole, he was glad that things were going to be back to the way that they once were. He couldn't stand COVID restrictions.

Mr. Abare dropped Joshua and Kendall off at the pool at 6:55. Having the 6 in the time made it seem even more earlier than it was. If there was a 6 in the time, then it was *basically* 6:00, right? It seemed so.

So, swim team began. They had their annual introductions, then they had some pool time. After Joshua and Kendall's practice, there was half an hour before Leah and Ava's practice. Then, Joshua coached their practice, and then he had to wait another half an hour for swim lessons to begin. During that half hour, he helped take out the lane lines and looked at his upcoming lessons. He read that he was going to have a Preschool Level 1, a Learn to Swim Level 4, and a Learn to Swim Level 3. First up was the Preschool 1. Joshua always liked preschoolers, in fact, at one point, he said he was going to be a preschool teacher...*then*...he taught this lesson. After his first class, he quickly changed his mind about being a preschool teacher. It's not that his students were bad, it was just that...they couldn't say their own name, they did not want to put their face in the water, they cried when their vocabulary failed them, and they were under the impression that they were the boss. Joshua didn't have to teach the lesson alone, but he honestly wasn't sure if that was better or worse.

After that, he went to his Learn to Swim Level 4, which was much easier because the swimmers were older and understood social cues better. Then, Joshua had Learn to Swim Level 3, where he knew one of the swimmers from swim team. Those swimmers had a lot of energy.

None of his lessons he had to teach by himself.

Finally, 12:00 came, and swim lessons were over. Joshua helped set up for public swim. It was opening day, so he stayed to watch the ribbon cutting, then he went home. When he got home, he was starving and tired. He ate lunch, as it was almost one o'clock by then, and afterwards, he fell asleep on the couch. He needed to go for a run that afternoon, for he needed to prepare for the cross country season, but he was too tired. And, his skin was in horrible agony.

The next morning, Joshua woke up, and his stomach and shoulders were crying. When he got changed into his bathing suit, he could see why. His skin was red: sunburnt. But it was only sunburnt where it had been white before; it was only sunburnt where his track uniform had covered. The rest of his skin had already gotten sunburnt.

Chapter 78: Overturned

A whole week of work went by, and Joshua was so tired. He struggled to get out for a run everyday. In addition, the pain of his sunburn was not going away. In fact, it was starting to look so bad. By Friday, it was starting to peel. When he decided to try aloe, it burned like crazy.

On Saturday, Joshua took Kendall out for lunch. It had been a while since they spent any time together, so they went to a sandwich place on their road.

They got their food once they had arrived and sat down, talking as they ate. When they finished, Kendall went to the bathroom to wash her hands, and Joshua waited out at the table. Kendall was in the bathroom when Joshua heard a ring, the sound of the door opening. He looked back and found his stomach spinning in circles.

"Joshua, funny seeing you here," Herman said, immediately seeing him alone at the table.

Joshua groaned. Herman walked over to his table and sat down in Kendall's seat. Annoyed, Joshua snapped, "My sister is sitting there."

"Oh, don't worry. I won't be long," Herman said. "It's been a while. How's it going?"

"It's been *a week*," Joshua pointed out.

"Right, but so much has happened since summer

vacation started. It feels like a lot longer. Hey, did you hear? Roe v. Wade was overturned."

"Yeah, I heard."

"I hope you're happy," Herman said through gritted teeth and squinted eyes.

"Why should I care? Honestly."

"What are you talking about? You don't like abortion."

"You're right! I don't! But how is Roe v. Wade being overturned going to prevent abortion?"

"Because Roe v. Wade is what allows abortion!"

"As a country, yeah. But each state gets its own rules. And Vermont is not going to take away anyone's ability to murder their own children."

"Augh!" Herman pushed Joshua from across the table, and Joshua cringed in pain as he had targeted his burn perfectly. Then, Herman walked away.

"Clearly I did *not* handle that well," Joshua said to himself.

Herman had gone up to the counter to order his sandwich when Kendall came back out of the bathroom. She came back to the table and found Joshua frowning.

"What's the matter?" Kendall asked, looking pretty confused.

Joshua nodded his head toward Herman at the desk. Kendall looked back at him, then she turned to face Joshua again and said, "Who's that?"

"His name's Herman," Joshua said.

"Oh. I get the feeling he's not very friendly."

"Not really."

"Well, I'm ready to go."

"Okay. Me too." Joshua made one last look at Herman, then they paid and left.

They were walking down the sidewalk, talking again, and Joshua was telling Kendall about some of the things that Herman had done when they saw a girl sitting on a bench outside of a coffee shop. She had her knees pulled up all the way to her face, which she was burying in between her knees. Joshua quickly recognized her smooth brown hair and her small stature.

Rowan.

"Oh no," Joshua thought to himself.

Joshua stopped walking when he got to her, and he said, "Rowan."

She looked up, tears streaming down her cheeks.

"What's the matter?" Joshua asked.

"Leave me alone!" Rowan snapped.

Kendall's eyes widened. She had no idea who this girl was. Joshua hadn't gotten to mention Rowan yet, so she didn't even have any clues.

"Are...are you okay?" Joshua asked.

"What do you want?" Rowan snapped.

"Nothing!" Joshua exclaimed. "I just wanted to see if everything was okay."

"Can't you see!? I'm not okay! Why do you care!?" Rowan shouted.

Joshua shrugged, then he started to walk away. Kendall followed. But then Rowan looked at him and cried, "Wait!" Joshua stopped walking, and Kendall, not expecting it, ran into him.

Joshua turned around to face Rowan.

"I'm sitting out here because I have no one to talk

to. I've tried to talk to people, but no one will listen to me. I slapped you because of what I'm crying about, but you *want* to listen?" Rowan asked.

When Rowan mentioned that she slapped him, Kendall's eyes widened again as she quickly turned her head to look at Joshua.

But Joshua didn't notice Kendall, and he replied to Rowan saying, "I mean...sure."

"Why? Do you *like* me?" Rowan asked.

Joshua's face turned red to match the sunburn hiding below his shirt, but he answered, "No. Not like that. I'm just being genuine."

"Okay," Rowan said. She looked at Kendall and said, "Who are you?"

Kendall opened her mouth, but Joshua answered, "This is my sister, Kendall."

"Oh," Rowan said.

"So...what's the matter?" Joshua asked, sitting down next to her. Kendall sat on the other side of him.

Rowan sighed and said, "It's Herman."

Kendall looked up at Joshua.

"He broke up with me," Rowan continued.

"Why?" Joshua asked, but he already knew the answer.

"Because Roe v. Wade was overturned, and he's worried he's going to get me pregnant. I tried to explain to him that we use protection and all, so it's safe, but he said he's not risking it, so here we are, broken up," Rowan said.

"He broke up with you over *that*?" Joshua asked.

"Yeah," Rowan replied.

"I'm not ready for high school," Kendall thought to

herself.

"That's a silly thing to break up over," Joshua said.

"I can't blame him too much. What else is there to dating?" Rowan asked.

"Um...you know...*love*."

"That *is* love."

"No, it isn't. I mean *real* love: the kind that comes from the heart, not the...augh... never mind!" Joshua covered his face in embarrassment and at a loss of words.

"You don't even seem real!" Rowan laughed a little.

Joshua laughed offhandedly and said, "What's that supposed to mean?"

"You've really never thought about *it* before?"

"I plan to one day get married and have kids...so...you can see..."

"Yeah, I've got the picture." Rowan paused, looking at the ground, then she looked back up at Joshua and said, "Why do you care so much about abortion? You can't get pregnant, but you seem to have a really strong opinion of the whole situation."

"My mom had two miscarriages, and although many abortion supporters believe that the unborn aren't human like us, I don't feel that way about my younger siblings. In fact, there is science and religion alike that both agree life begins in a mother's womb. If they can both agree, then how can I disagree?"

"What makes them alive?"

"For starters, at the second of conception, the zygote already has its whole DNA. Plus, unborn babies have heart beats and can feel pain, and they have so many other *human* qualities! I can't imagine ever wanting to kill one."

"But Herman says it's my body, my choice."

"And Herman *dumped* you, so why do you care what he says?" Joshua paused before continuing, "That's a pretty popular argument, but it's actually the baby's body, yet the baby doesn't get a choice. They need care, but they can't receive it when abortion comes into play. Don't these same people know how pregnancy works? Don't they know how babies are made? With all this knowledge, why do people need something to fall back on? And of all things, why this?"

"What about in cases of rape?"

"Rape accounts for less than one percent of abortions." Joshua took a deep breath. "And personally, I don't think abortion is going to help the woman very much. Did you know that a lot of women are actually more susceptible to mental illnesses like anxiety, depression, and suicidal thoughts after having an abortion? Rape or not, the baby is a baby, and it doesn't deserve to die for its dad's crimes, and the mom doesn't deserve a second trauma. Wouldn't it be better to care for the woman rather than persuade her to kill her child?"

"You must think I'm a really horrible person." Rowan's green eyes were filled with tears.

"No. Do you think I am? Most people don't agree with me, but I simply don't care. That probably makes *me* seem like a jerk."

"I *did* think so, but I don't anymore. Someone like you *shouldn't* care what other people think of your opinion. You have real logical and caring evidence and reasoning, meanwhile I just have pleasure behind my opinion. Well...*had*...I'm going to think about what you said. I'm *really* going to think about it."

Joshua smiled.

Rowan stood up and put her hand on Joshua's shoulder, saying, "Thanks, Joshua. I guess I've got to get home."

When her hand touched his shoulders, he squinted his eyes and clenched his teeth, cringing. She quickly drew her hand away once she realized and said, "What's wrong? Did I do something?"

"Sorry," Joshua laughed. "I've just got a really bad sunburn. That's all."

"Oh! I'm so sorry!"

"It's okay. It's my own fault. I guess I should have put on some sunscreen."

"Sunburns are horrible."

"Yeah, and I've never had one this bad."

"It's pretty bad," Kendall added.

"Oh yeah?" Rowan asked.

Kendall nodded.

"I'm going to go. And maybe you should go, too. It's pretty sunny out," Rowan said.

Joshua agreed, so the three of them all went home. Joshua and Kendall went one way, and Rowan went another. Joshua and Kendall walked home, but Rowan walked to her car, which was parked on the side of the road.

Chapter 79: Shoved

Joshua was waiting outside the pool after work for his mom to come pick him up. Public swim was in about 10 minutes. A small car pulled into the parking lot near him, and Joshua quickly recognized the people inside: girls from his school. They all got out of the car together, and one of them came over to him and immediately said, "Hey, Joshua. I've thought about what you've said."

"Hey, Rowan," Joshua said.

Rowan's friends continued walking to go inside, but Rowan stood in front of Joshua. One of her friends gave Joshua a stink eye.

But Joshua and Rowan ignored them, and Joshua asked, "What have you decided?"

"I think you're right," Rowan said. "I mean...I don't *think*...I *believe*."

"Oh yeah?" Joshua smiled. "I'm glad."

"Me too. I'm honestly horrified of what I used to think." Rowan sighed. "I just wish Herman would see it this way."

"*What* do you wish I would see?"

Joshua and Rowan jumped and looked behind them. Their eyes widened when they saw Herman standing there.

“*Herman!?* What are you doing here?” Rowan asked, her voice trembling.

“I came for a swim. I heard that the new pool was pretty sick, but I guess if it has you here, then it’s not all that great. And Joshua? Do you *work* here? If that’s so, I never want to step foot in this place again. And what are you doing talking to my *girlfriend*? You’re corrupting her! Are you doing this to get back at me for my beliefs? That’s just messed up,” Herman said, and he shoved Joshua.

“Ah,” Joshua cried, for Herman pushed his hands right into his sunburn.

“What’s the matter? Have you grown weak?” Herman asked. He pushed Joshua again, and Joshua cried again.

“Herman, please! I’m *not* your girlfriend! You *broke up* with me! And Joshua and I...we’re *not* a thing!” Rowan cried.

“Oh yeah? It sure looks like it to me,” Herman said.

“Just because a guy and a girl talk doesn’t mean that they’re a thing, but you’ve never seemed to understand that,” Rowan said.

“Shut up!” Herman shouted, and he pushed Rowan.

“Augh!” Rowan cried, surprised.

“Hey!” Joshua snapped, but he didn’t push Herman. Herman pushed him again, and he fell to the ground. Then, Herman kicked Joshua in his stomach, causing his sunburn to feel immense pain. A tear shed from Joshua’s eye because his burn was so bad he couldn’t help it.

“You’re all a bunch of losers! Get a life!” Herman said.

"You get a life!" Rowan cried. "You're the one who's coming around and pushing everyone! What kind of person does that?"

Herman looked at Rowan but didn't answer. They stared at each other for a moment, then Herman walked away, away from the pool.

Joshua stood up.

"I don't get it," Rowan said.

"What?" Joshua asked.

"You didn't even push him back once."

"Neither did you."

"No, but...he kept on pushing you, and I've seen him push you before, but I've never seen you push him back...*ever*."

Joshua looked at the ground and rubbed his arm slightly. Then, still looking at the ground, he said, "I *can't* fight back."

"You mean...you *won't* fight back?"

"No. I *can't*."

"Why not? Because you're weak? I thought you were a swimmer."

For a second, Joshua saw Maverick standing in front of him.

"No. It's not that I'm weak," Joshua said. "It's because fighting back will just make things worse. Believe me, I know."

"I don't understand you."

"That's fine. You don't have to. I don't need other people's reassurance. I make my own decisions."

"Augh!" Rowan walked away to the pool.

Joshua crossed his arms after she left, but only for a

moment because his arms pressed up against his burnt chest, and it made him cringe with horrible pain.

Chapter 80: Talk

Joshua had just clocked out and was leaving the pool the next day when he found Rowan sitting in the lobby. Initially, he was going to ignore her, until she said, "Joshua." So, he stopped walking, and he turned around to face her. She stood up and said, "I'm...I'm sorry."

"For what?" Joshua asked.

"Yesterday."

Joshua didn't respond. He was rerunning their encounter from yesterday in his head.

"I blew up at you after Herman came. I was upset because he was pushing us around. I wasn't mad at you. I was mad at him. But I took it out on you," Rowan explained.

"Oh, thanks Rowan. I get it."

"And I'm sorry that I didn't understand you."

"It's okay. It's hard to understand."

"Did something...happen?"

"Huh? You mean between Herman and me?"

"No. I *know* about you and Herman. I mean...did something happen that made you not want to fight back?"

Joshua shrugged.

"I talked to you; now you can talk to me. It must have been pretty bad whatever it was if it is preventing you from sticking up for yourself, and letting yourself get pushed around all the time by Herman...or anyone. I see you. You stand up for what you believe in, but it seems to fall short when it comes to yourself," Rowan said.

Joshua sighed, looking at the floor, all nicely mopped.

Joshua saw clearly the vision of Kole on the ground in front of him. Patrick, Maverick, Aiden, and Reese ran up behind him and held him in their arms. They all looked at Joshua with a frown. His stomach began to hurt in the present moment as he remembered exactly why he and Kole were both covered in blood. He remembered who started it.

"I've been in fights before," Joshua told Rowan, after a short silence where he relived that moment.

Rowan paused, then she said, "What happened?"

"Would you like to do the honors?" Kole asked Maverick.

"Sure," Maverick answered, with a huge smile.

Joshua reran the event again in his head. His body shivered as he remembered the cold park. It had been nearly four years, but still, every time it was brought to his attention, he relived the moment. He endured the fight all over again, and it ended the same way: with the final blow to his head. Then, he was back to reality.

Joshua said to Rowan, "I...I don't want to talk about it. And I certainly don't want to make it happen again. That's why I don't push back...because that's what started it all."

"Oh, you go to church?" Kole asked.

Joshua nodded.

"I'm not really into the whole church idea,*" Kole said.*

Their argument continued, the ending was what really pierced through Joshua's mind.

"Because I'm not gullible,*" Kole replied.*

"I'm not *gullible!" Joshua snapped, and he pushed Kole.*

"Okay, I won't ask you anymore about it," Rowan said.

"Thanks," Joshua said.

"Goodbye." Rowan started to walk away, going toward the parking lot.

"Wait!" Joshua said.

Rowan stopped and turned around.

"Aren't you going to use the pool?" Joshua asked.

"No."

"Oh. So...you came here just so that you could apologize?"

"Yeah."

"Oh. Wow, thanks." He stood still, and then he said, "Okay..."

Rowan took a step closer.

"In seventh grade..." Joshua began, "...I pushed this person because he insulted me. Well...I felt insulted, but everyday for four years I've wondered if I was overreacting. But it was about religion, and I'm sure that you can tell I care very much about that. I was just defending it. But...he got mad at me for it, and he wouldn't leave me alone. He used to beat me up, and although we both tried to make amends with each other, we could never quite do it. In the end, he nearly killed me. All I know is that now I never want that to happen again. He moved a few days later, and I haven't seen him again since, but his memory still haunts me to this day. *I* can't push again."

"How...how'd he almost kill you?" Rowan's heart rate had picked up.

Joshua laughed, and he said, "It's kind of pathetic."

"No, no. It's not," Rowan said.

"You're right. It's not pathetic. It's terrifying. It was an extremely cold day outside. I was writing a story, and one of the characters shared a name with one of his friends. So, they got mad at me, saying I couldn't use it, as if they *owned* it. But it's just a name. I wasn't feeling good, and they called me at my house. But I didn't want to talk, so I hung up. But then they showed up at my house, and they took me outside. I didn't have a chance to put on a jacket because they grabbed me and pulled me out. They beat me up in the park. I was too cold to fight back because I was in a t-shirt. Then, they knocked me unconscious and left me there in the cold. Some of my Church friends found me and took me to my house where I was able to warm up, but...I fear...what if they hadn't come? Would I have frozen to death? I mean, it was *really* cold that night, and I was in a t-shirt. I was laying off where no one could see me. I remember where they had brought me, and that's probably where they left me," Joshua said, holding back tears.

"Woah," Rowan said.

"Please," Joshua said. He looked at Rowan. "Don't

tell anyone about this. That was in middle school, and I'd rather not bring that reputation with me for the rest of my life."

"Your secret's safe with me," Rowan said. She pretended to zip her lips. "You have helped me in a way that no one has ever even tried to help me before. You have let me see clearly. I won't betray you."

"Thank you," Joshua said.

"I'll be going," Rowan said.

"Okay," Joshua said.

"If you ever need to talk...about that...or anything, just tell me. I will listen," Rowan said.

"Thanks," Joshua said. "Same for you. I will listen, too."

"I know you will," Rowan said, and she flashed a smile. Then, she turned around and walked away...for real that time.

Joshua stood still for a moment. The scene he had just described to Rowan played through in his head but was interrupted by: "Joshua! You're still here?"

Joshua jumped, for he had been in a different world. He turned around and there stood his boss, Isabelle. "I thought you left 10 minutes ago."

"Oh," Joshua said, looking at Isabelle. "I did...but...um...as I was leaving, I saw a friend, and we started talking. But I'm going now, goodbye."

"Goodbye, Joshua," Isabelle said.

Joshua walked away.

That evening, Mr. Abare's family was coming to visit. Both of his brothers were in town, for the first time since all of the cousins were born, so they were all going to get together at the Abare's house.

Chapter 81: Disappointed

Joshua got an invitation to National Honor Society (NHS), and he had to fill out a 14-page application form just to be *considered.* It took him a lot longer than he expected it would. In addition, he was running out of time to finish his summer homework. He had to read a whole book and write an essay, and he only had about one more week to do so. After that, he had to read another book, but he was going to wait until the swim season was done to do that.

But swimming was coming to an end quickly. The state meet came, and then it was over like a blink of the eye. Joshua still had one more week left of swim lessons, then he would hardly have a break, only three days (really two because he had to work at the "Pirate Party"), until cross country was going to begin.

Joshua was nervous about cross country. With swimming and work, even though he would get home between 12 and 1, he was always so tired when he got home. With that and the fact that he didn't run for about six weeks because he was sick, he hardly got out on any runs. Now that swimming was over and cross country was coming, Joshua knew that he needed to really focus on running. But he wasn't doing so well. He was dreading the first day of practice because he didn't want his coach to see all of the progress he had lost. He was running a 5k in 27 minutes, whereas he used to be able to run them in 19 minutes.

So, cross country began. The team was going to be a lot smaller that year.

Kendall was going to join the cross country team because she was now a freshman. That would be the first time Joshua and Kendall would be on the same team, for Kendall never did cross country when Joshua was in middle school.

The first few practices went just as Joshua had expected them to go. He did not run very fast. He and Kendall both missed the first meet because they were in Massachusetts. Then, school began.

***

Joshua saw Herman in the hallways when he arrived at school the first day, and when they locked eyes, Joshua could tell that Herman had *not* gotten over anything that had happened at the end of last year and beginning of summer. He also saw Rowan once, and although they didn't talk, they still acknowledged each other with a toothless smile.

After school, Joshua and Kendall both had cross country practice. It was hot out, with the sun shining bright overhead. It was interval day; they were going to run 400-meter repeats out in the open field, where there was no shade. Joshua got grouped with three other boys, and he could not stay with them, but the other ones were all running right together. They'd always wait for Joshua though, and they would never say anything to him about the fact that he was behind. In fact, they were probably the three most supportive boys on the team.

But Joshua was still disappointed that he couldn't stay with them.

When they got home that day, Leah was excited to tell Joshua and Kendall about her own first day of cross country practice. She was in fifth grade, so it was the first year that she was eligible. She said that she was able to run faster than a lot of people, so she couldn't wait for the first meet. She said she might even be able to beat Joshua. She was also excited to announce that she was going to start playing the glockenspiel.

***

Joshua and Kendall were standing together waiting to go to class when one of Joshua's worst nightmares came true. It was Herman entering the building with Bryan and Tucker at his side. He immediately saw Joshua standing there. Herman smirked and walked over to him. When he got to him, he pushed him, saying, "Welcome back, Joshua!" Joshua's hands flew up in the air as he hit the wall. Laughter filled his ears as he opened his eyes to see the three boys walking away while high-fiving each other.

Joshua couldn't look at Kendall, but she said to him

anyway, "So...I see that your rivalries didn't end in seventh grade."

"Nope, guess not," Joshua said, crossing his arms. But then he said, "But it's different now."

"Oh yeah? How's that?" Kendall asked. "Because they haven't tried to kill you?"

Joshua rolled his eyes. "Because I didn't push first this time."

"That's good."

"Yeah. It is."

It was time to go to class. Joshua and Kendall had the same one. They were both going to Latin I. When Joshua was a freshman, he didn't realize that he needed to take two years of a language for college, and now that he only had two years left, he had to begin. He also warned Kendall that she would need to take one and that she should take one as a freshman. So they both decided to take Latin, even though they took Spanish in middle school. Now, they were in the same class.

They walked into the classroom together, and one of their classmates, who was a first-time cross country senior, said, "Wow! Joshua and Kendall are in this class, too! The whole cross country team is in this class!" And although it was not completely true, it wasn't a very far-fetched exaggeration. There were two freshmen girls and a freshman boy that were both on the team. And there was also a freshman boy who was a part of the team but couldn't run, named Isaiah. Then of course the two Abares and the senior. Magistra Borden, the teacher, began doing attendance when the bell went off. She went in alphabetical order, which meant that she came to the

Abares first, but even though he wasn't the only Abare in the class now, Joshua was still the first one to be said.

"Joshua Abare," Magistra Borden said.

"Here," Joshua said, raising his hand.

"Salvē," Magistra Borden said. Next name: "Kendall Abare."

"Here," Kendall said. She was sitting behind Joshua.

Magistra Borden looked at Kendall, then at Joshua, then she said, "Are you two related?"

"Yeah, we're siblings," Joshua answered.

"Are you twins?" Magistra Borden asked.

"No," Joshua answered. "I'm a junior."

"And I'm a freshman," Kendall added.

"Oh, okay," Magistra Borden said, then she continued to go through the attendance. After that, she began to get on with Latin things.

Chapter 82: Application Accepted

Joshua's first 5k did not go as he had hoped, but after the meet he went to watch a college race that had some of his old teammates on it. The freshman Isaiah was also there, and Joshua ended up talking to him. They became friends at that meet, and they started to sit with each other in Latin. Kendall sat with them too because she wanted to sit with Joshua, since she didn't know anyone else in the class very well yet.

Joshua tried to work hard in practice because he knew that even if he couldn't get back to where he was when he was a freshman without much preseason work, he could at least improve from where he was the day before. He worked hard at practice, and after one day where he did intervals, he was feeling exceptionally proud of himself, but then that night, he began developing a sore throat, and he woke up the next day feeling really sick, so he didn't run.

***

"Joshua, you've got mail," Kendall said. He was laying on

his bed reading the Bible. It was his third time reading it all the way through since he started reading it during COVID in eighth grade. He had his door wide open, and Kendall stepped in and threw an envelope at his bed. It landed on the end, right by his feet.

"Thanks," Joshua said.

Joshua left it there until he had finished his chapter. Then, he set the Bible down and picked up the envelope. He opened it and unfolded the letter inside. It began with "Dear Joshua Abare." Then, he began reading: "Congratulations! You have been accepted into our chapter of National Honor Society! Included in this envelope is a paper with agreements to joining NHS. Please sign it and return it to the office by next Friday if you would still like to join."

"Yes!" Joshua exclaimed. He quickly pulled out his phone (which he had gotten since seventh grade) and texted his friend Ryan, who he had met during his AP U.S. History class. He had also applied. Joshua asked, *"Did you get a letter from NHS?"*

After about 10 minutes, Ryan responded, *"Yes! I did! I got in! Did you?"*

Joshua responded, *"Yes!"*

Joshua signed the paper after reading the agreement. At supper, he told his family the news, and they were all very excited. Joshua explained that he would need to complete at least one community service project each month, and he would need to attend a meeting at 7:30 every third Wednesday morning of the month.

Chapter 83: Too Much

Joshua woke up to the taste of paper. Groggily, he sat himself up and looked around. He was sitting at his desk. In front of him, his window showed that it was dark outside. On his desk was his pre-calc homework. He looked to his right and saw the clock, which read 2:36 A.M. He wasn't sure exactly when he fell asleep, but as he sat there trying to realize what was going on, he could remember doing his homework and hearing his parents telling him goodnight as they went to bed themselves. He must've fallen asleep shortly after.

That day had been a busy day. Joshua signed up for the PSAT at the beginning of the month. He spent all of his free time at school studying for that, so he didn't do any of his homework during enrichment (study hall). After school, he had cross country practice. When he got home, he worked out: strength training. He had been starting to do that because he thought if he could get stronger, he would get better at running. After being sick, he had not improved his 5k.

After working out, he took a shower. Then, he ate supper. After that, he studied more for the PSAT, then he started his homework. He had to read a chapter of a book about writing for his AP Lang class; and he had to pick out stocks for a stock market game in Personal Finance; and he had to write 10 metaphors for Creative Writing, which was a lot harder and more time consuming than he thought; then finally, he had to do his pre-calc homework. On top of that, he had to pray the Rosary and read the Bible. Now, it was 2:36, and he still had to finish his pre-calc (from the looks of it, he hadn't gotten very far before falling asleep), and he still had to pray and read the Bible.

He hadn't even had time to write or play his instruments, which was another thing—since he hardly played his instruments between seventh grade and freshman year due to "musician's block," he was falling behind. He was now trying to pick himself up from that too, but he wasn't going to play his instruments at 2:36 in the morning.

This wasn't the first day that he had fallen asleep doing his homework, either. This was the third time that week, and it was only Wednesday! He didn't know how he was going to manage. At the end of the month, he was starting swim team! That winter, he was going to do both swim team and Nordic! He had done that last year, but back then, he was only a sophomore. He wasn't a sophomore anymore—he was a junior—and he wasn't sure how to balance his work.

Joshua continued to do his pre-calc, his eyes fluttering open and closed. He wanted so bad to get it done. He finished it, not sure what exactly he had done. He prayed the Rosary, that day being the Glorious Mysteries, then he read a chapter of the Bible. He finished around 3:15. He set the Bible down and fell asleep in his bed without putting on his blankets, without changing into his jammies, and without brushing his teeth. He forgot to set his alarm, but he woke up at 5:00 when Leah and Ava got up and noisily walked past his bedroom, which he had left cracked open because he had been too tired to shut it after he finished reading the Bible.

Joshua laid awake for about an hour, then he fell asleep only for about another hour before Kendall came and opened the door to tell him that he needed to get up. A similar thing had happened the rest of the week.

Reluctantly, Joshua got up.

That night, Kendall told Joshua not to work out. She told him that he needed to get proper sleep, and that was more important than working out if he wanted to get better. Whenever she saw him in the hallways, he looked like a zombie because he was staring absentmindedly with his hands in his pockets. But he was overtired and just got mad instead of listening to her.

To make matters worse, the next day at lunch, Landon told Joshua, "I think I'm going to do Indoor Track this year."

"In *addition* to Nordic?" Joshua asked.

"No. *Instead* of Nordic."

"What!? No! You can't! Why can't you do both?"

"Because! I don't have the energy for that."

"Neither do I, nor the time, but I'm still doing two sports."

"Which ones?"

"Nordic and swimming."

"Oh yeah."

"I'm going to be sad if I don't get to do any sports

with you."

"Do Indoor Track."

"I can't! I already have two sports! I don't know how I'm going to handle them both. I can barely handle one!"

"Then don't do Nordic or swimming. Do Indoor Track."

"I can't do that, either. I've already committed, and even if I hadn't, I couldn't give them up. If I could do three, I would, but I can't."

"My mind's made up. I'm doing Indoor Track."

"*And* Nordic."

"No."

"Does this mean you're going to do Outdoor Track?"

"No."

"Why!?"

"Because I do lacrosse!"

"What event are you even going to do?" Joshua crossed his arms, thinking he'd won.

"Javelin."

"They don't even have javelin in Indoor." He knew it.

"They don't? Why not?"

"Because...you should do Nordic, that's why."

"I'm serious."

"Okay, okay. Seriously, it's probably to do with space. They don't have discus either, which is a rip-off because discus is my favorite. But it's probably because they don't have room for people to throw as far as discus and javelin," Joshua explained.

"Oh," Landon said. "I don't know what I'm going to

do, but I will find something."

"You can't leave me alone with Arthur!" Joshua cried. "Last year, he wacked me with his pole until I fell into the ditch just because I didn't want to take a break."

"Oh, that's aggressive, but I'm sorry. I'm not doing Nordic anymore. It's horrible," Landon said.

Joshua crossed his arms again, but he didn't say anything more. There was nothing that he could say. Landon had clearly made up his mind, and so had Joshua.

That night was Friday. Joshua was exhausted. He had less homework than usual, though he was going to a thing at the library with Ryan. He didn't have time to work out, and when he got home, he did homework. The next day was his birthday and a cross country meet, so he wasn't going to do any additional work.

Chapter 84: Hellos and Goodbyes

"You're moving!?" Joshua cried.

"Yeah," Teagan answered.

"When?"

"Next week."

"All the way to Florida!?"

Teagan nodded.

"Ah, man! But I'm going to miss you."

"Ah, Joshua. I'll miss you, too. But I certainly won't miss this upcoming season."

"Winter?"

"Yeah."

"We've got to hang out before you leave."

"I'm going to go watch the Homecoming and Powder Puff game this weekend, do you want to go, too? We can hang out then."

Joshua agreed to that. He had already been planning on it because he wanted to get *more involved.* When he got there, Teagan wasn't there yet. Landon was there, and Joshua wanted to sit with him, but there wasn't enough room. In fact, there wasn't anymore room in the student section at all. Joshua had to sit on the opposite side of the staircase, alone. There were a few people scattered on that side, but not many. Joshua felt so embarrassed. He sat alone, waiting for Teagan to arrive.

It was about 15 minutes before the game began that Teagan arrived. By then, the bleachers where Joshua was sitting had filled up compared to what they had been when Joshua first went over there. And at that point, everyone was standing.

Teagan was with a couple of his friends when he arrived, which made Joshua feel comforted. He couldn't stand being alone. Right after they arrived, the players all went onto the field, and they began to say their names. Joshua knew about half of the team.

After that, Joshua hardly paid attention to the game. He talked to Teagan most of the time, until Teagan went to get food. Joshua hadn't brought enough money to get food, so he didn't go with him. While Teagan was gone, a boy new to Joshua's enrichment, who was standing in the stands in front of him, turned around and said, "Hey, Joshua, right?" But when he said his name, he said it more like: *Yossua.*

"Yeah," Joshua replied. "Adrian?"

"Yeah."

"Hi."

"Do you have ChatChat or Instaface?"

"Yeah, I have both."

"Can I have it?"

"Sure."

Joshua pulled out his phone and added Adrian on both. By the time they finished, Teagan was back, but Joshua and Adrian talked a little bit more. They had talked once before during enrichment, and Joshua thought Adrian was nice. He was an exchange student from Spain.

At the end of the game, Joshua asked Adrian if he was going to go to the Powder Puff game, and he said he was, so they talked again then.

That week during enrichment, Joshua started to talk to Adrian. With the exception of one time, Joshua and Adrian used to sit at the same table but not talk to each other at all. Now, they started talking. One day, Joshua went to a going away party for Teagan during enrichment. That was Teagan's last day of school.

The Monday after Teagan left, Joshua started swim team. Both swimming and cross country were at Hard'Ack. So after he finished running, he walked over to the pool. He didn't get home until eight o'clock. He decided to finally listen to Kendall and not work out, but swimming was like a substitute for that. He still didn't get to bed until almost midnight.

He had swim practice again Tuesday, and he was on a similar schedule. This time, though, he was so tired from the lack of adequate sleep the night before that he fell asleep doing homework again. That time, he wasn't in his bedroom when he fell asleep. He was in the dining room, sitting at the kitchen counter.

To make matters worse, Joshua's first NHS meeting was the next morning. He had to be at school for 7:30 instead of 8:10. That was the time that he had gone to school last year, 7:30, but now, his body was adjusted to 8:10. And, he didn't get into his bed until after 2:30. He was so tired, and he was sore from getting back into the pool. He wasn't sure why. He never felt sore anymore after starting a new sport, but he did this time. His head hurt from being overtired and probably dehydration, and he forgot to eat breakfast that morning. His first class that day was pre-calc.

Joshua sat at his desk with a pounding headache, sore legs, and a grumbling stomach. His eyes struggled to stay open as he wrote endless equations on his worksheet. He used to enjoy math, but now he didn't really care about it. He needed a break.

Then, as if someone had poured ice-cold water over his head, he was awoken from his trance. The sound of creaking floorboards caused him to look up, and he saw *him* standing there. He was no longer falling asleep, but his stomach hurt worse, and he started to feel lightheaded.

His teacher looked up from her computer at the boy standing in the doorway and said, "Hi. Are you looking for Mrs. Childs?"

"Yes. I'm Kole. I'm supposed to be in pre-calc right now."

"Hi, Kole. Welcome to pre-calc!"

"Thanks. Sorry that I'm late. I got lost."

"It's okay; I understand. Find a seat, and I will get you a worksheet."

"Okay."

Chapter 85: Reaquainted

Joshua was no *longer in pre-calc but in his front yard. It was getting dark, and Kole stood in front of him. They were having a heated conversation, and Kole was saying, "Because I'm not* gullible.*"*

Joshua, upset, cried, "I'm not *gullible," and he pushed Kole. He quickly learned the mistake in that, as Kole pushed him back. Joshua hit the ground, and suddenly, he was nearing the end of the fight.*

He heard someone shouting, "HEY!" But he wasn't listening, and neither was Kole. He heard someone, multiple people, shouting, "BREAK IT UP! BREAK IT UP!"

Joshua was sitting on the ground, looking up to see Patrick, Kole, Maverick, Aiden, and Reese all standing in front of him. They all frowned and started to walk away.

It was the day after Thanksgiving, and he was sitting in his room, jamming on his saxophone, his bruised body still suffering from the fight, when he heard a knock on his door. It was Kendall to tell him that someone was there. When he came out, she told him it was Aiden.

Joshua answered the door, and he listened to Aiden tell him that he was sorry, unaware of the ulterior motive in his words as he brought him to Tony's Taco

Bar, acting sincere.

After a nearly silent walk, they arrived at the Taco Bar, and obliviously, Joshua asked, "Should we get a table?"

But Aiden wasn't himself. He was nervous, and Joshua quickly learned why as Kole stepped out in front of him. A shiver rushed down Joshua's back as he looked at Kole. Reese and Maverick were there all over again. Joshua found himself shouting at Aiden, "I thought I could trust you! You said you were sorry!"

Aiden gave the excuse, "I am *sorry, Joshua! I didn't know Reese was going to be here! I* really *am sorry!"*

It wasn't enough. Joshua relived his whole conversation with Aiden before he stormed out of the Taco Bar. But he didn't make it far before the others caught him and teased, pushed, and punched him.

Joshua remembered again finding Kendall in the staircase with Kole, tears streaming down her face. His stomach did somersaults as he remembered that Kendall now went to high school, too.

"Wow. Funny we would meet here," Kole said. It was the end of a long day, and Joshua was exhausted from Kole's torment. He was standing in the park near his house as the snow began to pick up and the sun began to go to bed. Joshua just wanted to go home, but Kole wouldn't let him. Instead, the event turned into a fight that even Carson got pulled into. He was saved by Daniel and Caiden.

Joshua remembered when Aiden showed up at his house

to rant about what Kole had done to him as if Joshua had never known Kole's falseness before. It was as if they thought they were bringing Joshua news, but they weren't. Joshua was already quite aware.

Joshua's head was pounding again, and he was laying on his bed. The phone was ringing, and Reese was on the other side. But Reese just wanted to hand him over to Maverick. Joshua wouldn't take it, so he hung up the phone, but they called again, showing him that there was no escape. After he hung up the second time, he took some Ibuprofen because he knew that he was about to suffer the consequences of trusting Reese.

He remembered opening the door to Kole and Reese and the others standing outside. The cold air slapped him in the face. Kole and Maverick grabbed his arms and pulled him outside where they dragged him to his eventual doom.

Then, Joshua was there, at the place, and it was the *fight,* the *final moment.*

"Would you like to do the honors?" Kole asked Maverick.

"Sure," Maverick answered, with a huge smile.

Joshua was on his feet. He stood shivering. He looked like he was going to run but wasn't able to move fast enough. Kole grabbed onto Joshua's arms, and Joshua thought he might be able to break free, but Kole squeezed him so tight that he couldn't.

"Wow, Joshua. I thought you were a swimmer. Aren't they supposed to be strong? Must be you're just not

one of that kind," Maverick said, standing in front of him.

Kole pushed Joshua, and although he stumbled, he didn't fall. Joshua tried to run, but he could hardly move. Kole grabbed onto his right arm, his dominant arm, and Joshua cried out loud, "No! Let me go! Please!"

But Kole didn't listen. He threw Joshua to the ground and kicked him. Maverick joined him. Joshua tried to crawl away, but they kept kicking him, and he lost all feeling. "Kole," he cried, but the boys didn't stop.

After a few seconds and many kicks, he was barely conscious. He heard Patrick say, "Come on, Kole! He's had enough! This is insane!"

Joshua felt a blow to his head, and everything went dark.

And that was Joshua's final memory with Kole. That was the last time that he had seen him until he saw him standing in the doorway of his pre-calc class. And that's where Joshua was brought back to. He was back to sitting in pre-calc.

Kole looked around the room. His eyes laid on Joshua, but just as quickly as they settled, they moved away again. It was as if they had never met each other before.

Joshua's mind was racing for the rest of class, dreading the bell—when everyone would be set free, making him vulnerable.

It finally came, and Joshua slowly picked up his papers and put them into his folder. When he looked up, Kole was leaving the classroom. He put his folder in his bag and left the room. Kole was nowhere to be seen, already gone.

Joshua's heart was pounding, butterflies were fluttering madly in his stomach, and his legs felt like they were about to collapse. He went to the bathroom and closed himself into a stall. He breathed heavily looking down at the water below. He thought he might throw up. Visions of his last fight were playing over and over again in his head. It was like he was there again, but this time, it wasn't happening just once, it was happening over and over again. Joshua could feel Maverick punch his face, feel his knuckles, feel the blood gushing. He could feel Kole's hands wrapped around his wrists. He could feel the cold air burning his bare skin. He was trapped in an endless loop of memories until suddenly he was lying on the floor of the bathroom. He looked up and saw Adrian standing there.

"Joshua? What happened?"

Joshua was still breathing heavily as Adrian helped him get to his feet.

"Are you okay?" Adrian asked.

"No," Joshua said, still breathing heavily, hardly back in reality.

"What happened?" Adrian's eyes widened.

Joshua was quiet for a second, then he said, "Sorry. I lost myself there for a second. I'm okay now."

But Adrian was holding Joshua up in fear that he might fall over because he was shaking so hard. "No, you're not," Adrian said. "I know we hardly know each other, but you can tell me what's going on. You're not a druggy, are you?"

"No! No!" Joshua exclaimed. "I'm not a druggy! I just...ah...it's...there's this person...and I knew him in seventh grade. We didn't exactly get along." Joshua stopped talking. His head hurt. He saw in his head vividly the reenactment of Kole arriving at his door that cold, cold day. Adrian couldn't tell what was going on inside Joshua's head, but he could tell by how much his body was trembling that he was deeply troubled. He thought maybe Joshua was about to pass out again, so he readjusted him in his arms in case he did.

Joshua looked at the bathroom wall, trying to focus on the present. "He wouldn't leave me alone...and one day, I almost died. Shortly after, he disappeared, and I never thought I'd see him again. Even to this day, I didn't think I had fully recovered from it, but when I saw him again, I realized I was right. I'm *not* fully recovered."

"Woah," Adrian said. "So you saw him again?"

"Yeah." Joshua felt a tear forming in his eye. "He..." His voice broke, but he continued his sentence, ignoring the cracking in his voice, "...walked into my pre-calc class. Oh, Adrian! He's in my pre-calc class! I don't know what I'm going to do!"

"What exactly did he do to you?"

"I'd really rather not talk about it. Not now, at least. Maybe another time and another place."

"Okay. I understand."

They both paused for a moment, then Joshua stood himself up. Adrian still thought he was going to pass out.

His face was white.

"I guess I should get to class," Joshua said.

"Are you ready to?" Adrian asked, raising one of his eyebrows.

"No. But what choice do I have?"

"Maybe you should go to the nurse or something."

"No. They would just give me a cracker and say I'm fine. It would be better to go to the guidance counselor."

"Oh. We don't have guidance counselors in Spain. Maybe you should go there, then."

"No. I don't want to. Then I have to talk about it."

"So, you really think you can go to class?"

Joshua shrugged.

"I can walk you there."

"Okay."

So, Adrian walked with Joshua to his class. Joshua told Adrian about some of the things Kole had done on the way. When they were almost there, Adrian said to Joshua, "Wow, that sounds pretty bad. Why won't you go see the guidance person?"

"Because I didn't want to bring that here. I wanted it to stay behind me in middle school," Joshua told him.

"But it seems like it's not behind you. You still seem very upset about it."

"Yeah, I am. But...it's all my fault, anyway. I pushed first. And it was Kole's birthday when I did it. Kole tried to be my friend, but I was just too stubborn. And it was just like...middle school. Everyone is awkward in middle school. They wouldn't understand. And plus, I'm fine. I can handle it on my own."

"Is that why I found you laying on the *bathroom*

floor?"

Joshua didn't respond.

"I'm just saying."

"Do you understand?"

"Yes, of course! My English isn't *that* bad!"

"No." Joshua laughed a little. "I don't mean because of your English. I mean because I wasn't always the most tolerable person. Do you understand my side?"

"Bro, he almost killed you! And it is *not* just because of middle school. And who cares if you pushed first? It sounds like he was pretty awful to you."

"Yeah, you're right."

"Listen, whatever happens between you and him, I'm here."

"Thanks."

"Um...for this year, anyway."

Joshua smiled, then he walked away because he had arrived at his class. His teacher probably would have asked him if he had a hall pass if it weren't for the fact that his face was still extremely pale.

His next class was band, and although he could hear Kole's antagonizing voice in his head as he set up his instrument, he knew he wasn't the musician he used to be in seventh grade, so that somehow made it better.

Joshua was always excited when he realized that he got to go to band next, except he was a little bit disappointed in himself everytime he got there. Due to his musician's block, he was starting to lose his talent. He got second saxophone (out of two), and he got third trumpet (out of three). It was a disaster, and he felt so bad about it. He tried to get better, but he just didn't have the time. He barely had the time to do the things that he was already doing.

***

Kendall was on her way to her enrichment. The hallways were so crowded, and people were always riding her heels. She walked aimlessly, as traffic was too slow for her to be concentrated in it. She was walking along when she suddenly froze. When she stopped, the person walking behind her ran into her and snapped, "Hey! What'd you stop for!?"

But Kendall didn't hear them. She was too busy staring at what caused her to stop. He was even taller than he was in middle school. He didn't seem to notice her, and if he did, he didn't acknowledge her. But she kept staring at him until he was gone. Once he was out of sight, Kendall sped to her enrichment. When she got to class, she sat down in her seat but didn't move. After a minute, her tablemate, named Kennedy, said to her, "Kendall, are you okay?"

"Huh? Oh, yeah. I'm good," she said, stumbling over her words. Then, she pulled out her math homework, but even though it lay in front of her, under her pencil, she didn't do any of it. She sat there, her mind back in fifth grade.

Chapter 86: Old Traumas

The Abares sat at their dining room table eating supper. Leah and Ava both spoke excitedly about their day, but Joshua and Kendall were both silent. Neither one of them had come to each other about seeing Kole during their day. Kendall was almost certain that Joshua had seen him because he had barely spoken since he got home. On the other hand, Joshua was unaware that Kendall knew anything about Kole being there.

After Leah and Ava finished telling of their day, Mr. Abare turned to Joshua and Kendall and said, "Joshua, Kendall, how was your day?"

Joshua didn't look up. He was pushing a piece of meat around on his plate with his fork. He had hardly eaten anything.

Kendall watched Joshua for a moment, then she looked at her dad and said, "Kole's back."

"Kole!" Mr. Abare exclaimed. "Oh, really?"

Joshua's head perked up, and he looked at Kendall. "You saw him?"

"Yeah," Kendall said.

Tears started running down Joshua's eyes. He couldn't hold them in any longer. They had been fighting him all day long, and now they had finally won. "I can still remember the fight, and all of his other torments, so vividly. It's as if it all happened just yesterday! And now, it could happen all over again tomorrow, or the next day, or any day because he's back." Joshua pushed himself away from the table and said, "I'm not hungry. I'm tired. I'm going to go lay down."

"Joshua!" Kendall cried.

"*Kendall*, it's okay. We'll take care of it," Mrs. Abare said quietly, as Joshua walked away.

"But..." Kendall cried. She looked at Joshua's plate, then she crossed her arms and sat still, staring at the table in front of her.

Chapter 87: Too Tired

The next day, Joshua made it through pre-calc. Kole sat in the back of the room, and Joshua sat in the front, so they didn't talk at all. In fact, Joshua hardly noticed that Kole was there since Kole was *behind* him. He'd have to look back to see him, which he decided not to do. Other than that, he saw Kole once in the hallway, but Kole didn't see him then. The reason for that was he was talking to Maverick. Maverick looked so happy, unlike any way that Joshua had ever seen him before. Following behind Kole and Maverick was a boy on crutches. That boy was totally unrelated to them; he just went along with the trend in the school—it seemed like everyone was on crutches. Mostly football and soccer players were the victims of sprained ankles and torn knees, but some of the injuries weren't from those sports.

That afternoon, Joshua nearly fell asleep during chemistry. It was his last class of the day, so he was always tired for it. Last night, he slept worse than normal. In fact, he didn't really sleep that much at all. He barely got any homework done, so now he had ruined his perfect *Transferable Skills* scores in two of his classes that he had that day. He couldn't do his homework because he was hungry, but whenever he tried to eat, his stomach hurt.

And then after he finally could eat, he couldn't do his homework because he kept playing reruns in his head from seventh grade when Kole was there. Then, he couldn't sleep because he refused to go to bed until his homework was done. He fell asleep a couple of times at his desk, but that was all the sleep he got until about five in the morning when he finally gave up and laid in his bed for an hour and a half.

Joshua didn't know how he was going to make it through cross country practice. Thankfully, it was not interval day, but still, he could barely stay awake to do his chemistry work, so how was he supposed to *run*?

When he got to practice, after changing, he talked to Isaiah. They started talking before practice every day ever since they talked at the college meet. Isaiah still wasn't running because of his own injury. It didn't require him to be on crutches, but he had to wear a giant boot on his foot.

Pretty soon, it was time to get running. First, the whole team would stretch, then they would go off and do their run. Some people would run with one or a few other people, whereas others would just run by themselves. Joshua was one of the ones to run by himself. He didn't listen to any music either, as many people did. He would just run in silence. He would take his phone with him in his fanny pack so that he would know how far he was running and how fast.

After stretching, he started his phone, then he began running. He was tired, and any progress that he had made over the season suddenly was lost. Every time he lifted his foot off the ground, it was like it was stuck in a giant wad of gum. Every hill he embraced was like a mountain. He had only gone a mile, and his ankles began to feel like rubber. He went on one of the middle trails that was covered in rocks. His mind must have gone astray, probably thinking about Kole...or his lack of sleep, which still had to do with Kole...because he suddenly found himself on the ground.

He had stepped on a loose rock and didn't realize it. Now, he was on his hands and knees. He picked his hands up off the ground and looked at them. They were dirty, of course, but the dirt was mixed with blood. He pulled himself to his feet, but as he began to put weight on his right side, he felt immense pain in his ankle, and he fell back to the ground. This time, he cringed in pain because his knees were all bloody, too.

His ankle...it was sprained.

Joshua opened his fanny pack and pulled his phone out. He called Isaiah. It rang three times before he answered with: "Hey?"

"Um..." Joshua said. He was now sitting on the ground with his legs out in front of him. Blood was starting to drip down the sides of his knees. His ankle was throbbing. "I can't walk."

"Good," Isaiah replied. "This is cross country running, not cross country walking."

"No!" Joshua exclaimed. He let out a small laugh. "I think I sprained my ankle. I *really* can't walk. Can you get Coach? Please!"

"Yeah, sure," Isaiah said, surprised. "Where are you?"

"I'm at the bottom of the massacre."

"I don't know where that is."

"That's okay; Coach does."

"Okay."

After a minute's pause, Isaiah said, "They're coming."

"Okay, thank you."

"Are you going to be okay?"

"Yeah, I'm fine, but I don't think I'm going to be doing much running for a little bit. I guess I will have to stand around all of practice with you."

"Yay!"

Joshua's mind was on the phone, so he jumped as he heard someone say his name: "Joshua."

He looked over, and he saw Avery (Arthur's friend), Jordan (Avery's brother), and Mac (their friend). They were walking towards him.

"What happened?" Avery asked.

"Gotta go," Joshua said into the phone. He hung up, then looked at Avery and replied, "I tripped."

"Are you okay?"

"Yeah."

"Then why are you still sitting on the ground?"

"I mean...no...I...um...I sprained my ankle. Isaiah sent Coach to come find me because I can't stand up."

"We can help you get to your feet until he's here."

"Thanks. The ground's not very comfortable."

"I agree."

All three of the boys came over to Joshua and grabbed him under his shoulders. They pulled him onto his feet and held him up so that he didn't have to put any pressure on his right ankle.

They had just gotten Joshua situated over their shoulders when they heard their coaches, Coach Michaels and Coach Trainer, coming towards them on a four-wheeler that they borrowed from the lodge. Joshua felt his face turn red. It was embarrassing to him for his coaches to see him like this, and the fact that they went this far was even more embarrassing. Joshua looked down at his feet, but that just made him feel more embarrassed because then he saw the blood.

"Looks like you've had quite the fall," Coach Michaels said, hopping off the four-wheeler.

"Yeah," Joshua said. "I can't walk. I can't even stand."

"I see that," Coach Michaels said.

Both of his coaches took his arms and put them over their shoulders, then they walked him to the four-wheeler. They cleaned up his knees and then drove him back. His mom was there when they arrived because Coach Michaels had called her.

The event ended in Joshua getting crutches.

Chapter 88: Bathroom Door

One of the first problems Joshua came across with crutches was opening the bathroom door at school. He would try to open the door, but once he would get a little bit opened, he would drop his crutch, and it would close shut. He was currently in the stage when his crutch fell to the ground, and he was about to pick it up when suddenly someone else picked it up for him.

Joshua looked up at the person holding his crutch, and his heart started pounding. There stood Kole Jackson with his crutch in his hand.

"Please, don't hurt me," Joshua cried. "Look, I'm already injured!"

"Relax," Kole said, smiling. He handed Joshua his crutch and opened the bathroom door. "Dude, you look awful."

"That's because I am...I mean...I *feel* awful," Joshua said.

But Joshua still hadn't moved, and Kole was still holding the door open, so Kole said, "You can go into the bathroom, isn't that what you were trying to do?"

"Yeah," Joshua said. He looked at Kole for a minute, his heart still racing, then he started to go into the bathroom.

They both did their business and finished at the same time. Kole helped Joshua with the door again. Kole walked ahead of Joshua, for he didn't go very fast on crutches yet. Just then, Kendall came up the stairs and saw Kole walking ahead of Joshua.

"Joshua?" Kendall asked. She rushed over to Joshua and said, "Are you okay!?

"Yeah, I'm fine." Joshua was watching Kole walk away.

"Really?"

"Yeah, really." Joshua looked away from Kole and at his sister.

"Did he bother you?"

"Who? Kole?"

"Uh...yeah!"

"No. He actually helped me open the bathroom door. That's all."

"Oh. That was...*nice*."

"Yeah."

They continued their own ways. Joshua took forever to get back to his class, but his teacher understood.

Chapter 89: The End to the Cross Country Season

Joshua didn't see Kole for the rest of the day, and the next day (Friday), he only saw him during pre-calc. Both days after school, Joshua went right home instead of cross country practice. He was taking the rest of the week off to get some proper rest. He was able to start his homework right away, and since he didn't have to fight sleep, he was able to get it done in less than an hour. By 4:30, he had finished his homework, prayed the Rosary, and read a chapter from the Bible. If he had gone to cross country and swim practice, he wouldn't even be home yet. Joshua decided to take out his instruments until supper, choosing the saxophone because that was the one he was doing the most in band. He played it for an hour, then it was time for supper.

The next day was the last race before States, and it was at a course that the team had never been on before. It was at a golf course, so Joshua imagined it was probably going to be pretty flat. Even though he wasn't able to run, he was still going to the meet because Kendall was still racing.

Ava was also running—in an elementary school race

that morning. The whole Abare family went in the morning before the team. When the team arrived, a couple of hours after the Abares had got there, it was almost immediately time to walk the course, so Kendall went with the team, and they all left Joshua alone. Even Isaiah went and walked the course.

Joshua sat on the ground while he waited for his team to come back. It took them almost an hour, and Kendall came over to Joshua with a red face to say, "This is the hardest course that I've ever walked. I can't believe I still have to *run* it."

"Oh, really?" Joshua asked.

"Yeah," Kendall cried. "It's all uphill. I don't get it. The uphills outweigh the downhills. How is that even possible? I'm telling you that this is a good race to miss. You chose a good time to sprain your ankle."

"Haha," Joshua laughed.

He then pulled himself to his feet, and the two of them went over to the rest of the team, for Kendall had to get ready for her race that was coming within just a few minutes.

When Kendall went to the start, Joshua and Isaiah together found a place to go watch. They chose to go to the top of the first hill. After all of their teammates had gone through, they went over to the finish where some of their teammates were coming to by the time they got over there with Joshua's slow movement.

When Kendall finally came through the chute, she looked like she was going to collapse, and after she crossed the finish and got away from the course, she laid down on the ground.

Joshua and Isaiah went over to Kendall, and after she had stood up, Joshua said, "It looks like this course was pretty hard, so I guess it *is* a good thing I can't run it. It would just prove to me another way that I have failed myself as a runner."

"Nooo," Isaiah said.

"Actually, I bet *you* would be pretty good at this course. I know what I said, but it was a joke," Kendall said.

"*Really?*" Joshua asked, surprised. "Why do you say that?"

"Because it just seems like a course you'd be good at. Sure, you're not running as fast as you used to, but there are still some strengths that you have held. For example, you are steady and determined. When you run, you treat the whole course the same. All of those uphills, people whine and complain, but you run up it like it's *just another part of the course,*" Kendall said.

"Yeah because it *is* part of the course. Kendall, believe me, my legs are burning just as bad as anyone else's. I'm just...slow," Joshua said.

"Really, you think you're slow? I don't," Isaiah said.

"No! No! You're not slow! And you keep the same pace, even on the uphills," Kendall said. "And that is what you need to do to get through this course. Believe me, as I was running, I was thinking about that...how *you* act as if it's all equal, and so because of that, I kept running."

"Really? *I* kept you running?"

"Yeah!"

"You're just saying that. I'm nothing inspirational."

"I'm *not* 'just saying that.' We all have times when we fall off our spot, but we can get ourselves back up there with a little bit of determination, grit, and patience. You have all three of those, even if you aren't seeing it right now, so I know that you will get back to where you once were running."

Joshua looked down at his ankle that was wrapped up and a little achy from being at the meet all morning. He wanted to make a point that it didn't look like he was going anywhere with his running right now, but he decided that Kendall didn't need more of his disagreement and negativity, so he just looked back up and said, "I hope you're right."

"Throughout my whole life, you have always kept me running. I see you run, and it inspires me," Kendall said.

"Wow," Joshua said, his face turning red. "Thanks."

***

The following weekend was States. Joshua went to practice every day that week and hung out with Isaiah, since it was the last week. They usually did some homework during practice. Afterward, Joshua went to coach the younger swim practice, as he had been planning to do before his injury, but he didn't stay for his practice because he couldn't swim and didn't want to be out late when he didn't need to be and needed rest. He also figured out a plan for himself once he got back to his sports so that he wouldn't be too tired and get injured again. He discovered better time management.

Joshua watched States, then the season was over for JV. That meant Kendall was no longer running, and Joshua didn't have a chance to get back into racing that season. November was upon them.

Chapter 90: Another Encounter

Joshua put his foot into his left sneaker as he announced to the house, "I'm going for a walk!"

"What?" His mom was sitting in the dining room with her back facing the door, but she turned around to face him.

"I'm going for a walk," he repeated.

"Why? You're on *crutches*."

"That's exactly why! I haven't gotten hardly any exercise lately! I need to get ready for Nordic...and swimming...when I am able to do it again."

"*Joshua*, if you want to get ready, then you need to let your ankle heal. That means rest."

"I *have* been resting! Every day! And look! It's not any better! That's why I need to go for a walk now! Last time I *rested*, I added a thousand minutes on my 5k."

"You added *three* minutes."

"Which is a lot when my time was only 19 minutes. Which is a lot when it means I don't get to be on varsity. Which is a lot when I continued to add time onto it throughout the season. Mom! I *need* to get in some exercise."

Mrs. Abare sighed, then she said, "You can't go by yourself."

"Why!? I've been going out by myself since I was Leah's age!"

"Yeah, you've been going out by yourself since you were Leah's age *when you were healthy*. But anything could happen to you when you have a sprained ankle."

"Augh." Joshua looked up at the ceiling.

"What if I go with him?" Kendall walked out from the living room and stood next to Joshua.

"Do you want to?" Mrs. Abare asked.

"I don't mind," Kendall said.

Now, Mrs. Abare sighed, and she said, "Okay. That's fine. But don't go too far."

"Thank you," Joshua said. He threw on his shoe, and so did Kendall, then they walked out the door.

After they had closed the door, Kendall said quietly to Joshua, "Are you sure that this is a good idea?"

"I've been getting pretty good with these, so yes."

"Okay. You're such a try-hard."

"I want varsity back, so yeah, I'm going to try hard."

Kendall smiled. "Yeah, that's why I agreed to go with you."

They had gone pretty far before Joshua said he wanted to turn around. They were on their way back when they found Kole sitting on a bench in front of a bakery. He was eating a cookie.

When Joshua saw him sitting there, he held his breath as he began to walk by, hoping that Kole wouldn't say anything.

But as they walked past, both Joshua and Kendall avoiding eye contact, Kole looked up and said, "Hey, Joshua."

They both stopped walking and turned around to look at Kole. He stood up and walked over to them, setting his cookie down on the bench. "Hey," Kole said again.

"Hey," Joshua replied back, his voice shaking.

The three of them all stood in silence for a moment, all staring at the ground before Kole finally looked up and said, "I...I have something I've been meaning to say. I've been wanting to tell you for about four years."

Joshua looked at him.

"I'm sorry," Kole said. "Like truly sorry."

Joshua raised his eyebrows, but he didn't say anything.

"Look, I don't expect you to believe me. I know that I've said sorry before and turned on you afterward, but it's different this time. I *really* am sorry, and I hope that I can prove that to you," Kole said.

Kendall looked at Joshua who was still quiet. It was just a few seconds, but it felt like minutes, and Kole said, "It's okay if you don't want to say anything. I don't expect that either. This probably comes as a pretty big shocker."

Joshua stared at Kole for a few moments more, then he said, "Thanks, Kole."

"You believe me?"

"We'll see."

"What can I do?"

"Don't beat me up, please." Joshua's voice trembled.

"My days of that are over, but I guess I'd better show you rather than tell you."

Joshua nodded.

Someone was walking toward them, as many people

did, since many people walked the streets throughout the day. This person, though, when she got to them, asked, "What's going on?"

Joshua, Kendall, and Kole looked up to see Reese standing there. Joshua looked toward the road and noticed that her house was within view. When he saw her standing there, he froze. She looked so much different than she did the last time he had seen her. Her hair was shorter, only going to her shoulders. It was a new color, too: black with blond highlights. She was taller than before, about Joshua's height. She was wearing gray sweatpants and a pink t-shirt.

Even though she looked different, Joshua felt goosebumps and said, "Guys, what's going on? Why are you both here? Is this another trap?"

"No way. I'm not here with him," Reese said, looking at Kole and squinting her eyes. She looked back at Joshua and said, "I came over because I could see you from my house, and being that you're on crutches, I thought maybe you were in trouble." Looking back at Kole, she asked again, "What's going on? Why are you two together?"

"We aren't together. I was just sitting here, and he was just walking by. That's all," Kole said.

"Then why are you talking to each other?" Reese asked.

"I'm just trying to apologize," Kole said.

"Really?" Reese asked, looking at Joshua. But Joshua was very pale, and he didn't answer. Reese looked at Kendall, whose eyebrows were facing downward toward her nose. Reese looked at Joshua's crutches and asked,

"What happened?"

"I..." Joshua started to say. He was unable to think because his mind was spinning.

"Cross country incident," Kendall answered.

"Oh," Reese said. "So, it *wasn't* Kole?"

"What!?" Kole snapped. "NO! I said I was trying to *apologize*."

"Come on," Reese said, looking at Kole. "Don't act like that's such a silly accusation. You know what I saw the last time that you were with Joshua. I personally don't think you should be allowed anywhere near him again."

"If I don't recall, you were there too, and you just watched," Kole snapped.

"There's a big difference! I didn't beat him up!"

"A bystander can be just as bad as the bully themself."

"So you admit it? You were the bully?"

"Yeah! At least I can admit that!"

Kendall looked at Joshua. His eyes were blank.

"Guys! Can we *please* not talk about this! You were both bullies! And you were both in the wrong! Now drop it!" Kendall snapped.

"I just want to make things better," Kole said.

"I think the door's closed for that," Reese said.

"Mind your own business!" Kole snapped. "Why'd you even come out here?"

"Because I thought you were going to hurt Joshua!" Reese exclaimed.

"Is that why you ignored him for the past two years!?" Kendall snapped.

Reese was quiet.

Suddenly, Joshua was falling over, and Kendall and Kole both rushed to catch him. As he fell into their arms, Kole exclaimed, "Woah! Woah! Woah!"

"Joshua," Kendall said.

"He's shaking," Kole said.

"Of course he is!" Kendall snapped. "He has P.T.S.D.! You guys bickering over history isn't helping!"

Kole didn't respond.

"Come on, Joshua, let's go home," Kendall said. She helped him stand up. He was still out of it, but he nodded his head. They started heading home, leaving Kole and Reese standing together. The two of them watched the siblings walk away, and after they had gone a good distance, Kole and Reese looked at each other. Kole had a frown, and his stomach hurt. Reese scowled, then she turned around and walked away.

Chapter 91: Changed

Patrick, Kole, and Maverick sat in the back corner of the cafeteria. Normally, Maverick was traveling around the cafeteria trying to impress different table groups with his scandalous behavior, but with Kole back, he chose to stay in one place.

"Maverick, did you know that Joshua has P.T.S.D. because of what we did to him?" Kole asked after a moment of silence where there was nothing else to talk about.

"No."

"Have you...talked...to him at all?"

"Just a little."

"I feel so horrible. I mean, at the time, I thought that I was doing the right thing...well...um...no, I didn't, but I didn't care because I thought he was stupid. But I was wrong. He wasn't stupid. He was *right*."

"He's kind of *different*."

"He's not really all that *different*, he's just more intense than anyone else I know. But I'm glad he is because he helped me learn...even if I put him through so much first."

"You might have learned from him, but I sure know that not everyone he meets has."

"What are you talking about?"

"Do you know Herman?"

"Herman who?"

"I don't know his last name, but I think there's only one Herman at this school."

"Oh. Yeah, I know him a little bit."

"He's not as bad as we were, but he's not exactly nice to Joshua."

"Oh yeah?"

Patrick butted into the conversation with a smile and said, "Did he call Joshua *gullible*? And did Joshua push him?"

"No, actually," Maverick said. "Joshua hasn't pushed Herman once."

"*Really?*" both Patrick and Kole asked at the same time.

"Really," Maverick replied. "In fact, a lot of people think poorly of Joshua because he won't ever push Herman back when he's always pushing him around."

"Why?" Kole asked. His voice was raised slightly.

"They think he's weak," Maverick said. "Are you okay?"

"I just don't get it," Kole said. "Why did Joshua push *me* if he won't push *Herman*? What did I do? I mean, sure...I was pretty bad...but not *before* he pushed me. And Joshua just won't trust me. I held the door for him, and he looked like he thought I was going to punch him if he walked through it."

"To be fair," Patrick added in again, "You were pretty cruel to him. Why should he trust you? You know you've changed, but he doesn't know that."

“Yeah, that’s true, I guess. Augh! I’ve made such horrible mistakes!” Kole cried.

“Why do you care so much? Joshua’s just one person, and there are eight billion other people in this world? So why him?” Patrick asked.

“I made *his* life miserable, not any of those eight billion other people. Well...no...that’s not necessarily true. I’ve made more than just Joshua’s life miserable, but out of everyone in the world, I think I’ve made Joshua’s life the most miserable. And...he’s the one that made me see straight. So, I feel I kind of owe it to him,” Kole explained.

“Owe what to him? I think the only thing you owe him is to leave him alone,” Patrick said.

“I *can’t*. I can’t live my life anymore being the bully. I don’t need to be his friend, but I just don’t want him to think of me as the one who constantly tormented him,” Kole said.

“Have you started by...I don’t know...saying you’re sorry?” Patrick asked.

“Yeah, I’ve tried that,” Kole said. “But...I know from experience...sorry is just a word. You can’t just say you’re sorry; you’ve got to prove you’re sorry. Well, I’m trying! But it’s not working!”

“I get it,” Patrick said.

“It’s going to take time,” Maverick said.

***

That very same afternoon, Joshua sat in the doctor’s office

as he watched the doctor unwrap his ankle. It felt like a sweet, sweet victory. Like he had finally been set free. It was a freedom he had never felt before. As soon as he got home, he went for a run, but it didn't go well. His ankle got tired quickly, as he hadn't been using it for a month, and he wasn't really supposed to run on it yet.

Chapter 92: Broken

Pressed up against the dirty bathroom wall, Joshua felt the medal chain of his necklace digging into the back of his neck as Herman tugged on the cross. Sweat built up on Joshua's forehead. He was stuck with nothing he could do. They were all alone, and if Joshua moved one bit, then his necklace was a goner anyway.

"Herman, please don't," Joshua pleaded.

Herman tugged the cross real hard, and the chain broke right off. Joshua stared at the broken chain for the split second that Herman held it in his hand before throwing it.

"No!" Joshua cried.

The cross necklace flew through the air. The chain detached from the cross, and they both hit the ground in different places. Herman had backed away from Joshua, so Joshua ran toward the stalls and searched inside. He opened one door, and he looked around the floor, standing on his feet. Herman came up behind him and pushed him. Joshua lost his balance and nearly fell right into the toilet. Joshua's ankle was still weak from his injury, being only three days off his crutches.

Joshua ignored Herman, as if he hadn't gotten pushed. He went to the next stall, and the cross wasn't there. Herman pulled on Joshua's arm, trying to pull him to the ground, but he wasn't successful. Joshua pulled away, but Herman was persistent. He pushed Joshua again. This time, Joshua wasn't in one of the stalls anymore, and he hit the stand in between the stalls. He was still for a minute after hitting it, his body in shock, then he continued to look for the cross. He went into the final stall, where he found it pushed up against the wall. Joshua bent over to grab it, and while he was down, Herman pushed him, and he lost his balance, falling to the ground. His forehead hit the toilet seat...*gross*.

Herman kicked Joshua, but Joshua didn't care. He now had the cross in his hand. He crawled under the stall into the next, then he stood up and darted out. Joshua heard the door open, but he paid no attention to who was there. He had one goal: to get out of there.

Herman, being closer to the door than Joshua, stepped out in front of him. But Joshua wanted to get out, so he pushed Herman out of the way. At first, he didn't even realize he did it. Herman was also shocked at this *new* behavior, and so he fell to the ground. Joshua had never pushed him before.

When Joshua saw Herman on the ground, he finally realized what happened, but he was in so much of a hurry to get out of there that he didn't think anything of it. He continued toward the door.

Herman wasn't too surprised that he couldn't come up with a plan in the moment. As Joshua was going for the door, Herman stuck his leg out in front of Joshua's feet, and he tripped. When he hit the ground, the cross flew out of his hand.

The shock delayed Joshua's comprehension for a moment. Once he realized he was on the ground *again*, he saw the cross out in front of him. He stretched his arm out trying to grab it, but he couldn't reach it from where he was. Behind it, he saw the pair of shoes belonging to the person who had just walked into the bathroom. He was about to move across the floor and grab the cross when the owner of the shoes' hand reached down and grabbed it. Joshua looked up and saw Kole standing there.

Kole stepped forward and reached his hand down to Joshua. For a split second, Joshua just stared up at him, but then he realized Kole was sincere, so he grabbed onto his hand, and Kole helped him to his feet.

"Leave him alone," Kole said, looking at Herman with a firm face. Herman still sat on the ground, now looking up at Kole, confused.

Kole walked Joshua outside and handed him the cross. The chain was gone, and Joshua wasn't going back into the bathroom to get it. He felt like crying, between his broken necklace, to being thrown around by Herman, to being saved by *Kole*, but he held it in. They started walking toward Joshua's class.

"I guess I'm not the only bully in town," Kole said.

Joshua's stomach dropped to the floor. "I thought you *aren't* a bully anymore."

"I'm not. But I used to be."

"Oh." Joshua's stomach bounced back to its place.

"Do you get beat up by *everybody* who differs in opinion with you?"

"No. I have a really good friend that doesn't think any of the same things as me."

"Oh. So you've got *one* person." Kole paused. "Sorry about your necklace. It's cool, when did you get it?"

"Beginning of freshman year."

"Oh, nice."

Joshua nodded.

"I saw you pushed Herman in there."

"I...I wasn't even thinking." Joshua frowned. "I just wanted to get out of there, and...he was in my way. I can't believe I did it."

"No, no, it's okay. I was just...observing. Maverick said that you don't push people, even when they push you first."

"Yeah. I *didn't*...but now...I just did."

"You must've been pretty upset."

"Yeah, I was."

"It's a pretty cool necklace and all, but it's just a piece of metal. Why did you get so upset?"

Joshua's voice shook as he spoke. "It represents my religious beliefs—that's why I wear it—so Herman breaking it felt almost as bad as saying he's not gullible."

"Hm..." Kole said, his face turning red. Joshua had never seen it that way.

"And...I was reacting in the moment...so I really wasn't thinking about any of the after-effects. I seem to do that a lot." Joshua's voice was still shaky as he finished speaking, but it was less so than before.

"I can't help but agree." Kole smiled.

"Thank you." Joshua's voice wasn't shaking anymore, but he had not managed to spread a smile across his face.

"Ah, no, *you* don't have to thank *me*. And...I'll be

going. My class is actually the other way."

"Oh, oops."

"One more thing, though."

"What?"

"I go to Church now."

"Really?"

Kole nodded.

"Oh." Joshua had a genuine tone.

Kole turned around, saying bye and leaving Joshua alone. Joshua looked down at the cross in his hand, and suddenly, he was swept away to another place and time.

"Because I'm not gullible,*" Kole said.*

"I'm not *gullible," Joshua said, and he pushed Kole.*

Joshua could hear clearly in his head the sound of his classmate saying, *"It doesn't matter. You still pushed him first. That makes you fair game,"* as if it were a narration to him pushing Kole. The words, all of the words, and Joshua pushing Kole, played over and over again in his head.

Then, Joshua heard Reese say, *"They were never going to inflict violence on you, but then you pushed Kole, so now, war is on."* That wrapped up the whole flashback.

***

Joshua and Kendall rode the bus to the middle school, then they walked home. It felt like the old days, when they were in middle school, walking home together. Whenever they didn't have any sports after school, that was how it went. Joshua was going back to swim practice, but that wasn't until a little bit later.

Joshua and Kendall walked into their house. Mrs. Abare was in the kitchen fixing Leah and Ava a snack. Kendall went and sat at the counter with them, but Joshua remained standing by the door.

"Hey guys," Mrs. Abare said.

They both replied with, "Hey."

"Mom, can I go to the store real quick?" Joshua asked.

"What store?"

"Kelly's Gift Shop."

"Why?"

"My necklace broke, and I need a new chain. I still have the cross, but..."

"We have to leave for swim practice in about an hour."

"I don't want to go."

"Why?"

"Because."

"But...I don't get it. Just last week, you were excited that you were going to be done with your crutches so that you could get back to sports."

"Yeah, I know, but I don't want to go today."

"Why? I still don't get it."

Joshua sighed, then he said, "Fine. I'll go."

"*Joshua.* If there's a reason you don't want to go..."

"No, it's okay. I'll go."

"Okay," Mrs. Abare said, but she didn't make a face like she thought it was okay.

"But...can I go to the gift shop first? Please. I'll be quick and back in time."

"Okay," Mrs. Abare said, still looking like it wasn't actually okay.

Joshua turned around and went back out the door. The gift shop was only a five-minute walk from his house. Joshua had to have help finding what he was looking for, but it didn't take him too long. He was back to his house within half an hour. He got home and put the cross on his new chain, and then he put it back on his neck. Afterward, he sat in the living room and did his homework.

***

Kendall's jaw dropped when Joshua took off his shirt to go into the pool, seeing a giant, blueish-purple bruise on the right side of his torso. He didn't look at her, but he knew that she had seen it. His swim friends also saw it, and they looked surprised, but they didn't say anything to him. He was glad because he didn't want to answer any questions. One of his coaches asked him if he was okay, but they didn't elaborate anymore. He told them he was fine.

Kendall held her question until the car ride home. Mrs. Abare started to drive her and Joshua home, and she said, "Joshua, what happened?"

"What are you talking about?" Joshua snapped.

"Yeah, what are you talking about?" Mrs. Abare asked.

"Don't even, Joshua! He has this giant bruise on his

side! Joshua! You don't need to keep things from me...or any of us! I've been there with you! We've *all* been there with you!" Kendall cried.

Joshua crossed his arms.

"Was it Kole?" Kendall asked.

"No," Joshua replied.

"Was it Herman?" Kendall asked.

"Who's Herman?" Mrs. Abare asked.

"A person," Joshua said, his arms still crossed, his eyes watching out the window.

"He's this person that likes to push Joshua around," Kendall said.

"This time was more than just that," Joshua admitted.

"Did he...*beat you up*?" Kendall asked.

"Um, not exactly. It got physical, but it wasn't exactly what I'd consider getting beaten up," Joshua said.

"Is that why your necklace broke?" Mrs. Abare asked.

"Yeah," Joshua admitted. "He doesn't like that I wear it, so he broke it off my neck *on purpose*. I grabbed the cross, and...I *pushed* Herman, and...he tripped me...and I accidentally threw the cross. And you know who picked it up? Kole. But he wasn't trying to take it. He helped me up, and stood up for me, and gave it back to me...surprisingly."

"Wow," Mrs. Abare said.

"I think...Kole's changed," Joshua said. "But I don't know. He's tricked me into thinking we were friends before, and then we weren't. But I don't know. This feels different."

"People *grow up* between seventh grade and junior year. Maybe Kole has," Mrs. Abare said.

"Yeah, maybe, but I'm still nervous around him. I don't want to get hurt again," Joshua said.

"That's okay. You probably should be. I hope he's sincere, but I'm weary about him, too," Mrs. Abare said.

There was a slight pause before Joshua said, "Kole told me he's been going to *Church*."

"Really?" Kendall and Mrs Abare both asked, at the same time.

"Yeah," Joshua said. "He told me that after we were walking away from the situation with Herman." Suddenly, Joshua's mood changed, and in a clearly distraught tone, he cried, "But...I *pushed* Herman! I've never done that before."

"Would you have any reason to have before?" Mrs. Abare asked.

Joshua paused, then he said, "Yes."

"How long has this been going on for?"

"Kole just got back, so..."

"No. How long has this been going on with you and Herman?"

"Oh...since last year."

"*Last year?* Why am I *just* finding out about it now, then?"

"Because...I was...I don't know...embarrassed."

"You don't have to be embarrassed! I'm your mom!"

"That's kind of why I'm embarrassed to tell you."

"Why?"

"Because...I don't want *you* to see me like this."

"Is this why you didn't want to come to swim

practice?" Kendall asked, chiming back in. "Because you didn't want anyone to see that nasty bruise?"

"Yeah," Joshua admitted.

"It's pretty bad," Kendall said.

"No, it's not that bad," Joshua said.

"It's like the size of my fist," Kendall insisted.

"Actually, it's like the size of Herman's shoe," Joshua admitted.

"He kicked you?" Mrs. Abare asked.

"Yeah," Joshua answered. "And...pushed me...and you know...those kind of things."

"I get it," Mrs. Abare said. "But...I don't want you to keep this from me."

"I know," Joshua said. "I'm sorry." A tear fell from his eye, but it was dark, and he was still looking out the window, so no one saw. For that reason, he let it slide all the way down his cheek and drip off before he wiped its streak away.

Chapter 93: More

Joshua stood the next day waiting to go to his class before school started. He had his new chain around his neck, with the cross dangling over his chest. Kendall had a cold, so she wasn't at school that morning. That left Joshua to stand alone because he didn't find any of his friends waiting.

He didn't like to be alone because it made him feel vulnerable, and pretty quickly, he realized that his feelings were real. He saw Herman walking through the crowd of students, toward him. He tried to walk away, but there was only so far he could go before he was trapped by Herman.

"Why do you run away from me, Joshua? It's like you know you're wrong," Herman said, standing close to him, causing him to back into the wall. "I see you got a new necklace. If you don't stop wearing that, I'm going to turn you into a pretzel!" Herman exclaimed.

Joshua threw his arms straight up into the air into streamline position, and he quickly said, "Look! I already am a pretzel! I'm a pretzel stick!"

"Augh," Herman said, rolling his eyes.

Herman reached his arm toward Joshua's necklace, but Joshua quickly dropped to the ground and rolled onto his side then back, smushing his bag under him, and he stuck his legs up in the air to stop Herman from grabbing onto him. But he knew this would only hold Herman back for a minute. Then, to his surprise, Kole was standing behind Herman.

Kole grabbed onto Herman's arm and pulled him away from Joshua. Joshua sat up but didn't get back onto his feet. He watched in shock and awe.

"What's going on over here?" Kole asked.

Herman spun around to look at Kole in the face. Herman was taller than Joshua, but Kole was taller than Herman. "Oh, you again," Herman said through gritted teeth.

"Leave him alone," Kole said. "He's gone through enough in his life already."

Herman, looking up at Kole, walked away, annoyed. Joshua stood up and looked at Kole. He wanted to thank Kole, but instead, he stood there, motionless and speechless.

"What does he want with you?" Kole asked.

"He wants me to stop wearing my necklace," Joshua said.

Kole looked at the cross hanging over Joshua's chest.

"Oh, you got a new chain?" Kole asked.

"Yeah. I know he won't leave me alone until I stop wearing it, yet I still went to the store and bought a new chain because I really want to wear it."

"Good! Wear it! Don't let someone else rule your life! You certainly never let me do that, so don't let Herman do it either!"

Joshua looked at Kole, but he didn't say anything at

first. People started walking past, and Joshua realized that they could go on to their classes.

"Thank you," Joshua said.

"I owe it to you," Kole said.

Joshua smiled, slightly. Then, the two of them parted their own separate ways. Joshua started to walk away when a memory stopped him.

"I'm not mad at you," Patrick said. "I've told Daniel about the fight, and he's not mad at you, either. He's just going to stay out of it. And as for me, it's not like I've never gotten into a fight with Kole before."

"Yeah," Daniel agreed.

"How do I know you're not trying to trick me like Aiden did?" Joshua asked.

"Aiden wasn't trying to trick you. Kole tricked him, too," Patrick explained.

*"Aiden should have known it was a trick when Kole said not to tell me that he'd be there. And...*you *were there," Joshua said, looking at Patrick.*

"Listen, Joshua. Why are you trying to make more enemies? You already have Kole, you don't need me as one, too," Patrick said.

"I'm not trying to make you into an enemy. I just don't feel like getting beat up again," Joshua said.

"I can understand that," Patrick admitted.

"I heard you pushed first." A voice was coming from behind Joshua. He turned around and saw a girl named Violet. She was standing with her friend Mandy.

"Yeah, that's what Kole said," Mandy said.

"Is it true?" Violet asked.

Joshua sighed, but he answered, "Yes."

"Wow, I'm surprised. I didn't expect that from you. You're kind of quiet, and I never thought you meant any harm," Violet said.

"I didn't! I don't!" Joshua pleaded. "I just...he was..."

"It doesn't matter," Violet said. "You still pushed him first. That makes you fair game."

Joshua opened his mouth to say something, but he was at a loss of words. He turned around and faced the middle of the table. Patrick had a neutral face, showing no emotion. Daniel had a frown.

Joshua came back to reality and continued walking. He went to his locker, then to Latin.

Chapter 94: Article 22

Joshua walked home alone that afternoon. Election day was right around the corner, so as he walked, he saw that people's front yards were crowded with election signs. He didn't know most of them because he didn't pay attention to political leaders. There was one sign that he recognized though, which wasn't to vote for a person. It was to vote for the ratification of an article. The sign said "Vote Yes Article 22: Reproduction Liberty." The article was meant to allow abortions for any reason during any part of the pregnancy term, but it didn't actually directly say that. Obviously, Joshua did not want that to be voted yes. There were some signs that said to vote no, but Joshua didn't think there were enough of them to make a no in the end. Although he tried to have faith in his state, he was pretty sure that the majority of people were going to vote yes.

***

The day after election day, Joshua refused to look at the results because he didn't want the heartbreak of finding out that the majority of people had voted yes. He tried to ignore the whole election, but other people didn't ignore it, so he found out anyway. That night, Joshua didn't have swim practice, so he and Kendall went to Donna's Diner after school, which was about half a mile away from his house.

Herman sat around a table at Donna's Diner with a group of boys. There were eight of them in all. They all picked up their drinks and had cheers. They all exclaimed, "Yeah!!!" Then, they all took a sip.

"Ah," Herman said, setting down his drink. Then, he looked at one of the boys at the table and said, "Hey, did you text Rowan?"

"Yeah," he answered. "She said she's coming. She has no idea."

"Great," Herman said.

"She should be here any minute."

Herman took another sip of his drink. Then, he turned around to face the door. Rowan was now there looking around, oblivious. Herman smiled and stood up. He walked over to her, and she looked up at him. Her face froze.

"Hey," Herman said, smiling.

"Herman!" Rowan cried.

"Did you hear the news?"

"What news?"

"Article 22."

"Of course I did." The middle of Rowan's eyebrows faced downwards.

Herman grabbed onto her hand. She tried to pull it

away, but he gripped it tight.

"I want to get back together," Herman said.

"No."

"Why not?" Herman grabbed Rowan's other hand and stood very close to her.

"Let go of me!"

"I want to get back together!"

"*I* don't!"

"Why not!?"

"I don't want a relationship that is based on the ability to murder an innocent baby!"

"Oh my gosh!" Herman let go of Rowan and backed away. "You sound like Joshua! He's corrupted you!"

"No! He hasn't! He's made me see the truth! I was wrong before, and so are you now!"

"Augh!" Herman pushed Rowan.

She came back and slapped him across the face.

The door to Donna's Diner opened, and there stood Joshua and Kendall. At this point, the other seven boys were standing up. They were behind Herman.

"*You,*" Herman said. He walked over to Joshua. Kendall's jaw dropped, and she stood in fear. "This is all your fault!"

"Woah," Joshua said. Herman grabbed onto him and dragged him outside.

"Herman! No! Don't touch him! He hasn't done anything wrong!" Rowan cried, her and Kendall following them outside.

"Herman!" Kendall shrieked.

The other boys also followed.

When they were all out there, Herman was pushing

Joshua. He pushed him three times, and Joshua didn't do anything.

"JOSHUA!" Kendall cried. "STAND UP FOR YOURSELF!"

As if he needed permission, Joshua pushed Herman on Kendall's command. He fell back, but he didn't fall to the ground. Instead, he pushed Joshua again. They kept pushing each other, until Joshua got sick of this endless back and forthness, and he punched Herman in the face. He had a flashback to him pushing Kole for the first time, and that allowed Herman to get the better of him.

Herman punched him in the face twice, and he would have done it a third time, but Joshua fell to the ground. Herman started kicking him, but Kendall and Rowan both ran over and grabbed Herman's arms.

The other boys came to Herman's rescue and pulled the girls away from him. Herman kept kicking Joshua, but now, he had regained his sense of time and place. That only meant that he was in a whole lot of pain. His face was bleeding and throbbing, and his side felt like mush. He tried to crawl away because at the moment, that was all he could do. He could hear Kendall crying behind him, and both Kendall and Rowan were trying to get away from the two boys (per girl) that were holding onto their arms, trapping them.

Joshua struggled to say, "Leave my sister alone." And he wanted to add Rowan too, but he could barely get those words out. He doubted Herman had any idea what he said.

One of the other boys came in front of Joshua and kneed him in the face. Joshua curled over onto the ground.

That same boy grabbed him under the shoulders and turned him around. Herman kicked him in the stomach. Joshua coughed, and spit came falling out of his mouth.

"LET HIM GOOO!" Kendall shrieked.

"Herman, please!" Rowan cried. "Let him go!"

"LET GO OF US, YOU CREEPS!" Kendall shouted.

One of the boys, who was only a bystander, said, "Come on, man. We don't have to do this."

"You don't know him," Herman said.

"Neither do you!" Rowan cried.

"What? Why do you keep defending him? Is he your new boyfriend? Is that why you won't get back with me?" Herman asked.

"NO!" Rowan snapped.

"DON'T LIE TO ME!" Herman yelled.

He kicked Joshua in the stomach again, and more spit came out of Joshua's mouth.

"I'm not!" Rowan cried. Now, she was crying, too.

"YES, YOU ARE!" Herman shouted. He kicked Joshua again, but this time, in the face.

To Joshua, the whole world was spinning, not just around its axis. There were three, four, five Hermans standing in front of him. What a nightmare.

Joshua felt himself being stood up by the person behind him. Herman grabbed onto him and flung him into the side of the building. Joshua's head smashed against the wall, and everything went dark to the sound of Kendall and Rowan shrieking at the same time, "JOSHUA!!!"

Patrick, Kole, and Maverick had gotten together for the first time since Patrick and Kole had moved back into town. It felt nice to be together again. They were choosing to go to Donna's Diner. It was new since they had been in seventh grade, so Patrick and Kole wanted to try it out. But they hadn't even arrived on the premises before they could see the fight that was happening. They arrived to the scene of Kendall and Rowan being held back by two boys. Maverick was the only one who knew the names of all the boys. Patrick didn't know any of them, and Kole just knew Herman and one other who was in his English class, which was the one holding onto Joshua. Herman was kicking Joshua in the stomach. Kole couldn't see the spit from where he was, but he saw Joshua cringe in pain. The three boys started running toward them. They heard Rowan shout, "I'm not!"

Then, Herman shouted, "YES, YOU ARE!"

Herman kicked Joshua in the face. Joshua looked completely out of it. His face was covered in blood, and his eyes were blank.

The boy holding onto Joshua stood him onto his feet, but Joshua had no strength left inside of him. He was motionless in the boy's arms. Herman grabbed onto Joshua and pushed him, sending him flying into the building. Joshua's head hit the side, and he fell to the ground. Kendall and Rowan both shrieked his name.

A vision of waking up in the middle of the night to his parents' wrath after they found out what he did to Joshua that cold December night in seventh grade ran through Kole's head. He remembered sitting up in his bed as they screamed and shouted at him. In the doorway, he saw Patrick standing there, but once he met Kole's eyes, he quickly slipped away.

Dozens of lonely suppers alone in his room, while his family ate together downstairs, danced through his head. The loneliness he felt during the months after the final fight still laid in his mind. In fact, even after four years, they still existed in the present.

He remembered the night he ran away, and someone found him and convinced him to go home. They told him his parents would want to see him, even though he persisted they wouldn't. Well, he was right. They didn't treat him any better once he got home. It had been almost a whole day, but there was no hugging with tears like in the movies.

Kole remembered going to the store and finding a box of Bible verse cards, and he thought to himself, "At least Joshua's family still loves him." *Initially, he just left the cards at the store, but it wasn't long before he went back for them. It was after a night where his parents snapped at him harsher than usual, for something that shouldn't have been a big deal, when he decided that he needed to seek comfort in someone other than his family.*

He had just made a new friend, but he was moving again, and so he decided to turn to God. He was reluctant at first, since he had never really thought highly of Christianity, but he thought if Joshua was willing to do all he did for his faith in God, then maybe there was more to it than what meets the eye. Kole saw that so many people believed full-heartedly in God, and he started to learn more about Him and His son, Jesus. He started to realize that all Joshua had said was true.

In all honesty, it was never that Kole didn't believe *in God, it was that he refused to accept Him because he didn't think he was good enough. But at the time being, God (and Jesus) were the only ones that he really felt like he actually was good enough for. And so his Church life began, and he rooted it all back to Joshua's persistence.*

Not long after, Kole was moving back to the area near where Joshua lived. He wasn't sure how he felt about it, but he told himself that he needed to make things right with Joshua. Although he had gone a long way in forgiving himself after he started going to Church and trusting in God, he also needed to show Joshua that he was sorry. He was going to need that if he was ever going to be able to fully forgive himself.

Patrick, Kole, and Maverick got to the fight. Patrick and Maverick went to the boys that were holding onto Kendall and Rowan and attacked them. Kole went to Herman and the boy who had been holding Joshua. Joshua was laying against the wall, completely out of it. He didn't move. Kole punched Herman across the face, and blood came out his nose. The boy from Kole's English class, named Mason, punched Kole. But Kole then punched him. Kole turned around and punched Herman again, but he made the mistake of putting his back toward Mason, and Mason pushed him. Kole fell an inch away from the brick wall that Joshua had hit.

Kole stood up, and when he looked back, Kendall was on Herman's back, and Rowan was standing in front of him. She punched him in the face.

The fight continued until a waiter stepped out of Donna's Diner and shouted, "Hey! What's going on out here!?"

Everyone froze as the waiter pulled his phone out of his pocket to call the police.

"We need an ambulance!" Kole cried, and he pointed to Joshua. Kole himself had blood on his face, but he also had it on his knuckles.

The waiter talked on the phone, and Herman and his boys ran. Kendall, Patrick, Kole, Maverick, and Rowan all stayed put. They went over to Joshua who had regained some consciousness, but he was still mostly out of it.

"Joshua! Joshua! Are you okay?" Kendall cried.

Joshua didn't say anything; he just moved his eyes around. The Abares arrived around the same time as the sirens did. They got out of their car and ran over to Joshua. They didn't even realize who was there. Leah and Ava were in the car, and they got out and stood by Kendall.

Joshua was lifted into the ambulance, and Mrs. Abare got in with him. They drove away, and Mr. Abare told the sisters to get into the car. He looked at the others to tell them he had room for them too, then he saw who was standing there and said, "*You!*" He walked over to Kole and Maverick. "Did you do this?"

"No! Dad!" Kendall exclaimed. "They're innocent! Like actually innocent! They *saved* Rowan and me! They would have saved Joshua too, but he was already unconscious by the time they got here!"

"Really?" Mr. Abare asked.

"It's true," Rowan said, softly.

"This is Joshua's friend," Kendall said, as her dad looked at Rowan with confusion.

"*Friend?*" Mr. Abare asked.

"We're *just friends*," Rowan assured him.

"Kendall, are you sure about what you said?" Mr. Abare asked.

"Positive," Kendall said.

"Okay," Mr. Abare said. He looked at Patrick, Kole, and Maverick, then he looked at Rowan, and he said, "If you guys would like, you can come with us."

They all accepted, and they all crowded into the car, with the exception of Rowan who drove herself. They got to the hospital and sat in the waiting room until they were allowed to go in.

Chapter 95: Sticking Around

Joshua laid silently in his hospital bed. His eyes were closed, and he hadn't been fully conscious since he hit his head. Patrick, Kole, Maverick, Rowan, and his family were all sitting around the room. Leah and Ava were having a quiet conversation with each other, and Patrick and Maverick were on their phones, but everyone else was sitting silently, staring at the floor.

Breaking the almost silence, Mr. Abare said, "It's been really nice of you all to be here for our son, but it's getting pretty late now, perhaps you should all go home to your families. They're probably wondering where you are. Have you called them?"

"Yeah, you're right," Patrick and Maverick said. "We will get going."

"Come on, Kole, let's go," Patrick said, standing up.

"Nah, it's okay. I want to see that Joshua is okay."

"Come on, Kole." Patrick's voice was quiet.

"No, I'm good. Really."

"Okay."

Rowan looked from Joshua to Mr. Abare to Patrick and Maverick to Kole. Then, she said, "I should be getting home, too. It's pretty late. But I really hope Joshua is okay."

"Thank you," Mr. Abare said. "Do any of you need a ride?"

"I can give you all a ride," Rowan said. "If you need one."

"We're good, thank you," Maverick said.

Patrick, Maverick, and Rowan all said goodbye to Joshua, but he was still out.

After they had left, Mr. Abare said to Kole, "Are you really sure you don't need to go home?"

"Nah, I'm not wanted there. After what I did to Joshua that night, my parents can't even look at me. They won't forgive me. So many people have forgiven me, and although my parents are my parents, I thought all of these other people could forgive me because they never knew me before—in seventh grade. But although I'm not so sure that you can forgive me, you have at least been kind to me and are able to look me in the eyes. So..." Kole's voice cracked a little. "It's just..." A tear fell from his eye. "...it's really ridiculous. They're my *parents*." More tears fell from Kole's eyes. "I'm sorry. I'm so sorry for everything. Everything that I put your son through. He didn't deserve any of it. I'm sorry."

"Kole, man, that's horrible," Mr. Abare said.

"I don't understand," Kole said. "How are you so understanding?"

"Listen, what you did to our son four years ago was wrong, but parents are parents. They should never abandon you. And what you have done for him today, and for Kendall, it shows a lot about where you have come. Sure, we will always *remember* what you did, but if you are kind to our son and daughters *now*, we will *see* you for what you are doing *now*," Mr. Abare said.

"I agree," Mrs. Abare said.

Kole wiped his eyes. He said, "Thanks. I'm sorry I'm getting emotional."

"Isn't that normal?" Ava asked. "Joshua *gets emotional* all of the time."

"*Ava*," Mrs. Abare scolded, but she had a smile.

Kole chuckled.

"Hey!" Everyone looked over at Joshua, as he spoke. His eyes were opened, and he said meekly, "I heard that!"

"Joshua!" everyone exclaimed, except Kole, who just looked at him, surprised. The Abares all rushed to his bed, but Kole remained where he was.

"I feel really dizzy," Joshua said.

"We'll get a doctor to come in," Mr. Abare said.

"Okay," Joshua said. He turned his head and saw Kole, and he said, "Kole?"

"Yeah...hi," Kole said.

Joshua looked at his own hand and cringed when he saw an IV sticking into the back of it.

"Don't look at that," Mrs. Abare advised him.

A doctor arrived.

Chapter 96: Back

Joshua didn't go back to school for a whole week. He had a horrible concussion, so even when he did go back, he wasn't going back to the full extreme. He only went to school for half the day. He was going to leave right before band. He didn't have to do much for work, since his teachers were pretty understanding of his condition. Herman was in a whole lot of trouble, but not with the school because this didn't happen there. In fact, it didn't even happen in the same town.

When Joshua arrived at school, he went looking for Patrick, Kole, and Maverick. He found the three of them standing together. As he was approaching them, Kole exclaimed, "Hey! Joshua! You're back! How are you doing?"

"Horrible, actually, but I could be doing a lot worse if it weren't for you. And Kendall...she could have a lot more than just a few black and blues if it weren't for you. I wanted to thank you...all of you," Joshua said.

"Oh, Joshua, that's kind of you," Kole said. "But it's nothing. We...well...*I* kind of owe it to you."

"Same," Maverick said.

"I'm still grateful," Joshua said. "So thank you."

The three boys nodded. Then, it was time to go off

to class. But Joshua and Kole stayed there and talked.

"Kole..." Joshua said. "There's something I owe *you*. I always thought you were the monster, but I was nowhere near perfect myself. I didn't handle things well in seventh grade. I'm sorry, too."

"No! No! No! You don't owe me that! I don't deserve that! I was awful! I was stupid! I shouldn't have beaten you up all of those times. I was just using that as an excuse," Kole said.

"I've been told that so many times, but I still feel so guilty. I think maybe it's my character, but I can't get rid of it," Joshua said.

"Wow, Joshua, thank you. That means a lot to me."

"I'm glad. You've really reproved yourself since you've come back, especially what you did last week. So, I really am sorry."

"Thanks." Kole rubbed his eye and said, "Wow. I mean, I'm sorry because I nearly *killed you*, and you're what...just sorry because you pushed me a few times? That's pretty powerful."

"There's a lot of things that I don't handle well, so although I didn't deserve everything you gave me, I still have my own faults."

"To be honest, I'm glad that you didn't stop fighting me. Even though I was a jerk to you, I learned from you."

"Really?"

"Really."

"Is that why you go to Church?"

"You're the one who made me consider it."

"Wow. I feel honored."

"Good. You should."

"But...sometimes, I feel like what I do is pointless. I always just get pushed around and nearly killed. All I do is make enemies. That's *not* what Jesus wants, is it?"

"Jesus would never want you to submit to suppressing your faith; He certainly never did and was nailed to the cross for it."

"You're right."

"Wow, I never thought I'd hear those words come out of *your* mouth."

Joshua smiled, then he said, "I just...I don't know what to do. Because I feel like I always just make things worse."

"Jesus didn't come to bring peace, He came to bring a sword. That is according to Matthew 10.34," Kole said. "Think about it. What would happen if Martin Luther King Jr. stopped fighting for equality just because he didn't want to *cause problems*?"

"Martin Luther King Jr. didn't *almost* die, he *did* die," Joshua said, his mouth falling open.

"No, no. That's not what I'm getting at. Listen, I wouldn't say that you should continue to have physical fights over it. For two reasons: one because it's immature; and two, you're just not that good at fighting. You wouldn't stand a chance at making it much past 20. You've already almost died twice now."

Joshua laughed, but it caused his head to pound, and he said, "That's true."

"I'm just saying don't give up on yourself, and certainly don't give up on God. Because you've helped me see, and even if you can't change the *world*, you can help people each one at a time in your life by your actions. Sure, you're not perfect, but you've forgiven *me*, and that's the greatest thing I could ask for. Keep being like that. Show, don't tell."

Joshua nodded. "I just...I feel so lost. I have no idea where I'm going to college or what I want to do for a living. I feel so busy and overwhelmed. That's getting better, but I still don't know what I'm doing after high school. I used to be a really good alto saxophonist and cornetist, but now, I get the second and third part because I don't practice enough anymore. My whole life is going downhill! Getting beat up because of my beliefs is the last thing that I want to worry about right now."

"I get it. My life isn't going so great, either. I didn't make the baseball team at my old school last spring, and my grades are plummeting. My parents won't even look at me. I have no one to turn to except God."

"You have me, too. Well, you do now, anyway."

"Thanks, Joshua."

"But...keep turning to God. Just me in *addition*."

Kole smiled. "Got it."

Joshua smiled, too.

"I've found peace in God," Kole told him.

"Maybe I could learn something from you," Joshua said.

"That's pretty hard to imagine, but maybe you can," Kole replied.

***

Joshua was sitting with a headache by the door to get picked up that day during passing time—the time in between classes. A long line of students were passing in both directions. Rowan was among them, and when she saw Joshua sitting there, she walked over to him and said, "Hey."

"Hey."

"How are you doing?"

"Fine. I mean, fine as I can be, considering."

"I get it. I'm really sorry."

"Thanks, Rowan, but it's all good."

"You want to hear something crazy?"

"Sure."

"Herman was trying to get back together with me."

"Why?"

"You know, with Article 22."

"Wow. That explains a whole lot."

"It really does."

A girl came up behind Rowan. She looked at Joshua, then back at Rowan and said quietly, yet Joshua could still hear, "Why are you talking to him?"

"Because he's my friend," Rowan answered.

The girl pursed her lips and crossed her arms, looking from Joshua to Rowan, then she said, "Really?"

"Yeah," Rowan said.

"Okay," she said, and she walked away.

Joshua looked at the ground, uncomfortably.

"Sorry about that, Joshua. I really am," Rowan said.

"It's okay," Joshua said, but he was still looking at the ground. He admitted that he probably looked pretty unfriendly. His face was black and blue, and pretty much the whole school knew about the fight. There were a lot of people involved, and Joshua wasn't at school for a week afterward. Rowan herself still had a little bit of black and blue, but not nearly as much as Joshua's. There was a difference between them, though. Before the fight, Joshua was nothing of much excitement. He wasn't popular; Rowan was. Joshua was just a nerd who got weirdly good grades, was in band, couldn't jump, and did all the weird sports where you'd run 5k every week and ski up hills. On top of all that, he was religious...deeply religious. And he didn't have a girlfriend, nor had he ever before.

"I'm sorry we had to end on an awkward note, but...I've got to get going. Have a good day," Rowan said.

"See ya, you too," Joshua said.

And with that, Rowan was gone. Joshua looked down at his phone, and he saw that he had gotten a text from his mom while he was talking to Rowan. She told him that she was there. So, he got up and went out to the parking lot where she then took him home.

Joshua had the rest of the day to do whatever he wanted. He didn't have any sports because of his concussion. He had just gotten off of crutches, and now he was out of sports *again*. He couldn't play his instruments either because the noise and exertion of air caused him to feel dizzy and have a headache. He couldn't even write because the screen and concentration (so even on paper) caused his head to hurt. Instead of doing all that, he slept.

Chapter 97: Forgiveness

It was about two weeks after the fight. At this point, Joshua was the only one of all 14 people involved in the actual occurrence to still be suffering the consequences. Everyone else's bruised faces, sore bodies, and cracked knuckles had healed. Joshua looked pretty back to normal, but he certainly didn't feel it. He now went to school all day, but he still got pounding headaches during band, lunch, when he looked at any type of screen, and pretty much doing anything except sleep. But he needed to move on with his life. He still didn't do everything normally, especially sports, but he didn't sit around all day, either. Joshua was falling way behind on his schoolwork, but his teachers were pretty understanding of his conditions and promised him an extension of the due dates. Joshua was sitting in pre-calc, talking to his friend Ryan, when he (Ryan) asked him, "Does your family go to St. Mary's Church?"

"No," Joshua replied.

"I heard they're closing," Ryan said.

"They are," Joshua answered.

Joshua looked back at Kole, who he knew went there. Kole looked up at Joshua, and he made a face like he was probably listening to what Ryan asked him.

Joshua heard more talk throughout the day about the Church closing. Some people were saying that they should take the Church and turn it into a parking lot for the school because the school didn't have great parking, but that wasn't right to Joshua. Then...there were some people...who showed sorrow for it. Not many people seemed deeply depressed about it, but they still felt bad about it. Joshua was surprised. Some of the people who seemed sorry were people that he didn't think paid much attention to the Church. Like Ryan. He seemed sorry about it. Of course, despite his views and beliefs, Ryan did once say that he thought if there's a God, then he would want to protect the Bible. It was a project they did in English class their sophomore year, and they had to choose five books *not* to burn. A surprising number of people chose the Bible, including Ryan...and Joshua, of course.

That afternoon, Joshua was walking out of the school at the end of the day with his friends: Adrian, Isaiah, Arthur, Landon, and Ryan. Kendall was also with them. They were walking away from the school when Patrick and Maverick came over running. Worry was spread across their faces.

"Joshua! Guys! All of you! Come quick!" Patrick cried.

"What's wrong?" Joshua asked, but Patrick and Maverick didn't answer. They were already turned around and running away. Joshua followed, and so did the rest of his friends.

When they got around the corner of the school, Joshua could see it clear. Herman and two of his friends, Bryan and Tucker, were gathered around a boy who was on his knees, covered in blood.

"Kole!" Joshua cried.

Joshua had never seen Kole like this before; he had never seen Kole as the *victim* of anyone.

Herman punched Kole, who then fell to his hands. The split second that Joshua stood watching the beating seemed like an hour. All eight of the boys and Kendall ran over to the situation. Now, Herman was outnumbered. But he hadn't realized yet and was repeatedly kicking Kole, who lay on the ground motionless. Joshua himself walked up to Herman and grabbed his right arm, saying, "Leave him alone."

Herman turned around and smirked when he saw who was standing there. "Joshua!" he exclaimed.

"Come on, Herman," Joshua said.

"Funny seeing you show up face to face with me again, seeing what I did to you last time we were like this," Herman said.

That was one way to put it. His head was pounding, he felt slightly dizzy every time he moved too fast or tried to focus on something, and he hadn't done much exercise since the concussion, so he was pretty out of shape. But Joshua said, "Last time, I was outnumbered; this time, I'm not...you are. But I don't mean any harm. All I want is for you to leave my friend alone."

"Really? He's your friend?" Herman asked. "Then why are you afraid of him?"

"I'm not."

"Yes, you are."

"No, I'm not!"

"I get it now. It all makes sense!"

"What makes sense?"

"I understand why the Church is closing. You're Christian, and he's Christian, but you're afraid of him. How should anyone think that the Church could stay together when the Christians that are a part of it can't even get along?"

Joshua clenched his fist like he was going to swing it at Herman's face, and he probably *was* about to do that if it weren't for the fact that he heard Maverick say to him, "Don't punch him."

Joshua relaxed his hands.

"And you're ill-tempered," Herman said.

"That might be true," Joshua said. "But that says nothing about God, and it says nothing about the Church, and it says nothing about Kole. It only says something about me."

"Oh yeah?" Herman asked.

"Yeah," Joshua replied.

"I guess I was wrong to be attacking Kole because I should have been attacking you," Herman said, and he pushed Joshua who fell to the ground since he hadn't been expecting the force.

"HEY!" That was Maverick. He dashed at Herman and punched him himself. Herman punched Maverick back, but Maverick stepped away.

Joshua sat on the ground, not getting up. His head was pounding and spinning. Maverick took over and said, "I would drop it, Herman. You're outnumbered."

Kendall, Patrick, Adrian, Isaiah, Arthur, Landon, and Ryan stood behind him. They all had stern looks on their faces. Bryan and Tucker stood there too, but their expressions were terrified because they saw it was true: they *were* outnumbered.

"I'm not afraid," Herman said.

"Come on, Herman," Bryan chimed in. "Don't be stupid."

"Relax, Bryan. They're not going to hurt me," Herman said. "They're too afraid to get into that kind of trouble."

"Oh yeah?" Maverick asked. He crossed his arms. "Why don't you ask Joshua there if *I* am afraid to get into *that kind* of trouble."

Maverick looked over at Joshua who was still sitting on the ground but replied, "Yeah, Herman. I'd drop it. Maverick's not afraid."

"I almost killed Joshua once," Maverick said.

Herman looked at Joshua, who nodded.

"Then...why is he *helping* you?" Herman asked. *Now*, there was fear in his voice.

"Because he's Catholic," Maverick said. "And so he can forgive us. And if you leave him...and Kole...and all of us alone right now, then perhaps one day, he will forgive you too for all that you have done to him."

Herman took a step back. Maverick thought maybe he had won, but then Herman took his fist and swung it at Maverick's face. It hit his cheek, and Maverick felt a lot of pain, but Herman quickly ran away before he could do anything back. So did Bryan and Tucker. Maverick was glad that they had run because he really didn't want to get into a fight again.

Joshua stood up now, only for a wave of dizziness to overtake him. When it went away, he saw Patrick and

Maverick trying to pick Kole up. Joshua went over and helped them.

The three of them got Kole onto his feet, but he was mostly out of it, so they put him over Patrick and Maverick's shoulders. Joshua did not take Kole on his shoulders because he was having a hard enough time keeping himself up. Kendall walked over to him and walked along as the boys walked Kole to Patrick's car. All of Joshua's friends walked with them, until they got to the car. By the time that they had reached it, Joshua was feeling so dizzy that he thought he might collapse. But he didn't say anything about it. The boys all got Kole into the car, then Maverick climbed into the car, and Patrick got into the driver's seat.

"Can I come?" Joshua asked.

"If you want," Patrick said. "But don't you have something better you'd rather be doing?"

"There's not much that I can do right now, so no, I don't have anything real important," Joshua said.

"Then come along," Patrick said.

Joshua looked at Kendall, who looked at him desperately, so Joshua looked back at Patrick and said, "And Kendall?"

"I don't care," Patrick said.

"Okay," Joshua said.

Kendall waited to get into the car until Joshua did, who was turning to the rest of his friends and saying, "Bye guys."

"Bye," they all said.

Joshua and Kendall climbed into the back of Patrick's car, next to Kole, who was still pretty out of it.

Patrick started driving as Joshua texted his mom that he and Kendall were going to Kole's house.

It was about 10 minutes before they arrived. Within that time, Kole started to feel better and was telling the others what happened upon Joshua's request. He was saying, "I left the school and was walking toward the car when I walked past Herman, Bryan, and Tucker. They were walking very slowly, and I wasn't, so I caught up to them. Not on purpose. When I reached them, I wasn't planning on talking to them, but they were talking about St. Mary's closing. They said a bunch of horrible things, and I felt really upset, so I told them to stop saying them. And they turned around and said some things to me, and then they started fighting me, and that's where everything went downhill. Anyway, now I know a bit of what it's like to be Joshua, and let me tell you, it's not pleasant."

Joshua made a nervous smile.

"Look, that just made me see how sorry I really am," Kole said.

"Oh yeah?" Joshua asked.

"Two reasons: one, I know what it feels like to be the victim of other people's unreasonably anti-religious comments and abuse; and two, you came and helped me and are going so far as to my house. I mean, maybe it was for a free ride, I don't know, but you still came and helped me," Kole explained.

Joshua laughed. "It's not for the free ride, for the record. And I helped you because you helped me. Sure, there were countless times where you and I were on different sides, but you have *proved* to me that you've changed. It seems like we have the same goal, and I think maybe we're not as different as we once thought."

"Thanks, Joshua," Kole said.

They arrived at Patrick and Kole's house. Patrick parked his car, and all five of them started to get out. Kole looked down at his clothes as he got out and saw that his shirt was covered in blood. He looked in the rear-view mirror and saw that his face didn't look much better. Maverick had a little bit of blood on his lip, but other than that, the rest was clean.

"Joshua and Kendall," Patrick said, looking at the two of them. "Would you like me to give you a ride home?"

Joshua opened his mouth to speak, but before he could get any words out, Maverick said, "Maybe you'd like to invite them inside?"

"Oh, so now you get to decide who comes into *my* house?" Patrick asked.

"Do you *not* want them to come inside?" Maverick asked.

Patrick looked at Kole and said quietly, "I just don't want him to get in trouble."

"I'll be okay," Kole said.

"Okay," Patrick said. He looked back at Joshua and Kendall and said, "Would you like to come inside?"

"Sure," Joshua said.

Kendall on the other hand, looked stiff like she was nervous about the idea, but she didn't say anything. Instead, she followed the boys toward the door.

As they walked, Kole said to Patrick, "It's not like they could say anything worse than they have before."

"Yeah, but now they are *seeing* him," Patrick said.

Joshua looked at Kendall with confusion, but she

didn't seem confused at all, so he looked back at Patrick and Kole and said, "Guys, what's going on?"

They all stopped walking, and everyone faced Joshua, and Patrick said, "After what Kole did to you four years ago, his parents have not forgiven him."

"Oh," Joshua said. He looked at Kole who was looking at the ground. "Oh, Kole. I'm so sorry."

"It's fine. I've gotten used to it."

"Maybe I *should* get going."

"No, no. It's okay, really."

The front door opened while they were all standing there, and a woman stood there. She looked to be in her early 30s, and Joshua knew exactly who she was: Kole's mom—Mrs. Jackson.

"What's going on out here?" Mrs. Jackson asked. "Are you all just going to stand by the door, or are you actually going to come in?"

"Come in," Kole said, quietly.

"Kole, why are you covered in blood? Did you beat someone up again?" Mrs. Jackson asked.

"Does it look like *he* beat someone up?" Maverick asked. "If he had beaten someone up, wouldn't *they* be the one covered in blood? Not *him*?"

"Maverick, I don't need this attitude from you," Mrs. Jackson said, crossing her arms.

Then, she looked at Joshua and Kendall and said, "I've never seen you two before. What're your names?"

Joshua, Kendall, Patrick, Kole, and Maverick all looked at each other with wide eyes, but then Kendall replied, "I'm Kendall."

Mrs. Jackson looked at Joshua, and he gulped

before replying, "Joshua."

"Joshua?" Mrs. Jackson asked. "Wait...you're not...wait...wait...oh...you poor thing."

"What?" Joshua asked, confused. His cheeks turned bright red like the color of his sunburn at the beginning of the summer.

"I'm so sorry," Mrs. Jackson told him.

"For what?"

"For what my son put you through. I'm truly sorry for you. I don't know where he went wrong. I've tried to send him to therapy and all, but..."

"Wait...wait...Kole didn't do anything to me."

"Wait...so are you not *the Joshua*?"

The Joshua? It sounded funny in Joshua's head. He had always just been *Joshua*, never *the Joshua*.

"No, no, Mom, he is *the Joshua*," Kole told her.

"Honey," Mrs. Jackson said, looking at Joshua. "He nearly killed you, so don't tell me that he didn't do anything to you."

"Oh," Joshua said. "That was four years ago."

"You can't just forget about a near-death experience. Four years ago or not, he still almost killed you," Mrs. Jackson said.

"I haven't forgotten about it, nor will I ever forget about it. But I've learned to move on. Kole isn't that same person anymore. In fact, he's like...the total opposite! I was tentative at first, of course! But Kole has proved himself worthy of my trust. In fact, Kole has now risked himself for both me and the Church, so I'm fine," Joshua said.

"And maybe you should be, too," Kendall added in.

"If Joshua can forgive Kole, certainly you can, too. You are his mom, aren't you?"

"Kole...did you bring them here just to clear your name?" Mrs. Jackson asked.

"No, I didn't," Kole said. "They helped me, so I thought it would be rude if I just sent them away. We're cool now, Mom."

Mrs. Jackson looked at Joshua and said, "I don't understand you, Joshua." A tone of sorrow was in her voice now, breaking the sternness that was in it just a few minutes ago. "You're so...so...*kind.*"

"If he's kind, maybe you should listen to him," Maverick said.

"I've about had it with your attitude, Maverick!" Mrs. Jackson snapped, like a switch had been flipped. "I'm this close to kicking you out of my house again! You're just as bad as Kole!"

"Oh, please. That was four years ago," Maverick said. He had a slight mocking tone, but he was sincere.

"Whatever!" Kole snapped. "I'm going to go clean up!" Then, Kole stormed inside.

Joshua looked at Mrs. Jackson after Kole had gone away and said, "I'm not upset with Kole anymore, and I'm the victim, so you don't have to be, either. He saved my life the other day, so how could I be upset with him?"

"That's just your character. Personally, I just can't do that. I'm embarrassed," Mrs. Jackson said.

"I wasn't perfect either."

"So, you deserved it?"

"No!"

"I'm just...confused."

"That's okay. You don't have to understand. Most people don't understand me."

"Can we go inside? We didn't bring Joshua here to be questioned," Patrick interrupted.

"Ah, yes, you can come in," Mrs. Jackson sighed. She went inside, and everyone else went in behind her.

In the dining room sat Kole's two younger sisters. They were a year apart, one of them being Ava's age. When Joshua, Kendall, Patrick, and Maverick walked into the kitchen, they both looked over but didn't say anything.

Maverick opened up the pantry and pulled out a bag of chips and began eating them. Kole was still cleaning up. Patrick went off to find him. Joshua and Kendall stood awkwardly in the kitchen of a house they had never been to before. Mrs. Jackson had gone into the living room, but after Patrick left, she came into the kitchen to scold Maverick for "eating all of the food." After Maverick apologized and put the chips back, Mrs. Jackson looked at Joshua and said, "You look uncomfortable. Are you sure that you and Kole are good?"

Before Joshua could respond, Maverick said, "He always looks uncomfortable."

"Kole and I really are cool. I know that's hard to believe, but it's true," Joshua said, ignoring Maverick.

"How?" Mrs. Jackson asked.

"When Kole first came back, I was terrified. But he kept being really nice to me. I continued to be skeptical, but a couple weeks ago, I was getting beat up by someone else, and he came to help me. Of course, by the time that he got over there, I was already unconscious, but if he hadn't come over, things probably would've gotten a lot worse. That's when I really knew that it wasn't another trap. And although this can never erase what happened, it certainly gives me a new perspective. And look, I get that you are ashamed and upset with him, but I really think he's changed," Joshua said.

"Wow," Mrs. Jackson said. "So...what happened today?"

"Kole was the one who got beat up. It was by the same people who have been bothering me."

"Truly?"

"It's true. You wanna know why it happened?"

"Why?"

"Because of religion."

"And...isn't that why he used to beat you up?"

"Yeah. He's changed."

"But how do *you* forgive someone who has treated you so badly?"

"Jesus was able to forgive those who nailed Him to the cross, so surely I can forgive Kole for what he did."

"You really follow the Bible."

"I try to."

Mrs. Jackson looked like she was about to say something, but she didn't because she heard Patrick and Kole coming down the stairs. They both walked into the kitchen. Kole had cleaned the blood off his face, but it was swollen around his left eye, and his bottom lip was puffed up. He had changed his shirt, too.

Mrs. Jackson looked at Kole's face as he stood at the bottom of the stairs with Patrick. It looked so different from the last time she had given it a good look. For one, it was four years older. And secondly, it was swollen. But there was so much more to it than just that. It showed maturity.

Mrs. Jackson left again, without saying anything to Kole. He didn't look at her. Instead, he walked over toward Joshua, Kendall, and Maverick. He said to Joshua and Kendall, "Thanks, guys. It means a lot that you had my back, after what I did to you both."

"Look, I'm just glad you've come to your senses," Joshua said, smiling.

"Ha," Kole said.

"We've probably got to get going," Joshua said, looking at Kendall.

Kendall nodded.

Joshua looked back at Kole and said, "I hope things work out for you."

"Thanks," Kole said.

They said goodbye, then Joshua and Kendall walked home. They had walked for about a minute in silence, then Joshua said, "I didn't know how upset Kole's parents were with him. Did you?"

"Yes."

"Am I really that oblivious? Augh! I feel so stupid!" Joshua covered his face with his hands.

"No, no. I just found out. But I didn't *figure* it out. He told us at the hospital when you were still out of it. That's why I knew, but you didn't."

"Oh. I still feel bad."

"Me too. I mean, what he did was awful, but even Mom and Dad cared for you when you told them you pushed first, and that was *before* Kole took it too far."

"Yeah. I guess it explains a lot about why he did

what he did."

"Yeah."

"He once told me that his parents couldn't look him in the eye, and I guess I didn't fully comprehend what he said. I just hope that after today, maybe they can start to heal...because Kole's really trying to do the right thing."

"I agree."

Chapter 98: Goodbyes

"Joshua, Jeneby, would you like to come join our group?"

"Sure."

The two of them walked over to a group of boys named Aaron, Toby, Sean, and Simon. They sat down and began talking about the assigned topic: their books. They were each reading their own independent book, and now, they got to share theirs to their group. Aaron went first, then Toby, then Sean, then Simon, then Jeneby, then finally Joshua. Joshua shared his book, then he opened it up to questions, as part of the way to get a perfect score was to ask other people about their books. His group mates asked him a couple of questions, then Toby, who had gone to middle school with him, asked, "How is your concussion doing?"

"Fine."

"Did Kole really come and *help* you?"

"Yeah, he did."

"That's pretty cool because I know how he was to you in middle school."

"Yeah, it is pretty cool."

"You know, Joshua," Simon began chiming in. "It's pretty cool how you defend your beliefs and religion. A lot of people aren't willing to be open about it, but you are. I respect that."

Joshua smiled and said, "Thanks."

Simon was Christian. He wasn't Catholic, just Christian, though Joshua didn't care because they still shared the same beliefs. Simon was pretty open about his religion too, yet somehow he managed not to get himself beat up for it. Simon's openness always encouraged Joshua because he knew that he wasn't the only high school boy to feel so strongly about his faith.

"I agree," Toby said in response to Simon.

"It takes guts," Aaron added. "And don't let Herman get to you. He's just a jerk."

"I agree," Simon said. "I've always got your back, if you need it."

"We all do," the other four said. Even Jeneby did, and she was Landon's ex.

"Thanks," Joshua said.

"It looks like we're all done," Toby said.

"Sweet," the others replied, and they all went back to their seats. Joshua sat down, feeling happy.

His group mates weren't the only people to appreciate him for his efforts, either. After the first week of Joshua being back from his concussion break, a lot of people had come up to him to tell him they were impressed. Some of these people Joshua hadn't even realized cared about religion or his values. Some of them didn't, they just admired his ambition. But others did care about his religion and values, like he did, and Joshua just didn't know that before.

***

"Do you want to hang out today after school?" Adrian asked Joshua during enrichment.

"Sure."

"Cool. What do you want to do?"

"You could come to my house. There's some things to do on my road, and maybe you could come to supper after. I'm sure my parents wouldn't mind, but I could ask them."

"Okay. Yeah, there's nothing to do on my road. My host family lives in the middle of a forest."

"What is it like where you live in Spain?"

"I live five minutes from the beach, so it's quite a bit different than here."

"Oh. Yeah, we don't have a beach. Well, we do have one on the lake."

"That doesn't count."

"Okay." Joshua smiled. "I do agree with that."

"Is there food on your road?"

"Yeah. Lots of it. There's a snack and smoothie shop that just got put in a few minutes from my house that I've been wanting to try."

"Okay then! Let's go there!"

"Okay."

"I love food."

"Okay." Joshua smiled again.

That night, they hung out, and Adrian stayed for supper, so he got to meet the rest of the Abares. He had met Kendall a little bit, of course, but he mostly just knew Joshua.

Adrian's host parents came to pick him up that night. In Spain, they couldn't drive until they were 18, though even though Joshua was 17 and living in Vermont where they could drive at 16, he still didn't have his license, either.

By the time Adrian left, the boys had already made plans to hang out on Sunday. They started hanging out every weekend, and sometimes on weekdays. Adrian tried out for basketball, but he didn't make it. He was told that he was really athletic, but he didn't know anything about basketball. He had never played before. So instead, he joined the Nordic team with Joshua! Joshua started out the season just sitting back and not doing anything, which proved pretty nice during the countless days of bounding. But when Joshua finally got to get into it, on their first day of skiing, he was really feeling the lack of exercise. Not only that, but his headache came back pretty quickly.

And you know who else joined the Nordic team? Kole! Patrick and Maverick stayed away from it, saying it was too cold and stuff, but Kole thought he'd give it a try.

Kole started hanging out with Joshua and Adrian a lot, too. Their three way friendship began in Nordic because they spent every afternoon suffering in the cold together. Joshua and Kole started to get pretty used to each other, so Joshua and Adrian started inviting Kole to hang out with them, too. The three of them would hang out almost every weekend, and sometimes, other people would hang out with them, too.

Joshua met Des again, who he hadn't seen since

that night. She was a lot different than back then, too. She had been pretty tall back in seventh grade compared to Joshua, but now, he was about her height. She hadn't grown much at all. She dressed a lot more relaxed than she used to. Her eyes looked tired from a constant lack of sleep and daily doses of caffeine. She wore more makeup than before. The biggest difference was that she no longer enjoyed seeing Joshua get teased, bullied, and beaten. That was mostly because she just followed whatever Kole implied interest in, but she said she was sorry for being a silent bystander and just walking away. Joshua appreciated that.

Kole tried to get Reese to hang out with them one day, but she told him she had to work. So, he tried again another day, and she had to work again. Joshua asked her one day, and she said that she had to work. So, one day, they surprised her at her work. At first, she was mad, but she ended up talking to Kole. One thing that did not go away about Kole over the past four years was his persistence.

Kole talked to some of his other old *friends* from middle school, but he never became *friends* again with any of them like he did with Joshua.

***

Springtime came, and Adrian's days left in the United States were coming to a close end. Joshua was devastated. He couldn't remember the last time that he had felt as happy as he did this past year.

Joshua and Adrian went to watch one of Kole's baseball games. (Kole made the team this year!) Afterward, they all went out for supper together. They had all ordered and were waiting for their food to come when Kole said, primarily addressing Josua, "There's something I need to tell you." He was looking at the table when he spoke, and his voice was quiet.

Joshua and Adrian both looked at him.

"I'm...moving this summer," Kole said. He looked up after he had finished speaking.

Oof! Joshua felt like he had just been punched in the stomach, and that certainly wasn't the first time that Kole punched him.

"What?" Joshua cried.

"I'm moving, Joshua."

"Where?" Joshua's voice cracked.

"Iowa."

"What!? That's like...hours away!"

"I know." Kole's voice was low and soft.

"WHY!?"

"Joshua, please, don't get mad."

Joshua's face quickly changed from what was tight and scrunched up to loosened. He looked at the table in front of him and said, "Sorry."

"It's okay. I figured you probably wouldn't take it well."

Joshua looked up at Kole, sighed, then looked back down at the table and said, "Sorry..." (again) "...It's just...now I'm losing *both* of you, not just Adrian."

"I know," Kole said. "But you're not just losing us,

we're losing you. And...if I had it my way, I wouldn't move either. I would stay here because I thought it was bad enough losing just Adrian too, but now I'm also losing you. So this is hard on me, too."

"That's true," Joshua said.

"I don't want to move. I mean, I've moved a lot before, but usually just around the state, at least nearby. I've never gone past New York before," Kole said.

"Me neither," Joshua said.

"That's funny. I have, and I don't even live in the United States," Adrian exclaimed.

"How about you be an exchange student, and I'll host you. Adrian, I'll host you, too," Joshua said.

"I can't," Adrian said.

"No, Joshua, it doesn't work like that," Kole said.

"I know." Joshua sighed.

Their food arrived, and they made a silent agreement to forget about what Kole said for the rest of the night, and when Joshua got home, it had still slipped his mind, so he didn't tell his family about it. It wasn't until the next morning when he woke up that he remembered. It was a Thursday morning, and even though the sun was shining bright through his bedroom window, the sun was not shining in his heart. It was the middle of May, and ever since the month had begun, Joshua was feeling dreadful about Adrian leaving. Now, it was twice as bad.

***

The school year ended, and that week, Adrian was boarding a plane to go home. Joshua and Kole both went to the airport to say goodbye, and so did many of Adrian's other friends. Beforehand, Adrian told Joshua and Kole that he felt like a celebrity. Only a celebrity would have so many people watching him board a plane.

Joshua and Kole both said goodbye, and they all stayed together until they couldn't anymore. Joshua cried a lot at the airport. He couldn't help it. He was an emotional person to begin with, and seeing his best friend get on a plane to go to a different country was not helping him in any way. Kole didn't shed any tears at the airport, he saved them for his bedroom that night. But that was only because he had learned to hide his tears until he was in the security of his room. Adrian cried too.

The next day, Adrian video-chatted with Joshua and Kole from the airport. He was having a seven-hour layover, so he had nothing to do.

After they ended their call, Joshua was to hang out with Kole in-person. Kole wasn't leaving for another two weeks. That whole two weeks was going to be spent primarily packing, but Joshua went over whenever Kole had a break.

The two weeks went by very quickly, and soon, it was time for another goodbye. Joshua could hardly bear it, and again, he started crying in front of everyone. He couldn't believe it. He was crying tears of sadness, but in seventh grade, he cried tears of joy when Kole left.

All of the progress Joshua had made seemed lost. Of course, it wasn't. He had still forgiven Kole, and he had made two amazing friends. But now, he felt so lost again. Herman had nearly forgotten about Joshua when Kole was there, but after he was gone, Joshua couldn't escape him so easily. Joshua still had friends, really good friends, but he missed Adrian and Kole who were irreplaceable. He called them at least once a week, but usually more than that. But that didn't make the days any better. Finally, he resorted to a therapist. He also became closer with Isaiah.

Epilogue

The morning of graduation, Joshua laid in his bed, looking through his yearbook. He was going through the senior section where he looked at everyone's picture, their quote, their thank yous, and whatever else they had put down. Joshua's picture was first. During the time that his picture was taken, he was feeling pretty bad. It was at the beginning of the school year, and Joshua was really struggling to be at school without Adrian and Kole. Summer was hard, but it felt like a normal summer because Adrian and Kole had never been a part of it. There wasn't an empty spot in his routine. Sure, he was sad because they didn't see each other anymore, but it wasn't unnormal. Sure, every weekend he wanted to call them and ask them to come over, but he couldn't. He still had swimming and family like every other summer. When school started, any healing he had was gone because then he was going back to the place where he had been with them, and there *was* an empty spot in his routine. So at the time of this picture, he was going through extremely tough times.

His senior quote was: "And when you stand and pray, forgive anything you may have against anyone, so that your Father in heaven will forgive the wrongs you have done" (*Good News Bible,* Mark 11.25).

Joshua continued to go through the yearbook, reading everyone's bios. He got to Herman's toward the very end, and his eyes popped when he read the thank yous. Herman had addressed a bunch of people by their initials, as Joshua had also done, but when Joshua read Herman's, he came across a very familiar initial, one that he himself had been writing down since he was in kindergarten! JA! That was his initials! But...no...it couldn't be him. Herman didn't like him. Even until the very last day of school, Herman was still on his tail. Certainly, he was still after him when he wrote these thank yous. Joshua tried to think if there was anyone else he knew in Herman's life whose initials were JA. But he couldn't think of anyone. *Must be a cousin or something.*

Joshua went downstairs to have breakfast. Afterward, he talked to Adrian and Kole. They were both coming up in July, which Joshua was really excited about. They couldn't make it for his graduation though, but he wasn't able to go to theirs either, so he wasn't upset with them. Adrian actually graduated two years ago because it was different where he was from. But he had important exams this time of year. Kole had his own graduation to be a part of. He said he tried to get out of it because he didn't even know half the people he was graduating with, but his mom told him he only got to have his senior graduation once, so he was going. She told him to be grateful for the opportunity because four years ago, people didn't get the same opportunity. Kole's mom, and the rest of his family, had gone a long way in forgiving him for what he did to Joshua, but they still tried to guide his life like he was five years old.

Even though Joshua was struggling through his senior year, he still somehow found something inside him to get better in his sports. In fact, it was probably all of his struggles that caused him to do so good. He made it back onto varsity for his final cross country season. In Nordic, everyone was on varsity because the team was just so small, but at States, the top four people from each team did a relay, and he got to be on that. During Track his junior year, he didn't accomplish his goal of doing the decathlon, but that made him realize how much work he was actually going to have to put into it. He improved his throwing a lot his junior year and went to States, and his senior year, he was able to do the decathlon. That wasn't going to happen until after his graduation, though. He also qualified for New Englands in discus, which took the top six people in the state at a qualifier meet. In swimming, he achieved times that would put him on the A relay team that summer.

***

So Joshua graduated. He was off to college to become a teacher and continue his swimming and throwing career. Joshua was talking with Arthur and Landon after the ceremony. The three of them and a few other people were going to hang out that afternoon, and then Joshua was going to have some people over at his house. Arthur and Landon walked away to say goodbye to some of their other friends, and when they did, Herman walked over to Joshua. Joshua's eyes widened, but Herman acted natural and said, "Hey, man. Congratulations."

"Thanks...you too," Joshua said, tentatively.

"Thank you...for...everything," Herman said.

Joshua wanted to say *what*, but nothing came out.

"And, I'm sorry...also for everything," Herman continued. "I hope you can find it within yourself to forgive me."

"I can." Joshua smiled.

Herman smiled back. "I hope college works out for you."

"Thanks. And I hope that your business works out."

"Thanks."

Herman reached toward the top of his shirt. Joshua noticed a chain going under his shirt. Herman grabbed the chain and pulled it out. A cross dangled from it. Joshua smiled slightly, then Herman put it back under his shirt.

They stood for a moment, then Herman said, "Goodbye, Joshua."

"Goodbye, Herman." Joshua smiled.

Then, Herman walked away. Joshua hadn't even moved yet when he was then approached by Rowan. She threw him into a hug, then she pulled away and exclaimed, "We did it!!!"

"Yes, we did!"

"Do me a favor. When you go to college, try not to get your butt kicked by anyone else."

"Um...okay, I'll try." Joshua laughed. "It'll be easier there because I'm going to a Christian college."

"That's great. That's where you belong," Rowan told

him.

They said goodbye to each other, though Joshua was going to see her later. She walked away.

Isaiah and Ryan both came over to Joshua, and they congratulated him. Joshua congratulated Ryan too, but Isaiah wasn't graduating yet.

After talking to them, Joshua had one more person he wanted to talk to. He found Carson standing with some of his own friends, and he walked over to him. When Joshua got to him, Carson turned his head and looked over at Joshua. "Hey," Joshua said when Carson looked up.

"Hey," Carson said.

"Congratulations."

"Thanks, you too."

"It's been a while, but I miss you."

"I miss you, too."

"I'm having some people over tonight for a graduation party. Would you like to come?"

"Sure."

"Cool. See you later, then." Joshua smiled.

"Yeah."

Then, Joshua found his family. Kendall, Leah, and Ava all handed him a small present, which he thanked them for. And his grandparents all congratulated him. His mom took pictures. Then, Joshua went to see his friends, and they all left to go enjoy their day.

***

Adrian entered the waiting room at the airport. He was tired and dragging a heavy suitcase, but it was much lighter than the last time he had walked through this airport. Adrian stood at the entrance, looking around. His eyes stopped when he saw two boys jump up and wave at him: Joshua and Kole. Adrian walked over to them, and they started walking too, meeting partway in the middle.

"ADRIAN!" Joshua exclaimed.

"HEY!"

Adrian looked at Kole, who had bags under his eyes and a cup of coffee in his right hand. It was clear that he had only just arrived in Vermont a couple of hours ago.

"Hey!" Kole said, with as much enthusiasm as he could due to the lack of sleep.

"Hey, man!" Adrian exclaimed.

"How was the flight?" Kole asked.

"It was fine. How was the ride?"

"Long."

"I can tell."

"Let's go."

The three of them walked out of the airport.

That's The End

Thank Yous

Thank you to Shakia, for being the first person to read my book all the way through and for giving me countless comments with advice. Thank you to my mom and grandmother for also reading my book.

Thank you to Mrs. Hebert because the Narrative Essay we wrote at the beginning of the year was what led me to write this book.

Thank you to my family for supporting me by allowing me to write. And thank you to you, the reader, for picking up my book and showing enough interest to read even my acknowledgments.

Made in the USA
Middletown, DE
03 May 2024